Growth, accumulation, and unproductive activity

Growth, accumulation, and unproductive activity

An analysis of the postwar U.S. economy

EDWARD N. WOLFF
New York University

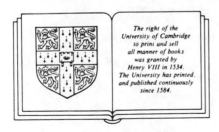

*The right of the
University of Cambridge
to print and sell
all manner of books
was granted by
Henry VIII in 1534.
The University has printed
and published continuously
since 1584.*

CAMBRIDGE UNIVERSITY PRESS

Cambridge
London   New York   New Rochelle
Melbourne   Sydney

Published by the Press Syndicate of the University of Cambridge
The Pitt Building, Trumpington Street, Cambridge CB2 1RP
32 East 57th Street, New York, NY 10022, USA
10 Stamford Road, Oakleigh, Melbourne 3166, Australia

First Published 1987

Printed in the United States of America

Library of Congress Cataloging-in-Publication Data
Wolff, Edward N.
Growth, accumulation, and unproductive activity.
Bibliography: p.
1. United States – Economic conditions – 1945–   .
2. Capitalism – United States.   3. Labor supply – United
States.   I. Title.
HC106.5.W58   1987   330.973'092   86–8260

British Library Cataloguing-in-Publication Data
Wolff, Edward N.
Growth, accumulation, and unproductive
activity: an analysis of the postwar
U.S. economy.
1. United States – Economic conditions
– 1945–
I. Title
330.973'092   HC106.5
ISBN 0 521 25151 6

To JANE
for her support and encouragement

Contents

Preface

This manuscript ties together and extends the work contained in five of my earlier papers. In 1971, I began working on the problem of concretizing and estimating basic Marxian value categories such as labor value, the rate of surplus value, and the organic composition through the use of input–output data. At that time, the two important theoretical contributions in the field were Francis Seton's "The transformation problem," published in the *Review of Economic Studies* in June 1957, and Michio Morishima and Francis Seton's "Aggregation in Leontief matrices and the labour theory of values," published in *Econometrica* in April 1961. During the course of my investigation, another major contribution to the theoretical literature appeared, Morishima's *Marx's Economics* in 1973. Between these three important theoretical works and the actual estimation of Marxian categories lay many unanswered accounting and other methodological issues.

In the early 1970s, I was working on a project developing two input–output tables for Puerto Rico for the years 1948 and 1963, the former year before a period of rapid industrialization and the latter after a period of significant change. This created the opportunity not only of estimating basic Marxian variables but also of seeing their movement over a period of major historical change. The results are contained in "The rate of surplus value in Puerto Rico," published in the *Journal of Political Economy* in October 1975, and "Capitalist development, surplus value, and reproduction: an empirical examination of Puerto Rico," published in *The Subtle Anatomy of Capitalism* in 1977. The first article represents, I think, the first systematic attempt to transform a Leontief input–output framework into Marxian categories and addresses many of the difficult accounting problems of the transformation. The second article proposes and tests several important hypotheses concerning the movement of Marxian variables over a period of rapid historical change.

In 1975, I began collecting input–output data for the U.S. economy. At that time, there were four compatible input–output tables – years 1947, 1958, 1963, and 1967. Now there is another official table, for 1972, and several more recent unofficial ones. I also began to extend the analytical framework in two directions. The first was to introduce the category of unproductive labor. The strategic importance of unproductive labor in advanced capitalism was first highlighted by Paul Baran and Paul Sweezy in *Monopoly Capital*, published in 1966. As I shall suggest below, even they may have understated the crucial (and contradictory) effect unproductive activity has on surplus generation, capital accumulation, and human welfare. On the accounting side, several formidable problems were presented by the introduction of unproductive sectors into the Leontief input–output framework. These problems were partially solved in "Unproductive labor and the rate of surplus value in the United States," published in *Research in Political Economy*, volume 1, 1977. This present manuscript resolves, I think, the remaining difficulties caused by the introduction of unproductive activity into an input–output framework.

The second direction was to extend the empirical analysis to the computation of Marx's prices of production and the general rate of profit and to reconsider Marx's law of the falling rate of profit on theoretical and empirical grounds. The results are contained in "The rate of surplus value, the organic composition, and the general rate of profit in the U.S. economy, 1947–67," published in the *American Economic Review*, June 1979. On both theoretical and empirical grounds, there seemed little support for Marx's law of the falling rate of profit, although an alternative view of the movement of the rate of profit over time was proposed.

This work makes three new contributions to the development of Marxian analysis. First, it develops a methodology by which standard accounting frameworks – in particular, the national income and product accounts and the Leontief input–output framework – can be transformed to provide an empirical basis for the categories of Marxian analysis. In this regard, it goes considerably beyond the previously published material and, in particular, develops in considerable detail the modifications to standard accounts occasioned by the inclusion of unproductive labor.

Second, a growth model is developed to assess the effect of unproductive activity on surplus generation, capital accumulation, and the growth in productivity. The model solves for the asymptotic equilibrium path of a two-sector economy, one of which produces productive output and the other of which is unproductive. The dampening effect of unproductive activity on capital accumulation and productivity growth is demonstrated.

The third and, perhaps, most important contribution of this work is the empirical evidence that is gathered about the role of unproductive activity in the postwar U.S. economy. The results suggest that the extent of unproductive activity in the postwar economy is a significant factor in the slowdown in the rate of capital accumulation, productivity growth, and the overall growth rate. Here, the villain is shown to be the gradual but persistent shift of resources to unproductive activities. The consequence has been a reduction in new capital formation and productivity growth and an erosion in the rate of growth in per capita living standards. Indeed, once non-use-values are netted out from personal and public consumption, average real living standards show an absolute decline during the 1970s. Moreover, the rise in unproductive activity is itself seen to be rooted in the logic of advanced capitalism. The forces of competition, which in the early stages of capitalism lead to rapid technical change and productivity growth, promote nonproductive and even counterproductive activities in its more advanced stages. The current stagnation in which much of advanced capitalism now finds itself thus appears to be rooted in one of the fundamental contradictions of the system.

Helpful comments were received from many colleagues during the course of development of this work. I am particularly grateful to Duncan Foley for his valuable suggestions, especially in regard to the theoretical work contained in Chapter 4. I also benefited greatly from conversations with Donald Harris, Thomas Weisskopf, and John Roemer. Useful ideas were also generated at seminars I gave at New York University, Columbia University, the New School, Stanford University, and the University of Massachusetts at Amherst. I am also grateful to Nancy Fernandez for her near flawless typing of the manuscript.

CHAPTER 1

Introduction

The paper entrepreneurs are winning out over the product entrepreneurs.
Paper entrepreneurs – trained in law, finance, accountancy – manipulate complex systems of rules and numbers. They innovate by using the systems in novel ways: establishing joint ventures, consortiums, holding companies, mutual funds; finding companies to acquire, "white knights" to be acquired by, commodity futures to invest in, tax shelters to hide in; engaging proxy fights, tender offers, antitrust suits, stock splits, spinoffs, divestitures; buying and selling notes, bonds, convertible debentures, sinking-fund debentures: obtaining Government contracts, licenses, quotas, price supports, bail-outs; going private, going public, going bankrupt. (Robert Reich, *New York Times*, May 23, 1980, p. A31. Copyright © 1980 by the New York Times Company. Reprinted by permission.)

François Quesnay (1694–1774) was the first economist to systematically analyze the relations among the following four elements of an economic system: (1) surplus absorption, (2) unproductive activity, (3) accumulation, and (4) productivity. In *Tableau Economique*, the French physiocrat traced through the generation of surplus in the productive sector of agriculture, its absorption in the unproductive activity of manufacturing, and its consequent impact on the expansion of the productive sector. Quesnay was aware that a certain level of productivity must exist in agriculture in order to feed the members of the sterile class. But, writing as he did about a precapitalist mode of production, he did not and probably could not foresee the immense gains in productivity that were to come and their impact on the economic system as a whole.

It is to Adam Smith's (1723–90) credit that he foresaw the central role to be played by productivity and capital accumulation in the development of modern capitalism. Writing at the dawn of industrial capitalism, Adam Smith managed to pierce the logic of the capitalist system in his brilliant treatise, *The Wealth of Nations*. Here he saw the central role played by capital accumulation in generating and increasing the wealth of nations. He also understood its connection with productivity increase and their reciprocal relation. Indeed, he was also aware of the competing goals of unproductive consumption and capital accumulation. What his work lacked was a telling analysis of the source of

1

the surplus that nourished both unproductive activity and the accumulation of capital.

It was for Karl Marx (1818–83) to fill in this gap. In *Capital*, Marx analyzed the source of surplus value as the difference between the time worked by labor and the labor time equivalent of the wages paid to labor in compensation for that work. This relation Marx called the exploitation of labor by capital. Marx saw the source of capital accumulation as the surplus value generated in the production process and the source of productivity increase in the process of capital accumulation. More than this, though, Marx recognized that the logic of competition among independent capitals (firms) led to capital accumulation and increased productivity. The reason is that any cost-cutting technique introduced by one firm that was not soon adopted by others in the industry would lead to their being undersold and eventually driven out of business. One impediment to this constant "revolution" in the means of production was an increased absorption of surplus value in unproductive activity. This might lower the rate of capital accumulation and thereby the rate of productivity advance. This analysis was foreshadowed in volume 2 of *Capital* and in *Theories of Surplus Value*, but perhaps because unproductive activity was relatively unimportant in mid-nineteenth-century Britain, the analysis was never completed.

Paul Baran and Paul Sweezy in their now classic work, *Monopoly Capital* (1966), returned to the issue of unproductive activity. Working within a Marxist tradition, they argued that one of the major characteristics of advanced capitalism was not only a significant level of unproductive activity in the economy but also a tendency for its relative level to rise. In fact, they proposed a law of the tendency of the surplus to rise in contradistinction to Marx's tendency of the rate of profit to fall. Their reasoning and analysis we shall go into later. However, one element that was missing in their analysis was an assessment of the impact of a rising level of unproductive activity on capital accumulation and productivity. Indeed, it is this missing connection that shall be the focus of this book.

A.   Four elements of the economic system

Let us now briefly consider the four elements cited in Quesnay's analysis and their relation with each other.

1.   Absorption of economic surplus

Almost all societies have generated some amount of economic surplus. The surplus is the difference between the total net product of an economy and the amount of product necessary to maintain the productive class. The meaning of these terms depends on the social structure and, more specifically, the mode of production of which they are a part. However, in general terms, the net product is the total product produced in a given period less the portion of the product required to replace the means of production used up during the period. The necessary cost of maintaining the productive class refers to the level of consumption of the working class required to both physically and socially sustain and reproduce it. It can be thought of as the subsistence level, where it is understood that subsistence is determined not only biologically but also historically and socially. Moreover, this level must allow the working class to reproduce and, in some historical contexts, expand its numbers. This may mean that children, adults who help in child rearing, and, in some instances, adults too old to work must be supported out of this subsistence level.

Implicit in the notion of the surplus is a distinction between a productive and an unproductive class of workers and, more generally, between a productive and a surplus class of people. In regard to the first distinction, suffice it to say that a certain set of activities in society produces *use values* – that is, output that serves a real function and satisfies a real need or want – whereas another set of activities maintains a given *distribution* or *set of rights* to these use values. The first set of activities is productive and their producers the productive class, and the second set is unproductive and their producers the unproductive class. Both classes consist of workers. The surplus class, on the other hand, consists of all groups that have rights to the economic surplus. This class consists not only of unproductive workers but also of various functionaries of the state and, in a capitalist society, owners of the means of production.

The total economic surplus produced each period is absorbed in three activities: (1) surplus consumption, (2) unproductive activity, and (3) capital accumulation. The first component is the consumption of use values by the surplus class. The second consists of the absorption of part of the product in activities that produce no use values themselves but instead serve to maintain an existing set of entitlements to the total product. The third, only relatively recently, has become a major component of the economic surplus. This component consists of that part of the surplus product used to increase the net product of society in future periods. It primarily takes the form of new means of production – that is, plant and equipment. It is primarily in capitalist economies that this disposition of the surplus has become of both quantitative and qualitative importance.

It is now apparent that a certain level of productivity – that is, output per labor hour – must be attained before a society can generate any surplus. If each worker could produce only his subsistence level of consumption, the total net product must fully be absorbed in maintaining the (productive) labor force. It is only after output per worker increases beyond the subsistence level that a surplus class can develop. Anthropological studies suggest that even in the most primitive forms of society some form of surplus class exists. This class usually performs one or more of the following three functions: ruling, warfare, and religion. All three functions, as we shall argue in Chapter 2, are unproductive. More advanced societies devoted part of their surplus to some form of capital investment – for example, the great road and aqueduct network of the Roman Empire. For such massive investment programs, the level of productivity must have been substantially above the subsistence level. Under capitalism, the entire logic of the system becomes geared toward capital accumulation. An even higher level of average productivity must have been reached in order that so much of society's total product can be absorbed in ways other than immediate consumption.

2.   Unproductive activity

Unproductive activities are those that use labor power but produce no directly usable output (use value). Instead, they serve to maintain and reproduce an existing set of entitlements to the social product. The particular forms such activities take vary from society to society. But, generally speaking, they serve four principal functions: ruling, warfare, religion, and controlling circulation. Ruling entails the maintenance of a set of rules or procedures that govern the distribution of society's product. Its most direct form is the apparatus of the state or ruling authorities. This includes, among other elements, the administration of these laws and rules (executive bureaucracies and a police force), the means to alter existing laws and rules (the legislature and its peripheral activities), and procedures to settle disputes arising over interpretation of these laws (the judicial system). A large array of unofficial services whose function is to influence the official procedures would also be included. Examples are the legal profession, lobbying groups, and providers of information to the state (consultants).

The second function, warfare, guards a society's distribution of its product against an external threat. Almost all societies have devoted part of their resources to this function. This may have taken a very simple form, such as producing implements of warfare like spears, or a much more complex form, such as maintaining a standing army and developing advanced military hardware.

The third function, religion, is similar to the first function and, in many primitive societies, indistinguishable from it. Religion attempts to ground the somewhat arbitrary and capricious rules of a given social formation in a "higher authority." Particularly in societies where the level of economic or political inequality is high, the need for a transcendental principle to justify the existing social order is great. During the Middle Ages, the church was a major recipient of the surplus in Europe, as evidenced by the great cathedrals. In more recent times, the importance of the church, as well as its share of the surplus, seems to have fallen considerably.

The fourth function, controlling the circulation process, has only in recent history, with the development of a complex exchange economy, assumed considerable importance. In earlier economies, when most output was consumed by the producer, circulation of goods was of relatively minor importance. With the development of industrial capitalism, the vast majority of production has become for purposes of exchange rather than for the use of the producer. As a result, vast exchange systems have evolved within and between capitalist economies, and their attendant costs of circulation have risen. Part of these expenses are productive in that they modify the use value of the product. Transportation, for example, is by and large productive since the use of a commodity depends on its spatial proximity. However, most of these expenses are unproductive since they are concerned almost exclusively with establishing title to goods in circulation. Contracts, inventory financing, and real estate brokerage fees are some examples. One of the most important changes in postwar America has been the rapid relative rise of these kinds of circulation costs.

Indeed, as we have suggested above, the earliest disposition of the economic surplus was largely confined to the first three functions of unproductive activity. In most primitive societies, some group came to form a warrior class, if only to protect the society from extinction. Anthropological studies also show the presence of a ruling class or classes in many, if not most, primitive societies, with special rights to the social product, as well as a priesthood or shaman class, also with special privileges to the societal product. In more advanced but precapitalist societies, cursory evidence suggests massive unproductive expenditures. In fact, the physical remnants of these societies are precisely these great unproductive products – the Great Wall of China for defense, the pyramids of Egypt and the Mayans for both religious and political purposes, and the great cathedrals of the Middle Ages. The size of these projects suggests the existence of not only considerable economic surplus but also considerable unproductive employment of this surplus. Early capitalism seems to have channeled its surplus primarily into capital accumulation, but in more advanced forms of capitalism, particularly that of the postwar American economy, unproductive activity has been absorbing an ever-increasing share of the economic surplus.

3.   Accumulation

Capital accumulation as a major outlet of the economic surplus is a relatively recent historical phenomenon, traceable to the industrial revolution. All societies devote (and devoted) part of their product to the construction and production of new means of production – that is, structures and implements used in the production of goods and services. In primitive societies, it took the form of simple tools used in agriculture and weapons used in hunting as well as implements for processing raw materials. In more advanced societies, the tools and structures became more complex, requiring more labor time for their construction. With the coming of the industrial revolution, hand-driven tools gave way to machines powered by running water and eventually steam. The liberation of the tool from the limitations placed on it by the capabilities of the human body set the stage for the immense increases in productivity that followed the industrial revolution.[1] This revolution in the means of production is continuing today, with the limitations on production from the human mind being transcended by computer-controlled production.

It should be apparent that a certain level of productivity over and above the subsistence level is required for society to devote part of its labor time to new capital formation. In primitive societies, where the tools were simple and their production required a minimal amount of labor time, the level of productivity required was not much greater than the subsistence level. As capital goods became increasingly complex and their production came to require more and more labor time, the level of productivity needed to sustain such capital formation became increasingly greater. At the same time, the increased stock of capital goods increased the level of productivity. Thus, a postive-feedback cycle of increased capital *accumulation* followed by increased productivity and followed in turn by increased productivity was established, as evidenced by the economic history of Western Europe and North America.

The battle over the disposition of the surplus, which raged primarily

---

[1] See Landes (1969), for example, for an excellent treatment of the change in technology that characterized the industrial revolution.

between unproductive uses and surplus consumption, was joined by a third claimant about the time of the industrial revolution. This was the burgeoning capitalist class, and its interest was to use the surplus for capital accumulation. Many of the political battles of nineteenth-century Britain, such as the Enclosures Act or the Corn Laws, were fought over ways to increase the size of the surplus and/or to alter its distribution. Indeed, many of the political fights today are over exactly the same turf, except that the main combatants are now the promoters of unproductive expenditures and the promoters of capital accumulation. The recent cries to lower government expenditure in order to raise the rate of capital accumulation is a manifestation of this battle. The truth of the matter, as the "neoconservatives" correctly recognize, is that increased unproductive expenditure will lower the rate of capital accumulation. Moreover, this in turn will lower the rate of productivity growth, which in turn will further depress the amount of surplus available for accumulation.

4.   Productivity growth

The fourth element is productivity growth. The causes and sources of productivity growth have been the subject of considerable debate in recent years, with no clear consensus emerging. There are many factors involved in productivity growth, but for the purposes here, there are two of particular interest.

First, the development of new techniques can lead to higher productivity. The growth in scientific and engineering knowledge over the past 200 years is one of the most extraordinary accomplishments in human history. The translation of this new knowledge into new technology has been no less extraordinary. The most apparent manifestation of this accomplishment has been the appearance of new *products* – automobiles, airplanes, radios, televisions, and missiles. But perhaps of even more importance has been the development of new industrial *machinery* to produce both existing and new products – the cotton gin, the steam engine, and electric motors. Throughout most of history, the creation of new technology was an informal process: the independent inventor working in his own workshop developing new products and improving old ones. In the past 30 or so years, this process has become institutionalized as *research and development*, and research and development departments are now a standard feature of most large corporations.

Second, new investment is needed in most cases to translate new techniques into functioning plant and equipment. Aside from minor innovation, new techniques must be embodied in new capital equipment. And for new capital equipment to be installed, capital accumulation is necessary. The dissemination of new technology largely depends on the rate at which new equipment can be purchased, which in turn depends on the rate of investment. Moreover, new investment, by increasing the capital–labor ratio, will thereby enhance labor productivity even if no new technology is embodied in the capital goods. These two factors establish a direct linkage between productivity growth and capital accumulation and, by extension, a linkage between productivity growth and the level of the economic surplus.

One of the outstanding social accomplishments of competitive capitalism, as Marx argued in *Capital*, was the fantastic increase in labor productivity that it engendered. Indeed, viewed from the outside, the system as a whole could be considered one designed precisely for this purpose. Each individual capitalist in an industry has an incentive to introduce new technology since it thereby reduces the unit cost of the output. The innovating capitalist can then sell his product at a slightly lower price, make the same or a higher profit per unit sold, increase his share of the market, and thereby obtain a higher total profit (per capital advanced). His competitors, as a result, would be eventually forced to make the same or a superior innovation simply to survive. There would be great incentive in the system for new techniques to be quickly disseminated throughout an industry and for increasingly more productive technology to be introduced. Moreover, there would also be great incentive in the system for the economic surplus to be used for capital accumulation, since it is only in this way that new capital equipment can be purchased.

With the coming of monopoly capitalism, the incentive structure shifted. It no longer became necessary for one company to match a rival's technological advance since either there were no rivals or a working agreement had been established among competitors. It was, of course, still advantageous to introduce new cost-cutting techniques since this would raise the firm's profit margins, but the survival motive no longer existed. Scale of production had so expanded that problems in demand management were becoming increasingly difficult. This, together with the risks and uncertainties of new technology, made other avenues for increasing the firm's profits cheaper and more desirable and set the stage for the central thesis of this book.

5.   *The logic in brief*

Precapitalist societies whose productivity surpassed the subsistence level tended to dispose of their surplus for nonproductive functions.

Traditionally, the functions were threefold: ruling, warfare, and religion. With the emergence of capitalism, a major new outlet of the surplus appeared, which was for *productive investment*. Of course, earlier societies like the Romans had used part of their surplus for such investment, particularly in the construction of buildings, roads, aqueducts, and other forms of social overhead. Moreover, even handicraft production, as characterized in most precapitalist societies, required some investment in tools and other implements. However, what was peculiar to industrial capitalism was the change in the *scale* of investment in both physical and financial terms. There was thus a *qualitative* change in the disposition of the surplus.

Yet, a contradictory force was set in motion by the emergence of industrial capitalism, the development of a complex exchange economy. In earlier economies, there was, of course, some trading of goods. However, with the development of industrial capitalism, the level of worker productivity and the scale of production changed dramatically, and a vast system of exchange was built up with its attendant costs of circulation. Most of these new expenses were unproductive since they were concerned with maintaining or changing title to these use values. A fourth form of unproductive expense, the so-called costs of circulation, thus emerged as a major drain on the surplus. Indeed, as productive investment increased the level of productivity and the scale of production, the expenses of circulation seemed to increase concomitantly.

It is at this juncture that we can now introduce the Baran and Sweezy thesis. They argued that an essentially new era emerged in the history of capitalism, which they call "monopoly capitalism." Though it is hard to date its beginning, it was firmly established in the postwar American economic order. There are two complementary implications of this development. First, it meant that the need to innovate or to adopt a technologically superior innovation was vastly reduced. In competitive capitalism, as Marx argued, there is constant pressure on the individual firm to introduce new technology. For the innovator, his total profits can be substantially increased. For the others in the industry, their survival is placed in jeopardy if they do not match the innovation. In monopoly capitalism, there is no such pressure since, by definition, there are no competitors. Even in an oligopoly, the survival pressure is much less severe since price is usually considerably above average cost (and there are often working agreements among competitors). Second, new forms of competition emerged that proved more profitable. These involved controlling the circulation process through sales promotion, advertising, and "tied-in" merchandising outlets. In addition, corporations started to control credit access and other financial instruments as well as legal resources. In addition, as American corporations expanded abroad, they came to realize that the use of political and military resources was a more effective way of controlling the market than through the technological innovation.

On the aggregate level, the Baran and Sweezy thesis continued, there was an increasing emphasis on demand management to ensure full employment. Indeed, Keynes had once suggested that full employment could be guaranteed if the government could buy up surplus product and throw it into the sea. Moreover, the expansion of American capital abroad created pressures on the federal government to maintain an extensive military presence around the world. Thus, the combination of imperialism and Keynesianism led to a huge increase in the military establishment. Baran and Sweezy reported that defense spending as a fraction of GNP increased from 0.7 percent in 1929 to 10.3 percent in 1957 (p. 152).

B.   Unproductive activity in postwar U.S. economy

My own computations concerning the increases in unproductive expenses during the postwar period are shown in Table 1.1. At the outset, it is necessary to introduce some new terminology when referring to the outcome of unproductive activity since, by definition, unproductive activities do not produce any output. On the other hand, standard national accounting frameworks, including input–output data, do generate output figures for sectors that I will classify as unproductive activities. I shall refer to these output figures as "*conventionally measured output*" or "*standard output measures*" (or, sometimes, simply as "*output*" in quotations). Likewise, I will also talk about unproductive output or expenditures in *real terms* or in *constant dollars*, where again this should be understood to refer to conventional measures. These measures will prove useful for documenting the rise in unproductive activity, though we shall abandon such output figures in later chapters.

The results here indicate that there was a rapid buildup in unproductive expenses during the years 1947–58. During this period, the conventionally measured output of unproductive sectors increased more rapidly than total output. In constant-dollar terms, the standard measure of final output of unproductive sectors indicated a growth rate of 4.8 percent per year and the corresponding gross output figure a 4.9 percent growth rate, whereas total final output grew by 2.9 percent per year and total gross output by 3.6 percent. A breakdown by type of unproductive output helps reveal the sources of its relative growth.

Table 1.1. *Percentage average annual growth rates of conventionally measured unproductive output in constant dollars by sector, 1947–76[a]*

| | 1947–58 | | 1958–76 | |
Component	Final output	Total output	Final output	Total output
Unproductive sectors:				
1. Trade	2.71	3.56	4.99	4.08
2. Finance and insurance	4.11	3.49	4.12	3.85
3. Real estate and rental[b]	3.40	3.42	1.93	3.28
4. Business and professional services	−0.73	5.63	3.95	5.21
5. Federal government (unproductive portion)	9.25	9.25	−0.87	−0.87
6. State and local government (unproductive portion)	7.04	7.04	5.39	5.39
Total unproductive sector	4.83	4.85	3.31	3.65
Total gross output	—	3.55	—	3.68
Total final output	2.91	—	3.41	—

[a] Total output is gross domestic output. See Chapter 3 for details on definition and adjustments of the various components of total output.
[b] The output of the real estate and rental sector excludes imputed rent to owner-occupied dwellings.

Unproductive output is divided into six components (see Chapter 2 for details on the classification scheme). Of these, the largest growth was in unproductive federal government. This growth, in turn, was led by defense spending, which increased at an annual rate of *9.9 percent in real terms*. The remaining unproductive portion of federal government activity increased at an annual rate of only 4.7 percent. The other major growth in unproductive activity was in state and local government. Since the unproductive portion of state and local governments' spending remained an almost constant percentage of total state and local spending, the growth in this unproductive expenditure was due to a very rapid increase in the size of overall state and local government between 1947 and 1958.

The total conventionally measured output of business services also grew considerably faster than total gross or final output during this period. The major spurt came from the increased use of business services by intermediate users (that is, other industries) since the final "output" of business services actually declined during the 1947–58 period. This trend reflects, in part, the rapid increase in the use of advertizing and other sales promotion services. The total standard measure of the output of the trade sector and the finance and insurance sector increased at rates slightly above that of total gross output, while the total output of the real estate sector grew slightly slower than total gross output.

The sharp rise in the relative size of unproductive activity that occurred between 1947 and 1958 was thus due primarily to the big buildup of the defense establishment. A secondary factor was the growth in state and local government expenditure (though *not* in the share of unproductive expenditures by state and local government, as will be seen in Chapter 2). A third contributory factor was the growth in business services, including advertising and legal services. The Baran and Sweezy thesis seems fairly well substantiated by these results. It was the combined effect of militarism on the national level and demand management on the *firm* level that led to the expansion in unproductive expenditure during this period.

The rate of growth of the total conventionally measured output of unproductive sectors slowed down from 4.9 percent in the 1947–58 period to 3.7 percent in the 1958–76 period. Moreover, the rate of growth of unproductive final output was a shade lower than that of total final output in the later period. The growth in total output accelerated in the trade and finance and insurance sectors and slowed down slightly in real estate and business and professional services, though this sector had the highest growth rate in total output among the four. Unproductive state and local government expenditures also increased at a very high rate, though almost two percentage points below the sector's 1947–58 growth rate. The major change was that the federal government's unproductive expenditure in constant dollars actually *declined* between 1958 and 1976. Defense spending, which had amounted to 85 percent of federal expenditures and 10.1 percent of GNP (in current dollar terms) in 1958, fell to 67 percent of federal expenditures and 5.0 percent of GNP by 1976. In 1972 dollars, national defense spending actually fell from approximately 79 billion dollars in 1958 to 65 billion dollars in 1976. The years from 1958 to 1976 were characterized not only by a relative decline in the importance of defense spending but also by an absolute decline in real terms.[2]

---

[2] The data on national defense are from the *Economic Report of The President, 1983*, Tables B-1, B-2, and B-3. The official national defense expenditure figures represent the budget of the defense department. Related national defense spending by other agencies, such as NASA and the CIA, are not reflected in these figures.

C.   Effects of unproductive activity on labor absorption and
        productivity growth

From 1947 to 1958, unproductive output in the United States grew at
a significantly greater rate than overall output. From 1958 to 1976,
unproductive output increased at almost exactly the same rate as total
gross output (3.7 percent), and the final output of unproductive sectors
increased at about the same rate as total final output. Thus, the Baran
and Sweezy thesis of an increasing relative size of unproductive activity
was true in the early postwar period but not in the later. In the more
recent period, unproductive activity remained more or less proportional to overall economic activity – a "fixed coefficient," as it were,
in the economic system.

There are several important economic consequences of increasing
relative size of unproductive activity and several from proportional
growth in unproductive activity. However, before these effects are
considered, it is important to establish another characteristic of unproductive activity, namely, its slow rate of "productivity growth."
The term *productivity growth* may appear to be a misnomer when applied to unproductive activity, like output, since unproductive sectors
do not produce use values. However, the term productivity growth will
be used in the conventional sense as the rate of change of the ratio of
conventionally measured real output to real inputs. (As with "output,"
this will be indicated by the terms conventionally measured or standard
measure or the use of quotation marks.) In a moment, I shall drop the
term productivity growth in reference to unproductive activity and,
instead, speak of the unproductive labor *absorbed* per unit of (productive) output. It might be noted, in passing, that government statisticians have always had a difficult time measuring the output of
sectors that I have designated as unproductive – in particular, finance,
insurance, real estate, professional services, and government services.[3]
Indeed, the difficulty the statisticians have in defining, let alone measuring, the output of these sectors is one indication that they are
unproductive.

The low rate of productivity growth of unproductive sectors is not
endemic to the category of unproductive activity but rather is related
to the fact that they tend to be labor-intensive services.[4] In an argument

[3] The output of these sectors (with the exclusions of finance and insurance) is essentially
measured by the total inputs used in official national accounts. The output of finance
and insurance is equated to the net interest received.
[4] They are not exclusively services since the production of military hardware is also
considered an unproductive activity.

Table 1.2. *Percentage average annual rate of conventionally measured labor productivity growth by sector, 1947–76[a]*

Component	GDO/*L*	TLP
Unproductive sectors:		
1. Trade	1.65	0.99
2. Finance and insurance	−0.11	0.41
3. Real estate and rental[a]	1.09	0.95
4. Business and professional services	−0.13	0.38
5. Government (unproductive portion)	0.22	0.12
Total unproductive sector	0.60	0.64
Total productive sector	2.65	2.27
Overall: GNP	2.18	—
Total final product (CFP)[b]	—	1.75

[a] The output of the real estate and rental sector excludes imputed rent for owner-occupied housing.
[b] See Chapter 3 for adjustments.

originally advanced by William Baumol in 1967, the contention is made that activities that are labor intensive and whose output is essentially the labor service itself are condemned to low rates of labor productivity growth. Such activities include not only unproductive sectors such as most government services and professional services but also productive areas such as education, personal services, repair services, domestic servants, and many forms of entertainment as well. In general, however, the officially measured rate of productivity growth in the unproductive sector might be expected to be lower than that of productive sectors.

This is generally confirmed by the estimates shown in Table 1.2. Two different indices are used to measure average annual rates of labor productivity growth over the 1947–76 period. In the second column, the labor productivity measure is the ratio of gross domestic output (GDO) in constant dollars to employment. GDO, an input–output concept, is equal to the gross value of a sector's output or sales deflated by the sectoral price deflator (see Chapter 3 for more details). The third column uses an input–output-based measure of labor productivity, called total labor productivity (TLP). TLP is defined as the inverse of the direct plus indirect labor requirements per unit of final output. A standard Marxian accounting framework is used, where capital, as a produced means of production, is valued by its rate of depreciation (see Chapter 3). Two measures of total output, each corresponding to the measure of sectoral output, are used to measure overall labor productivity growth: (i) gross national product (GNP) and (ii) adjusted total final product (CFP).[5]

The results are fairly consistent across the two measures of labor productivity. Overall growth of labor productivity averaged about 2 percent per year from 1947 to 1976. Among the five unproductive sectors, the annual rate of conventionally measured productivity growth was highest for the trade sector and second highest for the real estate sector. The rates of labor productivity growth of the finance and insurance sector, business and professional services, and government services were all substantially lower, under half a percent a year. Altogether, the unproductive sector experienced an average rate of productivity growth of about 0.6 percent per year, whereas the corresponding figure for the productive sector was between 2.3 and 2.7 percent per annum.

I shall now introduce new terminology when talking about the ratio of output to unproductive labor. In particular, since unproductive sectors do not produce use values, it is necessary to look at the ratio of productive output to unproductive labor. Moreover, since unproductive labor, by definition, produces no output, it is now necessary to speak of the unproductive labor *absorbed* per unit of productive output. This concept (which will be formally defined in Chapter 6) is roughly the ratio of the unproductive labor employed to productive output in constant dollars. Thus, the unproductive labor absorbed per unit of productive output, or ULA, is the inverse of a labor productivity measure. Instead of speaking of a slow rate of labor productivity growth of unproductive activities, one can instead talk about a slow rate of *decline* of ULA. It follows directly that if conventionally measured unproductive output grows at the same rate or faster than productive output and the rate of conventionally measured productivity growth is lower for unproductive sectors than productive sectors, than the rate of decline of unproductive labor absorption per unit of productive output will be lower than that of productive labor absorption. In fact, in the framework to be developed in the ensuing chapters, one cannot refer to unproductive output and productivity in the unproductive sector since these terms no longer exist. All that is observed is that the rate of decline of ULA is less than the rate of decline of productive labor absorbed – that is, less than the rate of growth of productive

---

[5] CFP is essentially the net national product with the exclusion of owner-occupied rent and several other minor adjustments.

Table 1.3. *Percentage average annual rate of growth of employment by sector, 1947–76*

Component	1947–58	1958–76	1947–76
Unproductive sectors:			
1. Trade	2.85	1.86	2.23
2. Finance and insurance	6.11	2.99	4.17
3. Real estate and rental	1.63	2.61	2.24
4. Business and professional services	5.70	5.41	5.51
5. Government (unproductive portion)	5.25	2.51	3.56
Total unproductive sector	3.61	2.44	2.88
Total productive sector	−0.22	1.47	0.83
Total employment	0.91	1.82	1.47

labor productivity. From this it follows that unproductive employment will rise relative to productive employment.

This is shown in Table 1.3. Between 1947 and 1958, total employment increased at an annual rate of 0.9 percent, and the annual rate of growth of unproductive employment was 3.6 percent. During this period, employment in finance and insurance grew at 6.1 percent per year, that in business and professional services at 5.7 percent per year, and unproductive government employment increased at 5.3 percent per year. Overall, unproductive employment increased from 25 to 34 percent of total employment, and productive employment actually declined in absolute terms. In the 1958–76 period, unproductive employment grew at 2.4 percent per year and total employment at 1.8 percent per annum. Business and professional employment had the highest growth rate among the unproductive sectors, at 5.4 percent per year, followed by finance and insurance at 3.0 percent and the real estate sector at 2.6 percent. Unproductive government employment grew at 2.5 percent. Overall, unproductive employment rose from 34 to 38 percent of total employment between 1958 and 1976.

Another implication is that a relative shift in labor input toward the unproductive sectors will cause, ceteris paribus, the conventionally measured overall rate of labor productivity growth to decline. It can be demonstrated as a general proposition that if the rate of labor productivity growth in the productive sector and the rate of decline in ULA are both constant over time and the former exceeds the latter, the standard measure of overall labor productivity growth will fall over time. The evidence is somewhat mixed on this score since many factors outside the analysis here influence the rate of productivity growth. In particular, neither the rate of labor productivity growth in the productive sector nor the rate of decline of ULA has remained constant over time. The results do indicate that in the period from 1958 to 1967, when employment in unproductive sectors grew 0.6 percentage points faster than total employment, traditional labor productivity growth averaged 3.1 percent per year. In the 1947–58 period, when employment in unproductive sectors grew 2.7 percentage points higher than total employment, traditional labor productivity growth was 2.0 percent per year, 1.1 percentage points lower than in the 1958–67 period. Finally, in the 1967–76 period, when the growth of employment in unproductive sectors exceeded total employment growth by 1.4 percentage points, traditional labor productivity growth fell to 0.2 percent per annum. This precipitous drop in overall productivity growth was, of course, also due to many other factors.

There is another important trend that occurred during the postwar period, which shall be briefly mentioned at this point. Activities that produce productive output, in general, use unproductive inputs. These are of two types. The first consists of purchases made by productive sectors from unproductive sectors that are recorded in conventional input–output tables. Almost all goods-producing sectors make use of trade services in their wholesaling and retailing operations.[6] Moreover, most productive sectors also buy services from the finance and insurance sector and the business and professional service sector. The second are workers directly employed by productive sectors who engage in unproductive work. Examples include lawyers, accountants, supervisors, managers, night watchmen, and clerical workers directly employed in the automotive sector. It is interesting to note that the Bureau of Labor Statistics, in its official statistics, divides workers in manufacturing establishments into two groups: *production* and *non-production* workers. These categories loosely correspond to my division between productive and unproductive workers.

Since 1947, purchases made by productive sectors from unproductive sectors have remained more or less constant as a percentage of the output of productive sectors in constant-dollar terms. During the same period, there was a marked increase in the ratio of unproductive to productive workers employed in sectors producing productive output. Indeed, many manufacturing companies have become primarily white-collar employers. The evidence suggests two factors: First, it is easier to substitute capital goods for productive workers than for un-

---

[6] By input–output convention, all wholesaling and retailing activities, whether external or internal to the corporate entity that produces the output, are recorded in a separate trade sector.

productive workers. Second, technological change has been much more successful in reducing the input requirements for productive workers and capital goods per unit of output than in reducing the input requirements for unproductive workers. Two implications follow immediately. First, the share of the labor force involved in unproductive work within sectors producing productive output will increase over time. Second, insofar as unproductive labor represents a fixed coefficient in sectors producing productive output, the conventionally measured rate of labor productivity growth in these sectors will decline over time. The reason is that as unproductive labor increases as a share of employment in productive sectors, the reductions that can be made in total labor requirements per unit of productive output will correspondingly fall over time.[7]

In summary, there are two sources for the increased absorption of labor in unproductive activity. The first is the increasing share of labor directly employed in sectors that engage in unproductive activities. The second is the rising proportion of labor employed in productive sectors who are included in unproductive work. Yet, even this is not the full story. As will be argued in Chapter 3, labor employed in producing productive output that is purchased by unproductive sectors can also be considered to be unproductively engaged. When this last factor is considered, the results show that the full net increase in employment between 1947 and 1967 was either directly or indirectly absorbed in unproductive activity.

D.   Implications for capital formation

There are two factors involved in the determination of the level of capital formation in an economy. The first is the size of the surplus. The second is the disposition of the surplus.

In regard to the first factor, it is perhaps helpful to take note of Baran and Sweezy's law of the tendency of the surplus to rise. Karl Marx, of course, had proposed in Chapter 13 of volume 3 of *Capital* the law of the tendency of the rate of profit to fall, which states that the mass of surplus value will decline relative to the value of constant capital over time. This law was argued on theoretical grounds and assumed a

---

[7] More specifically, the fixity of both unproductive intermediate and labor input coefficients in productive sectors will cause the growth rate of total labor productivity (TLP), defined as the inverse of the direct plus indirect labor requirements per unit of output, to decline over time in the productive sectors. The reason is that as direct productive input and labor requirements are reduced over time, the direct unproductive inputs represent an increasingly greater share of the total costs of producing productive output in labor value terms. This result is formally demonstrated in Chapter 4.

competitive economy and (implicitly) a negligible amount of unproductive activity in the economy. Recognizing the dominant role played by monopoly power and the growing importance of unproductive activity in the American economy, Baran and Sweezy (1966, p. 72) proposed a new law of the tendency of the surplus to rise. The theorem is that "the surplus tends to rise both absolutely and relatively, as the system develops." The Baran and Sweezy concept of surplus includes not only enterprise profit but also government expenditure and unproductive consumption. They did not attempt a systematic exposition of the concept of unproductive activity but included such items as advertising and other sales costs, planned obsolescence, expense accounts, and litigation costs. My own results, reported in Chapters 5 and 6, do indicate that the ratio of surplus value to total labor value increased from 0.80 in 1947 to 0.86 in 1976. However, the ratio of the surplus product to conventional final output rose from 0.76 in 1947 to only 0.77 in 1976.

Surplus value is allocated to three uses: (i) the consumption of the surplus classes, (ii) capital formation, and (iii) unproductive activity. The first component has little correlation with the rate of capital formation. However, the results show a very strong inverse relation between the level of unproductive activity as conventionally measured and net capital formation. In the 1947–58 period, when the rate of growth of conventionally measured unproductive final demand exceeded that of total output, new net investment in capital formation was actually lower at the end of the period than in the beginning. In the 1958–67 period, when the converse was true, the rate of growth of new investment was not only positive but also far exceeded that of total final output. Finally, in the 1967–76 period, when the growth rate of unproductive final output again exceeded that of total final output, the rate of growth of net investment was again negative. On the surface, at least, there is strong evidence that investment and unproductive activity move inversely. Indeed, unproductive activity is the only component of the traditional net product that is consistently related to investment.

A similar inverse relation emerges when the rate of growth of the capital stock is compared to the relative growth of unproductive output. In the 1947–58 period, when conventionally measured unproductive output expanded considerably faster than productive output, the rate of growth of the capital stock was 3.1 percent per year. In the 1958–76 period, when unproductive output and productive output grew at the same rate, the capital stock grew at 3.8 percent per year.

Yet, this is not the complete picture, since a portion of new investment will be absorbed by unproductive sectors for their own capital expansion. As suggested above, because of technological differences, it is easier to substitute capital for labor in productive sectors than in unproductive ones. As a result, the capital–labor ratio tends to increase in productive sectors but tends to remain more or less constant in unproductive sectors. If conventionally measured output were growing at the same rate in the two sectors, capital stock would grow faster in productive sectors than in unproductive activities. Such was the case during the 1958–76 period, when the capital stock of the productive sector grew at 4.1 percent per year and that of the unproductive sector at 3.2 percent per annum. On the other hand, if the unproductive sector were expanding sufficiently more rapidly than the productive one, then capital stock could grow faster in the former than in the latter. This was the case in the 1947–58 period, when capital stock in the unproductive sector grew at 3.6 percent per year and productive capital stock at 2.9 percent. In later chapters, we shall introduce different terminology and speak about the unproductive capital absorbed per unit of productive output. In the long-term growth model developed in Chapter 4, it is demonstrated that if the unproductive capital absorbed per unit of productive output is fixed and if productive capital and productive labor are substitutable, the rates of growth of productive and unproductive capital stock will asymptotically converge to the same constant level. In addition, it is shown that overall labor productivity growth will fall over time and asymptotically approach zero.

E.   Unproductive activity and its effect on well-being

The growth in unproductive activity has produced a substantial drag on the growth of productivity in the postwar U.S. economy. This is particularly evident during the period after the mid-1960s. This, in turn, has caused the rate of growth of real labor earnings and other measures of the standard of living to decline. In fact, between 1968 and 1981, median family income actually fell in real terms.[8] Indeed, one of the great potential ironies of the capitalist system is that it is a system that originally advanced itself by the progressive improvement of technology but ultimately develops by increasing the level of useless activity in society. As a result, the great gains in real per capita income that had characterized capitalism for over 100 years may now be drawing to a close.

Unproductive activity has two effects on living standards. First, it

[8] The source is *Economic Report of the President, 1983*, Table B-27.

leads to the gradual but persistent shift of employment to unproductive activities. This causes the overall rate of productivity growth to decline, which, in turn, produces an erosion in the rate of growth of real income. Second, part of the income that workers receive is spent on unproductive expenditures. If unproductive expenditures increase as a share of total consumption, then the growth in the "effective" real wage will thereby be reduced.

The traditional measure of the real wage increased by 2.7 percent per year from 1947 to 1958, when unproductive employment increased most rapidly; by 3.0 percent per year from 1958 to 1967; and by 2.3 percent per year during the productivity slowdown period of 1967–76. In constant-dollar terms, unproductive expenditures increased as a share of total consumption from 0.37 in 1947 to 0.39 in 1958, 0.42 in 1967, and 0.44 in 1976. As a result, the rate of growth in the effective real wage was lower than that of the traditional real wage: 2.4 percent in 1947–58, 2.5 percent in 1958–67, and 1.9 percent in 1967–76. Perhaps the best measure of average individual well-being is the sum of private and public consumption of productive output per capita. By this measure, average welfare grew by 1.5 percent per annum from 1947 to 1958, 3.1 percent per annum from 1958 to 1967, and 1.9 percent per annum from 1967 to 1976. Probably the best measure of average social well-being is the sum of the last measure and the per capita net addition to the capital stock since investment provides for future consumption. By this measure, social well-being increased by 0.1 percent in 1947–58, 3.8 percent in 1958–67, and 0.9 percent in 1967–76.

By all four measures, the rate of increase in well-being was greatest in the 1958–67 period, when both productivity growth was high and the growth in unproductive employment was lowest. In 1947–58, the rate was lowest because of the extraordinary rate of growth of unproductive activity, whereas in 1967–76, the rate was low because of the low rate of productivity growth.

F.   A comparison with Baran and Sweezy

The indictment against unproductive activity is *not* that it is irrational from the standpoint of individual capital. Indeed, almost all of the unproductive expenditures, such as advertising, trade, and finance expenses, are *absolutely necessary* for the individual capital to function and survive in advanced capitalism. However, from the *social* point of view, the resources absorbed in such unproductive activity represent *wasted resources*. They provide no use value to final users. Moreover, unlike other intermediate inputs, unproductive inputs do not make a tangible contribution to real output (and the production structure could be rewritten without them). Most of unproductive activity is involved with the realization of surplus value or the division of surplus value among competing entitlements. Thus, from the social point of view, these unproductive activities are *irrational*.

It might be useful to contrast the Baran and Sweezy argument at this point. For them, too, unproductive activities represent social waste. However, from the social point of view, unproductive expenditures *are rational* in that they provide necessary effective demand for full capacity utilization or a full employment level of output. It should be noted that *Monopoly Capital* appeared in 1966, almost at the end of one of the longest uninterrupted periods of productivity and output growth in world history (the period 1945–65) and during the reign of Keynesianism. Thus, their argument, to some extent, reflects the Keynesian emphasis on *demand management*. As a result, they tend to see unproductive expenditures, particularly defense, as a means to fill the slack in effective demand. Unproductive spending therefore becomes part of a demand management strategy to ensure full employment. By implication, unproductive expenditures provide a direct stimulus to output growth and hence capital formation and productivity growth.

The argument here contrasts rather sharply with Baran and Sweezy's. Whereas the emphasis of their argument is on the *realization* of surplus value, the one presented here is on the *disposition* of surplus value. In particular, an increase in unproductive activity must reduce, ceteris paribus, the amount of surplus product available for capital formation. So, even if unproductive expenditures should stimulate production by closing the effective demand "gap," their effect on capital accumulation is, at best, indeterminate and, most likely, negative. Moreover, in light of more recent evidence, particularly that of the 1970s, and the deep recession of the early 1980s, it is hard to place much credence in the notion that unproductive spending has been an effective demand management policy device. In general, unproductive activity reduces the resources available for capital accumulation and therefore exerts a deleterious effect on productivity and overall growth. The approach here emphasizes the supply-side consequences of unproductive activity, whereas the Baran and Sweezy approach emphasizes the demand-side effects.

Another way of contrasting the approach here with that of Baran and Sweezy is that this one looks at the *dynamic* implications of unproductive expenditure, whereas theirs looked at its static implications. Their approach also reflects the Keynesian bias of considering the short-term effects of inadequate demand on the *current level* of output. The approach here, in contrast, is more concerned with the long-run implications of the effect of unproductive activity on capital formation and thus the *growth* of output.

G.   Plan of this book

It should be noted at the outset that the intent of this work is not to conduct a thorough historical treatment of the rise of unproductive activity in the U.S. economy. The scope is limited to two major concerns. First, the book will document the importance of unproductive labor activity in the postwar American economy. Second, it will trace out analytically and document empirically several important implications of the presence of unproductive activity. The analysis thus proceeds on four levels: (i) the classification of productive and unproductive activities; (ii) the accounting framework; (iii) a dynamic growth model with unproductive activity; and (iv) estimation and empirical documentation.

Chapter 2 develops, in some brevity, the Marxian category of unproductive labor. Comparisons with Quesnay and Smith are provided. Based on this discussion, a classification scheme for productive and unproductive activities is proposed.

Chapter 3 introduces the accounting framework to be used in the empirical analysis. The basic data are input–output tables of the U.S. economy for the years 1947, 1958, 1963, 1967, 1972, and 1976. The chapter shows how a standard Leontief framework can be transformed to a Marxian framework with unproductive labor. New measures are developed for standard Marxian categories such as the rate of surplus value and the rate of exploitation.

In Chapter 4, a growth model of the economy is developed with unproductive activity. Assumptions roughly based on the postwar U.S. experience are made concerning the production structure of the economy in regard to both productive and unproductive inputs. Limiting solutions are derived for the growth in productivity and the real wage, the rate of capital accumulation, and the rate of surplus value.

In Chapter 5, documentation is provided of the growth in unproductive activity from 1947 to 1976. Various calculations are first made of the share of unproductive labor in the total labor force over the period. Then, percentage breakdowns of final output are provided using both traditional components and those from the new accounting framework developed in Chapter 3. Other breakdowns are constructed using alternative definitions of final output.

Chapter 6 concentrates on the absorption of resources in the various components of final output. Measures are provided of both the direct and indirect allocation of labor and capital to various final uses. In addition, estimates are made of the rate of labor productivity growth in the provision of final-use commodities. Finally, various measures of the ratio of surplus value to total value are computed.

Chapter 7 focuses on the growth in living standards during the postwar period. Various concepts are developed of average welfare and computations made of their rate of growth. Changes in average living standards are then related to the disposition of newly added resources in the economy. Decompositions are made of the distribution of newly added labor value among final demand components into productivity effects and real growth effects.

Chapter 8 provides both conclusions and speculations. A review of the evidence is made first. Long-term implications concerning capital accumulation, productivity growth, and the increase in living standards are then drawn. The issue is then addressed whether the growth of unproductive labor is a necessary condition of advanced capitalism. Finally, some broader issues are considered, particularly in regard to the implications of this work for economic analysis in general.

Unproductive activity in a capitalist society

At the same time, the complexity of litigation seems to be increasing. Even if a case is settled without trial, preliminary motions and discovery procedures may occupy much time of judges and attorneys. Moreover, the country has experienced a marked growth in statutes and administrative regulations; the number of federal agencies jumped from twenty to seventy in the last two decades while the pages of federal regulations tripled in the 1970s alone. Paralleling these trends, the supply of lawyers has doubled since 1960 so that the United States now boasts the largest number of attorneys per thousand population of any major industrialized nation – three times as many as in Germany, ten times the number in Sweden, and a whopping twenty times the figure in Japan. In sum, though there may not be more court cases, the country has more legal work to do and many more attorneys to do it. Just what society pays for this profusion of law is hard to guess. Lloyd Cutler has put the figure at $30 billion a year, but the truth is that no one has bothered to find out. Be that as it may, legal costs are primarily people costs, and if we mark the growth in the total number of lawyers and the average compensation of attorneys, it is clear that legal expenditures have been climbing more rapidly than the gross national product for many years. (Derek C. Bok, "A flawed system," *Harvard Magazine*, May–June 1983, p. 40.)

A.   Historical background

The concept of unproductive labor has a long history in economic thought. It should be emphasized at the outset that unproductive activity is coterminus neither with governmental activity nor services. Since the concept of unproductive labor is central to the thesis of the book, it is, perhaps, useful to give some historical background to this idea. The historical sketch will begin with Quesnay because he was probably the first to give a systematic treatment of the concept and end with Baran and Sweezy since the work contained here derives in large measure from their work. However, it should be noted at the outset that the intention here is to give only a brief historical grounding of the concept of unproductive activity.

1.   Nature and reproduction

Quesnay developed a fully embellished theory of material and social reproduction. On the one hand, he illustrated the material flows necessary to ensure a continuous flow of inputs to the sectors in the economy. On the other, he showed the distribution network and consumption patterns required to preserve the three social classes. The distinguishing mark of the entire reproduction process is the role played by natural regeneration.

It is natural reproduction that distinguishes the productive sector, agriculture, from the sterile sector, manufacturing: "Ainsi l'origine, le principe de toute depense, et de toute richesse, est la fertilité de la terre, dont on ne peut multiplier les produits que par ses produites mêmes" ("Second dialogue," p. 892).[1] Nature is viewed as a self-sustaining system, capable of its own internal maintenance and rooted ultimately in the soil since all life depends on plant life. Agricultural production is but one form of this natural cycle, where labor may intervene in an ancillary way to aid the process but where nature itself is responsible for life. In this sense, the fertility of the soil is the basis of all production and wealth. For this reason, manufacture is unproductive: "Les production de nos terres doivent être la matière des manufactures" ("Fermiers," p. 459). "La terre . . . fournit les sucs nécessaire à leur [manufacturers'] vegetation et a leur accroisement" ("Grains," p. 473). Thus, *Les travaux d'industrie ne multiplient pas les richesses*" ("Grains," p. 496). Manufacture transforms what is already produced in agriculture. It does not add to the production of output but simply modifies the product by much the same logic that the home cooking of meals is not included in gross national product in modern income accounting. Agriculture supplies manufacturing with its raw materials, and nature supplies agriculture with its raw materials (seed). Thus, nature is the source of all production.

Moreover, nature is the source of human subsistence. Agricultural products "favoriseraient la propagation et la conservation des hommes, surtout l'augmentation des habitants de la campagne" ("Fermiers," p. 452). "Les hommes se multiplient donc à proportion des revenus de biens-fonds" ("Grains," p. 497). Agriculture supplies the products necessary for human preservation. Labor also consumes manufactured products, as Quesnay described in *Tableau Economique*. But these are comforts and not necessary and hence auxiliary to subsistence. Moreover, the size of the agricultural output determines the number of people that can be supported in the nation. The extent of nature's bountifulness thus controls the population size and "c'est la source de la

---

[1] All page references in this section refer to Institut National d'Etudes Démographiques, ed., *Francois Quesnay et la Physiocratie* (Paris, 1958).

subsistence des hommes, qui est la principe des richesses" ("Grains," p. 496).

Natural regeneration leads to a third property of production, the creation of a physical surplus. This surplus arises in agriculture because of the peculiar ability of one seed to produce many. The difference between the food harvested and that required to feed the cultivator and his farm labor and that withdrawn for next year's planting is the net product. The surplus is appropriated by the landowning class in the form of a rent. This rent is partly spent on manufactured goods, and the surplus thus supports the unproductive sector. Biological reproduction becomes tantamount to the formation of a surplus, and the creation of a surplus becomes a defining characteristic of production.

The circulation patterns that ensure a renewal of activity in the two sectors and the maintenance of the agricultural, manufacturing, and landowning classes are described in *Tableau Economique*. The accounting is a bit puzzling but seems as follows: The "reproduction totale" – the total agricultural output – of the year is 5 billion, and the total output in manufacturing is 3 billion. The landowners receive 2 billion in rent from the farmers, with which they buy 1 billion in agricultural goods and 1 billion in manufactured goods. The farmers exchange 1 billion in agricultural goods for 1 billion in manufactured goods with the artisans. With the 1 billion received from the landowners, the artisans buy 1 billion of agricultural goods. Thus, of the 5 billion produced in agriculture, 1 billion is sold to the landowners, 2 billion to the manufacturers, and 2 billion remains in the sector. Of the 3 billion produced in manufacturing, 1 billion is sold to the cultivators, 1 billion to the proprietors, and 1 billion remains in the sector. Of the 2 billion in food remaining in the agricultural sector, part is consumed directly by the farmers and part is reserved as seed for the following year's planting. The 1 billion in manufactured goods in the farming sector is used presumably to replace worn-out implements. Of the 2 billion in agricultural products bought by the manufacturing sector, part is directly consumed by the artisans and the remainder used as raw materials in the production process. The 1 billion in manufactured goods kept in the sector is used to replace worn-out tools. The goods received by the landowning class are directly consumed.

The reproduction process is thus complete. *Fixed capital* is restored in both sectors, and raw materials are available for the following year's production. Production can thus continue in both sectors. The three classes – cultivators, proprietors, and landowners – receive their required subsistence goods and are maintained, and the exchange relations between the three classes are preserved since the distribution of output at the end of the year is precisely as it was at the beginning. The key to the reproductive process is the 3 billion physical surplus in agriculture (a total output of 5 billion less 2 billion required for seed and food for the farmers). This surplus allows for the subsistence of both landowners and artisans and for raw materials in manufacturing. The expanding character of natural reproduction thus supports the material and social reproduction of the economy and became for Quesnay the defining mark of production.

2.   *Circulation and reproduction*

Though vestiges of physiocratic thought appear in the work of Adam Smith, his major accomplishment was to advance the analysis of production and reproduction from the characteristics of an agrarian, precapitalist economy to the conditions of capitalism. There are inconsistencies that arise in *The Wealth of Nations*,[2] and two rather distinct principles of unproductive labor emerge in the work.

The first principle of production is the reproduction of capital:

There is one sort of labour which adds to the value of the subject upon which it is bestowed; there is another which has no such effect. The former, as it produces a value, may be called productive; the latter, unproductive labour. Thus, the labour of the manufacturer adds, generally, to the value of the materials which he works upon, that of his own maintenance, and of his master's profit. The labour of the menial servant, on the contrary, adds to the value of nothing. Though the manufacturer has his wages advanced to him by his master, he, in reality, costs him no expense, the value of those wages being generally restored, together with a profit, in the improved value of the subject upon which his labour is bestowed. But the maintenance of the menial servant never is restored. A man grows rich by maintaining a multitude of manufacturers: he grows poor, by maintaining a multitude of menial servants. (p. 314)

Furthermore:

Whatever part of his stock a man employs as a capital, he always expects it to be replaced to him with a profit. He employs it, therefore, in maintaining productive hands only; and after having served in the function of a capital to him, it constitutes a revenue to them. Whenever he employs any part of it in maintaining unproductive hands of any kind, that part is, from that moment, withdrawn from the capital, and placed in his stock reserved for immediate consumption. (p. 316)

[2] All book, chapter, and page references in this section refer to Adam Smith, *The Wealth of Nations*, Modern Library Edition, 1937.

A man in possession of a given stock (of goods or value) can hire labor for one of two purposes. First, he can hire labor to produce a commodity for exchange. When the commodity is sold, the initial wage advance and the advance on raw materials is restored, together with a profit. The recovery of the advance through the sale of the product normally leads to a resumption of production as labor is rehired and new materials purchased. The stock put forward in this case is capital and the labor employed is productive. Alternatively, the man can use his stock for consumption. He can hire labor, servants for example, to service his immediate needs. No product is sold, the wages expended on the servant are not returned, and no profit is generated. The stock in this case functions as a revenue, and the labor is unproductive.[3]

The exchange cycles in which productive and unproductive labor are involved are thus quite distinct. The capitalist advances a wages fund to hire productive labor, who transform the raw material inputs into a finished product owned by the capitalist and sold at a price sufficient to cover the costs of labor and raw materials and to provide a profit. The value of the stock advanced to the workers is restored to their employer, who can use the receipts to rehire the workmen. On the

---

[3] This principle has given rise to a wide range of interpretation. According to Marx, the labor of productive workers is exchanged against capital, whereas that of unproductive workers is exchanged against revenue. As stated in *Theories of Surplus Value*, Part I, 1963, p. 157, "The former's labour produces a surplus-value; in the latter's revenue is consumed." According to Eric Roll (1956, p. 168), productive labor is defined as that which creates both value and a surplus for the employer. Hla Myint (1962, p. 73) argues that productive labor reproduces itself by putting into motion an additional quantity of productive labor. These three interpretations are relatively consistent. Mark Blaug (1968, p. 50), on the other hand, argues that the distinction boils down to one between "activity that results in capital accumulation and activity that services the needs of households." Smith (1937) argues that productive labor will generate a profit, but this profit need not necessarily be accumulated. Moreover, government workers are unproductive by this principle but fall in neither of Blaug's two categories. Blaug has failed to distinguish between this principle and Smith's second principle (see the text). Schumpeter (1937) proposes an interpretation compatible with Marx's but claims that the creation of a profit and the sale of the product constitute two "inconsistent" theories of productive and unproductive labor: "Productive labourers reproduce the value of the capital that employs them with a profit; unproductively employed labourers either sell their services or else produce something that does not yield profit. From another cognate standpoint the distinction is between labour that does and labour that does not produce something that must be sold in order to complete the transaction: when a personal servant has sold his services to his employer and has received payment *out of the latter's income*, there is no further step in the process; if the same man secures employment in a shoe factory he is paid out of capital and the process in which his work is an element is not completed until the shoes have found a buyer" (p. 192n). Yet, the whole point of Smith's analysis is that a profit is not realized until the product is sold, and the sale of the product and the generation of a surplus are both moments in the reproduction of capital.

other hand, the money advanced to the servant is not restored by his activity, and the relation between employer and servant cannot be internally self-reproduced. That is why a person can grow "poor by maintaining a multitude of menial servants." For the servant to maintain his employment, the employer must continue to earn elsewhere. In this context, therefore, production is equivalent to the self-reproduction of capital.

But to say that this principle is equivalent to the reproduction of capital may be overstating the case and reading too much into Smith. What Smith seemingly had in mind was the circulation of exchange value that characterized capitalist production. The value (exchange value) advanced by the capitalist is retrieved by him by the sale of the product. But this is not all: The value is not only restored but also expanded. (For why else would the capitalist put forward an advance?) Thus, Chapter 3 of Book II is entitled "Of the accumulation of capital or of productive and unproductive labour." Not only is the preservation of exchange value a necessary condition for production but so also is the self-expansion of the capital. Here we notice, as in Quesnay, the creation of a surplus built into the definition of production. Whereas for Quesnay the surplus arose from outside the social system – that is, from the bountifulness of nature and the properties of natural regeneration – for Smith the surplus is a property of the social character of capital. Expansion is not an act of nature but a characteristic of the capitalist relations themselves. Yet, this idea is only in embryonic form in *The Wealth of Nations*, and Smith was perhaps not even aware of the tremendous conceptual breakthrough he forged. Almost 100 years were to pass before this analysis, begun by Smith, was completed by Marx. It was Marx who analyzed capital as self-expanding value, who equated production with the generation of surplus value, and who traced the complex pattern of reproduction that this gave rise to, including the intervention of money, and uncovered many of the pitfalls and shortfalls of the process and the eddies in which the circuit of capital could become lost.

The second principle of productive labor develops as a derivative of the first in the same chapter:

But the labour of the manufacturer fixes and realizes itself in some particular subject or vendible commodity, which lasts for some time at least after that labour is past. It is, as it were, a certain quantity of labour stocked and stored up to be employed, if necessary, upon some other occasion. That subject, or what is the same thing, the price of that subject, can afterwards, if necessary, put into motion a quantity of labour equal to that which had originally produced it. The labour of the menial servant, on the contrary, does not fix or realize itself in any particular subject or vendible commodity. His services generally perish in the very instant of their performance, and seldom leave any trace or value behind them, for which an equal quantity of service could afterwards be procured. (pp. 314–15)

This principle reduces to a distinction between goods and services, which, in turn, are differentiated on two grounds. First, goods are durable and last over time, whereas services are not reexchangeable for goods or labor. The menial servant, "the sovereign with all the officers both of justice and law under him and the whole army and navy," and "churchmen, lawyers, physicians, men of letters of all kinds, players, buffoons, musicians, opera-singers, opera-dancers, etc." are all unproductive workers (p. 315). Their common characteristic is that "like the declamation of the actor, the harangue of the orator, or the tune of the musician, the work of all of them perishes in the very instant of its production" (p. 315). Second, a good can "put into motion a quantity of labour equal to that which originally produced it." It can be reused in production or exchanged for labor or some other commodity. Services, on the other hand, are not reexchangeable and "seldom leave any trace or value behind them, for which an equal quantity of service could afterwards be procured."

This principle is likewise based on differences in circulation patterns. Goods continue to circulate after they are produced. The original buyer may use the good for a while and resell it. The good may pass through a chain of owners before it wears out or is no longer of use. Goods retain their exchangeability and the effort of their producers is, in this sense, not wasted. Services, on the other hand, do not circulate after their original performance. A meal cannot be reeaten or a play (at least, a particular performance) reseen. Services lose their exchangeability and cannot command additional labor. The effort put forward by their producers, in this sense, disappears, and they are considered unproductive. Production, from this viewpoint, is equivalent to exchangeability and thus the ability to command future labor.

The difference between the second and first principles may be illustrated by a few examples. First, a cook employed in a restaurant would be productive by the first principle and unproductive by the second. Second, dancers and singers hired by a profit-making theater company would likewise be productive by the first principle and unproductive by the second. Third, a clothes maker, in the private employ of a patron, would be unproductive by the first and productive by the second. Fourth, road-building activities of the government would be unproductive by the first and productive by the second.

The difference between the two principles is founded in the dual nature of the commodity, as fusion of use value and exchange value. The former expresses the usefulness or utility of a good, the latter that it is embodied labor and can therefore command other labor in exchange. By promulgating, though unintentionally, two distinct principles of productive labor, Smith effectively ruptured the dialectical relation between use value and exchange value. The circulation of exchange value leads to a consideration of the mechanism by which the capitalist recoups his advance of wages and material; the circulation of use value leads to a consideration of the physical properties of the commodity output. The dialectical tension between use and exchange values that will stand at the heart of Marx's *Capital*, permeating his entire analysis from the development of the categories of capitalism to the causes and forms of crises, is severed by Smith in this passage. A consideration of exchange value tends to one principle of production, a consideration of use value to another.

There is also a notion of reproduction embedded in the second principle, but it is not the reproduction of the conditions of production but that of the conditions of circulation. In fact, the reproducibility of goods is immaterial. Goods may appear from any source or in any fashion, be it homemade, imported, factory produced, or simply found. As soon as they enter circulation, they become items to barter, and the more durable they are, the longer they circulate. The principle of production in this case is, ironically enough, circulation proper, and production is subsumed under circulation.

3.   Capital and reproduction

In contradistinction to Smith, whose first principle of productive labor emerged from an analysis of the circuit of an individual unit of capital, Marx argued that "the metamorphosis of the individual capital, its turnover, is a link in the circuit described by social capital" (p. 352).[4] Moreover, "the circuits of the individual capitals intertwine, presuppose and necessitate one another, and form, precisely in this interlacing, the movement of the total social capital" (p. 353). The possibility of an individual capitalist to retrieve his initial advance of capital and to plough it back for further production presupposes that other capitalists recoup their advance and use it for new production. The reproduction of any unit of capital thus depends on the circulation of the aggregate social capital. And it is just this circuit of the total capital

---

[4] Page references in this section refer to Karl Marx, *Capital*, vol. 2, International Publishers, 1967 edition.

that is the reproduction of capital and hence the reproduction of the capitalist economy.

The process of reproduction is "the replacement of the *value* as well as the *substance* of the individual components of C', the total product" (p. 393, emphasis added). In general, the reproduction of any economy must preserve both the social relations of production and the forces of production. In capitalism, the social relation between capitalist and labor leads to commodity production, where a commodity is a fusion of use value and value (that is, exchange value).[5] The forces of production take the form of the concrete means of production and the composition of labor power. Therefore, reproduction must guarantee the preservation of the material elements of production, including labor power, and that of the capitalist and labor classes, which takes the form of the restoration of the value of capital.

Part III of volume 2 of *Capital* details the reproduction requirements of capitalism. The first is the preservation of labor power. This is necessary because labor power is an essential ingredient in the production process. Labor must therefore be assured of the requisite necessities of life (as socially determined). Since there is a division of labor in capitalist production, with different units of capital producing different commodities, a worker must normally exchange with capitalists other than the one who employs him to obtain the necessary subsistence goods. Therefore, labor is normally paid in money wages, and "by spending his wages and consuming the purchased commodities, the labourer as a buyer of commodities maintains and reproduces his labour-power" (p. 446). The second is the maintenance of the capitalist class. This, too, takes the form of individual consumption. But whereas the worker consumes out of money wages, the capitalist consumes out of the surplus value generated in production. Thus, "the movement of that portion of the social commodity-product which is consumed by the labourer in expending his wages, and by the capitalist in expending his surplus-value . . . forms an integral part of the movement of the total product" (p. 393).

The third is the reproduction of constant capital. Constant capital consists of the means of production required for production – raw

---

[5] Production in all economies takes the form of use values. The peculiar characteristic of capitalism is the existence of a class of "free" labor who own no means of production but are dependent on the capitalist class who own the means of production. The interchangeability of labor and its ability to work in different sectors gives labor its "abstract" character. The fact that labor is involved in all production in capitalism gives commodities the character as embodiment of abstract labor. Finally, the fact that commodities must be exchanged under capitalism makes labor both the measure and substance of exchange value (see *Capital*, vol. 1, pp. 35–46).

materials, intermediate goods, machinery, and plant. Since an enterprise will rarely produce all its requisite inputs, exchanges of capital goods will normally occur between units of capital. In the case of circulating capital (raw materials and intermediate goods), a constant supply must be on hand for production to occur. In the case of fixed capital (plant and equipment), capitalists must accumulate a sinking or depreciation fund. When the fixed capital wears out (or becomes obsolete), new equipment must be available for replacement.

The fourth requirement is the maintenance and expansion of the value advanced as capital. The value advanced by capitalists must not only be embodied in a commodity for sale but must also be realized (retrieved) by the exchange of the product. The completion of the circuit of capital restores the capitalist's ownership of capital and thus the reproduction of the capitalist's social role as owner of capital. Moreover, the circuit of capital allows the resumption of production and, in particular, the renewed purchase of labor power. The circuit thus restores the capitalist's function as employer of labor and labor's function as employee of the capitalist. Furthermore, not only must the value advanced in production be realized in the sale of the product but the surplus value generated in production must also be realized. This restores the capitalist's role as appropriator of surplus value and makes possible his additional function as accumulator of capital.

Marx's two-department scheme of Chapters 20 and 21 of volume 2 illustrates the process of capitalist reproduction as a whole, much the same way as Quesnay's *Tableau Economique* did for the agrarian economy. Department I consists of producers of means of production and department II of producers of articles of consumption. The sales among the capitalists of department I and those of department I to those of II show how the constant capital in material form is restored each year to the individual capitalist. The sale of consumption goods produced in department I to the workers and capitalists in each of the departments accounts for the maintenance of working and capitalist classes. Moreover, the value advanced in each of the departments may be divided into a constant and variable component and the value produced in each into a constant, variable, and surplus component. The exchange between capitalists in the two departments and between workers in both departments and capitalists in department II illustrates how the value advanced by an individual capitalist is retrieved together with a surplus portion. Reproduction for Marx, as for Quesnay, is an aggregate phenomenon. The reproduction of individual units is subservient to and dependent on the reproduction of the whole.

Marx's principle of productive labor is a logical correlate of his analysis of capitalist reproduction.[6] The principle is rather simple: Productive labor is involved in commodity production, whereas unproductive labor is not. The implications, however, are rather complex. As for Smith, a commodity has both a use value and an exchange value. The former refers to the material properties of an item or action that make it desired for consumption. The latter refers to the item's ability to exchange against an item, or money, representing a similar exchange value. The value (exchange value) of a good or service is proportional to the amount of labor, both present and past, required for its production. Commodities are produced for exchange (except where they can be used directly in production, as seed in farming), though they might not necessarily be sold, as, for example, in times of glut.

This principle leads to two major divisions of activities. The first falls between production proper and circulation. Both are part of the reproduction cycle and necessary to it. But unlike production, where commodities are produced, circulation activities are necessary for the exchange of commodities or their transfer of ownership but themselves produce no use value. Circulation activities are therefore unproductive. Under "costs of circulation," Marx includes services like merchandising, bookkeeping, storage, money and credit, and the like (pp. 129–52). Wholesaling and retailing, though necessary for the realization of the exchange value contained in commodities, does not itself create a use value or modify an existing one and hence does not produce a commodity. Transportation, on the other hand, does modify the use value of a commodity by changing its location and is therefore productive. Guards and protection services, though they may be required to prevent pilfering, do not alter the use value of a good and are hence unproductive. Banking, finance, insurance, and credit operations, though greasing the wheels of circulation, do not themselves create a use value. Communications – that is, the transmission of messages – on the other hand, are productive since they alter a use value by changing the spatial location of information. This distinction follows directly from the reproduction schemes. For production to be renewed, the commodities produced must be distributed where needed: raw materials, intermediate goods, and plant and equipment to producing units and articles of consumption to workers and capitalists. The circulation process is even more complex, involving the mediation of money and credit instruments and sometimes a chain of exchanges before a commodity reaches its final destination. Circulation, however, is not an end in itself but only a means to ensure continual production and the

---

[6] Marx's discussion of productive labor precedes that of reproduction in volume 2. For heuristic reasons, the argument is presented in reverse.

subsistence of labor and capitalist. It "performs a necessary function, because the process of reproduction includes unproductive functions" (p. 131).

The second split occurs between production proper and production for immediate use. This division is very similar to that formed from Smith's second principle and develops from Marx's critique of the inconsistencies in Smith's theory of productive labor.[7] Household servants, for example, though wage labor, like manufacturing workers, produce a service that is directly consumed by their employer. They produce a use value but no exchange value, since their product is not exchanged, and are therefore unproductive. All household labor time, whether paid or unpaid, would in fact fall into this category. Though chores like cooking, washing, cleaning, and child rearing are essential to the maintenance of the labor force, they are not exchanged and embody no value. This second distinction is also a logical consequence of the reproduction schemes. Reproduction requires a continuous production and circulation of commodities to restore the conditions of production. Payments to servants and food and subsistence goods shared within a family are leakages from the reproduction process. They are transfers outside the scheme and are not internally self-reproduced. These transfers can be replenished only by the continued appropriation of surplus value by capitalist or the continued receipt of wages by productive labor.

The dialectical tension between use value and exchange value severed by Smith in his first and second principles is restored in Marx's principle of productive labor. It is the reproduction of the commodity as concatenation of use and exchange values that defines productive labor and that stands at the heart of the reproduction of the system as a whole. From this dialectical relation, Marx constructs the whole complex of material and social reproduction for the capitalist mode of production in much the same way as Quesnay did for his fabricated agrarian mode. Whereas for Quesnay the reproduction cycle was based ultimately on natural reproduction, for Marx it was ultimately based on the social relations of capitalist production. Whereas for Quesnay the surplus generated in reproduction emanated from natural regeneration, for Marx it resided in the capitalist's exploitation of labor.

4.   Unproductive labor and advanced capitalism

As noted in Chapter 1, Baran and Sweezy did not attempt a systematic development of the category of unproductive activity in modern cap-

---

[7] See *Theories of Surplus Value*, Part I, pp. 152–74.

italist society. They were, however, very acute in noting the major structural changes that had occurred in capitalist economies since Marx's time. Of particular relevance for their thesis were the domination of the private economy by huge, oligopolistic corporations and the tremendous growth in government. The development of oligopolistic industries resulted in large increases in the share of costs devoted to sales, marketing, and related circulation expenses, whereas the growth of government resulted in an increasing share of GNP that was absorbed by the state.

In *Monopoly Capital*, Baran and Sweezy noted that Marx included in his catalog of unproductive expenses the wages paid to public officials, the clergy, and domestic servants as well as the costs of circulation (p. 112). In their treatment of the absorption of the surplus, both government spending and circulation expenses are included. Yet it seems that only circulation costs are treated as unproductive costs. In regard to government spending, they did argue that the state makes a "direct contribution to the functioning and welfare of society" (p. 152). Such expenditures include those in public education, roads and highways, health and sanitation, recreation, and housing. Whether such "useful" government programs constitute unproductive spending remained ambiguous.

In defense of Baran and Sweezy, it should be noted that their primary interest was in the formation of effective demand, so that whether government spending was unproductive or not was not directly germane to their argument. However, for our purposes, this issue is crucial since the effects of unproductive activity on capital accumulation and societal welfare are of primary concern.

There is little consensus among Marxian economists on the proper definition of productive and unproductive labor. Part of the problem lies in the fact that Marx himself proposed two conflicting principles in his own work, as noted above. One principle, which emerges in *The Theories of Surplus Value*, is that productive activity is identical with capitalist production. Therefore, household servants and most government activity would be unproductive since no commodity is exchanged on the market. A second principle, which emerges in volume 2 of *Capital*, is that within capitalist production, activities that produce use values are productive whereas those involved in "circulating" those use values are unproductive. Thus, food production is productive, but cereal advertising is unproductive. That there is a conflict between these two principles should be apparent. There are many government activities that provide use values, such as garbage collection, and there are many circulation activities that involve capitalist relations of production, like an advertising firm. Most of the subsequent interpretations of productive and unproductive labor stem from one or the other of these alternative avenues. [See Hunt (1979) for a good review of the controversy. Also see Gilman (1957), Baran (1957), Mage (1963), Becker (1971), Gough (1972), Harrison (1973), Bullock (1973), and O'Connor (1975) for particular interpretations.]

It is not proposed here to develop the definitive principle of unproducive labor but rather to provide a definition that is consistent with the objectives of this work. I shall therefore adopt Marx's second principle that the expenses of circulation are unproductive, where circulation is understood to refer to the selling of goods and services and the transferring of titles to and claims on productive output. Productive activity creates both use value and exchange value and hence commodities. Unproductive activity affects the disposition of commodities but creates neither use value nor exchange value. Productive labor creates surplus value; unproductive labor absorbs surplus value:

The general law is that *all expenses of circulation, which arise only from changes of form, do not add any value, to the commodities.* They are merely expenses required for the realization of value, or its conversion from one form into another. The capital invested in those expenses (including the labor employed by it) belongs to the dead expenses of capitalist production. They must be made up out of the surplus product and are, from the point of view of the entire capitalist class, a deduction from the surplus value or surplus product. (*Capital*, vol. 2, p. 149)

The apparent problem with this principle is the classification of government expenditures. Many government activities, of course, do not produce use values and can be construed as expenses of circulation. These include most of general government activity, what is concerned with establishing procedures to determine rightful claims, such as general legislation and the court system, and police and defense, which help to preserve the system of property rights. These activities are unproductive by Marx's first and second principles. Yet certain governmental activities, such as education, health, water and sewer services, garbage collection, and fire protection, provide direct use values to identifiable recipients. Yet, on the surface at least, it appears that these services are not commodities since they are not exchanged on the market.

However, further reflection suggests that it is not the form of *ownership* that is material but rather the form of reproduction. First, there are many nationalized industries, particularly in Western Europe, that behave like privately owned companies in almost all respects. They both sell their output on the market and undergo expanded reproduction over time. The mere fact of government ownership should not hide the fact that both exchange and surplus values are generated. Second, many "public" services provided by government in the United States are sold on the basis of use. These include local transit systems, publicly owned utilities, the federal post office (now a quasi-government agency), and many highway systems. These also undergo expanded reproduction over time, like comparable private companies. Third, other government services, such as public education, that are not paid directly on the basis of use are nonetheless paid in the form of taxes. Indeed, government reproduces itself over time by collecting taxes in exchange for providing such services. It is true that these services do not have a market price. Yet, here too, there are many private, profit-making companies that sell comparable services on the market, such as privately owned carting services, protection services, and even educational services. The mere fact that these government services are paid indirectly through taxes rather than directly through market exchanges should not disguise their fundamental similarity to comparable, privately provided services. As a result, government services that provide identifiable use values should be treated as productive, just like their privately owned counterparts.

Nonprofit institutions should be treated in similar fashion and categorized on the basis of function. Nonprofit hospitals, for example, are almost indistinguishable in behavior and function from profit-making hospitals. Private, nonprofit educational institutions behave in almost identical fashion to profit-making educational institutions and to public institutions. Here, too, differences in organizational form should not hide fundamental similarities in the process of (expanded) reproduction.

The classification of self-employed persons presents another kind of difficulty. Self-employed activities are precapitalist forms of activity since there is no capital–labor relation in the production unit. Yet, the output of, for example, a self-employed farmer is normally sold on the market and the exchange value realized. The crucial issue is whether surplus value is generated in production. In principle, one could separate out the revenue received by the self-employed person into a wage component (a payment for labor power) and a return on the advanced capital. Moreover, in a perfectly competitive economy, the wage portion and rate-of-profit portion must be equal to that obtained in capitalist production (for, otherwise, capital will shift toward or away from the self-employed sector). Moreover, if a self-employed person sells his or her capital to a capitalist but continues to work as before, the material conditions of production will be unaltered, though the *dis-*

position of the surplus may alter. Here, again, differences in the form of ownership should not be relevant in classifying unproductive activity but rather the nature of the output.

The final problem is caused by domestic servants. Though domestic workers are labor, there is no corresponding capitalist class. Moreover, though use value is created, no exchange value is produced since the services are not directly sold on the market. This case falls squarely in the middle since productive activity produces both exchange value and use value and unproductive activity produces neither. For a solution, it is again possible to rely on the principle of comparability. There are, for example, capitalist firms that sell cleaning and catering services directly to households. Their output would be classified as productive. If domestic servants were to be employed by a capitalist firm instead of directly by a homeowner, the material conditions of production would remain unaltered. The only change would be in the circuit of exchange, whereby the homeowner would pay the capitalist firm, which would, in turn, pay the domestic workers.[8] By the logic of this argument, domestic servants should be classified as productive workers.[9]

It is necessary to bear in mind the distinction between activities that are *productive* and those that are *necessary* to the functioning of modern capitalism. Circulation activities such as advertizing and sales promotion are by and large necessary in advanced capitalism. As Marx argued, it "performs a necessary function, because the process of reproduction includes unproductive functions" (*Capital*, vol. 2, p. 131). The reason is that capitalism is itself characterized by competition and

---

[8] There is a subtler issue that concerns the generation of surplus value. Domestic servants employed by a capitalist firm would, of course, generate surplus value, and the capitalist would receive a normal rate of return on the capital advanced. Moreover, the wage received by the domestic servant would be, in competitive equilibrium, unchanged by the switch in employer. The major difference is that the homeowner is now paying more for the domestic servants, and this increment is the profit that the capitalist firm is charging on the capital advanced. Yet, this is not the full story since part of the homeowner's exchange value that was formerly locked up in the form of wage advances, vacuum cleaners, and the like when he directly employed the domestic servants is now freed up and available for investment in the financial capital markets. In perfectly competitive equilibrium, there is no net gain or loss by the homeowner by the change in employer.

[9] There is an opposite argument that is sometimes made that if domestic servants are considered (productive) labor, unpaid housework performed by family members should also be considered production. Some national accountants, for example, propose that household work activity such as cleaning and cooking be added to the measure of national welfare [see, for example, Kendrick (1976), Eisner (1978), and Adler and Hawrlyshyn (1978)]. However, for the purposes here, this argument can be dismissed since unpaid family members are not labor, and the housework they do is not a labor activity.

a lack of social planning, which makes the sale of commodities difficult for the individual producer. Indeed, one of the major problems facing most producers is how to dispose of the vast quantity of output they can produce. To the individual capitalist, then, sales and other circulating expenses are necessary for continued reproduction. On the social level, they are unproductive expenses since they do not materially add to the product. Police are also necessary in a society characterized by great inequality, poverty, and social injustice. They too create no use value. The same is true of defense expenditures, which for the United States are necessitated in large measure by a need to protect American business interests abroad. It too may be seen as a necessary expense of maintaining and expanding American capital overseas but certainly not as a productive expenditure.[10]

B. Classification of unproductive labor by industry

The application of a definition of unproductive labor to the concrete economy is, perhaps, as difficult as its formulation. This is particularly true when it is necessary to work from a classification scheme that is used for national accounting or official employment statistics. In some cases, official categories combine productive with unproductive activities. Therefore, there is some degree of arbitrariness involved in classifying activities into productive and unproductive categories. However, generally speaking, when there is some ambiguity about the classification of an activity or when it contains both productive and unproductive elements, it has been placed in the productive category. In this manner, an attempt has been made to consistently understate the degree of unproductive activity in the economy.

The term *activity* must now be made operational. Labor activity can be classified in two directions: first, by the industry in which it takes place and, second, by the type of work performed or occupation of the worker. A *productive industry* or a *productive sector* will be defined

---

[10] A related line of reasoning was pursued by Hunt (1979). He argued that unproductive labor is "that labor which is necessary only because of the irrationalities (from a socialist, normative perspective) of the capitalist social structure" (p. 318). Thus, for example, advertising and sales promotion expenses would be unproductive in a capitalist economy since in a socialist economy with national planning the disposition of the output would not be subject to such uncertainty. The same is true of many forms of legal services, whose aim is to ensure that private contracts are obeyed. Though this principle leads to a similar classification of unproductive activities, it does suggest that there would be no unproductive labor in the ideal socialist state. This is not likely the case. Even in the best ordered society, some level of police and legal services would be required to enforce some form of property law, and this labor would still be unproductive.

as one whose *output* is productive. An *unproductive industry* or *sector* is one whose output performs a circulation function. All labor activity in unproductive sectors is unproductive since the product of the labor is unproductive. However, in most productive sectors, there are workers who perform unproductive labor activity. In the automobile industry, for example, there are accountants, lawyers, salesmen, and managers who are engaged in the process of circulation. This labor activity is also unproductive since the tasks performed are themselves part of the costs of circulation. *Productive labor* is therefore defined as workers employed in productive sectors who perform productive labor activity. *Unproductive labor* is defined as either workers who are employed in unproductive sectors or who perform unproductive labor activity.

The first categorization of labor is by sector of employment. The basic data source used in this work are 87-sector input–output tables for the United States. The standard Bureau of Economic Analysis classification scheme is followed (see the Appendix for a detailed list of sectors). The proposed classification scheme for productive and unproductive sectors is shown in Table 2.1. Agriculture (1–4), mining (5–10), construction (11–12), and manufacturing (13–64) all produce tangible use values and are therefore productive (sector numbers are shown in parentheses). Transportation (65) is generally productive since it creates a use value by altering a good's spatial relation to its purchaser (Marx, *Capital*, vol. 2, ch. 6). However, insofar as the transportation of goods is generated by the peculiar trade patterns arising in capitalism, including cross-shipping, it is unproductive. Likewise, warehousing (65) is productive insofar as it is part of the normal operation of moving goods (Marx, *Capital*, vol. 2, ch. 8). Insofar as it is necessitated by the uncertainties associated with the transfer of ownership (that is, realization) within a capitalist economy, it is unproductive. Since transportation and warehousing (65) are primarily productive in nature, the whole sector is classified as productive. Communications (66) is productive since the flow of information is a necessary ingredient in production and provides use value to consumers. Radio and television broadcasting (67), though paid for largely by advertizers, is also productive since it provides entertainment to households. Utilities (68) like water, sanitation, and power companies are productive.

Wholesale and retail trade (69) is a cost of circulation and is unproductive (Marx, *Capital*, vol. 3, ch. 17). The geographic movement and storage of goods is largely productive, but this is already captured in

Table 2.1. *Classification of productive and unproductive sectors*[a]

Productive	Unproductive[b]
Agriculture (1–4)	Wholesale and retail trade and rest of world (69, 85)
Mining (5–10)	Finance and insurance (70)
Construction (11–12)	Real estate rentals (71)
Manufacturing (13–64)	Business services (73)
Transportation and warehousing (65)	Government (84b)
Communications except broadcasting (66)	
Radio and television broadcasting (67)	
Utilities (68)	
Hotels, personal and repair services except automotive (72)	
Research and development (74)	
Automotive repairs (75)	
Amusements (76)[c]	
Medical and education services and nonprofit institutions (77)	
Federal government enterprises (78)	
State and local government enterprises (79)	
Allocated imports (80)	
Business travel (81)	
Office supplies (82)	
Scrap (83)	
Government (84a)	
Household industry (86)	

[a] Sector numbers from the standard Bureau of Economic Analysis 87-order input–output tables are shown in parentheses.
[b] Inventory valuation adjustment (87) is distributed proportionally to gross domestic output across sectors.
[c] Industry purchases of amusements are transferred to surplus final consumption.

sector 65. Moreover, some display of goods and transmittal of information to customers serve a useful function, but this is likely a very minor part of the role played by the trade sector in modern capitalism. The trade sector performs three main functions. First, trade workers try to sell their merchandise. In a capitalist economy, this function is particularly important because of the uncertainties and vagaries associated with the marketplace and competition. Second, they collect payments. In modern capitalism, this may involve credit and financing arrangements. Third, personnel in this sector also function as guards, preventing the merchandise from being stolen (imagine what would happen if stores had no sales people). Thus, the activities of the wholesale and retail trade sector are almost entirely costs of circulation.[11]

Financial, insurance, and real estate services (70, 71) are unproductive since they involve the transfer of titles to and claims on property. The hotel, personal, and repair service sectors (72, 75) have two components. The first is the output that is sold to final consumers, like households. This portion of the output is productive since it provides useful services to consumers. The second is the portion that is sold to firms (interindustry flow). Of this, repair services are productive expenses since they contribute directly to production. The remainder consists of hotel and personal service expenses. Though recorded as an interindustry flow in input–output accounting, these expenditures may in actuality be a hidden form of final consumption. These expense account items provide use value to the recipients and thus fall in the productive category. Properly speaking, however, these expenses should be recorded as part of surplus income (and the corresponding intermediate flow as part of final consumption).[12] Unfortunately, this adjustment is not possible for sector 72 since it contains both entertainment expenses and repair services.

The business service sector (73) includes advertizing, legal, and other professional services (except health). These are unproductive since they are involved with settling, establishing, or changing claims on goods and property.[13] Sector 74, research and development, though not contributing to current output, may lead to the more efficient pro-

---

[11] In input–output accounting in producer prices, wholesaling and retailing activities of all sectors are grouped into a single trade sector. The trade sector thus includes all workers involved in sales activities and all wages paid to sales workers, irrespective of their actual sector of employment. Thus, the earnings of a car salesman working for General Motors would be recorded in the value added of the trade sector. The actual markups on input costs in a producing sector are then recorded as a purchase made by the producing sector from the trade sector. This accounting technique is quite appropriate for the purpose here, since it is necessary to separate out the markups from the production costs.

[12] This is what the Internal Revenue Service would like to do in any case. Becker (1977) took another approach to the issue of unproductive activity, which he equates with consumption out of the surplus. Thus, restaurant expenses of the capitalist class would be unproductive since they are ultimately paid for our of surplus income. Likewise, Rolls Royce and Cadillac production would be unproductive. In my classification scheme, restaurant services are productive – use values are created and literally consumed – even though they are paid for out of the surplus. The same would be true of Rolls Royce and Cadillac production.

[13] Lawyers work in other areas of the law besides contract, real estate, and tax law. However, many of these other areas, such as criminal, divorce, and even civil rights law, are ultimately concerned with the disposition of real property or the maintenance of a set of rules to protect and secure ownership.

duction of use values or to improved use values. This activity is therefore productive. The amusements sector (76), like hotel and personal services, has two components. The first is the portion that is sold directly to households. This provides use values and is thus productive activity. The second is the portion purchased directly by firms. This portion also provides use values to individuals and is hence productive. However, as with interindustry flows of hotel and personal services, these expenses should be treated as final consumption. This adjustment was made by including such expenses as part of surplus consumption since such expense account items are a form of extra income to managers and executives. Firm purchases of amusements will correspondingly be treated as part of the firm's profit.[14]

Medical and educational services (77) are also purchased by both firms and households. Medical services and, in the main, educational services are use values and are therefore productive activities. Medical services provide a direct use value to their recipient. Educational services, particularly those purchased by the firm, can improve worker efficiency and productivity and are therefore productive. Another portion of educational services, that purchased directly by households and state and local governments, can be viewed as providing consumption benefits.[15] Therefore, sector 77 is classified as productive.[16]

Federal and state and local government enterprises (78, 79) include such activities as the post office, local utilities, and local transit systems, which sell services directly to the public. Since their activities produce use values, these two sectors are classified as productive. Noncompetitive imports (80) consist of items imported but not produced in the United States, such as rubber. This is classified as productive since most of the imports are raw materials or manufactured goods. Business travel (81) is productive insofar as it is required for the coordination of production (see *Capital*, vol. 3, ch. 23), but insofar as it is related to sales, is it unproductive. Since it is difficult to separate the two components, the sector is classified productive. Office supplies

---

[14] Part of these expenses may be incurred by salesmen and other workers. This portion would be treated as part of employee compensation rather than as surplus income. I am guessing that this portion is small relative to executive expense accounts.

[15] The educational system also serves to maintain and transmit the dominant social and political ideology. This function is unproductive since it is aimed at justifying and securing existing property relations and ownership. Since it is difficult to separate the two components, education will be treated as productive.

[16] There is a third component to sector 77 – nonprofit institutions. Since they perform a myriad of functions – some productive, like education and medical research, and some unproductive, like sheltering income from taxes – this sector will also be treated as a productive activity.

(82) and scrap (83) provide material inputs into the production process and are therefore productive sectors.

The government sector performs a variety of functions, some productive and some unproductive. In the input–output tables, there are both an endogenous government sector (84), which consists of wages and salaries paid to government workers, and two government expenditure columns, one for the federal government and the other for state and local governments, in final demand. The government expenditure columns in final demand record both the direct purchases of goods and services from the private sectors and the employment of labor, the latter as a purchase from the endogenous government sector. It was first necessary to combine the government purchases of goods and services with government wages and salaries, thereby creating an endogenous federal government sector and an endogenous state and local government sector. Government final demand was then recorded as a purchase from each of these two endogenous government sectors.

Each of these two endogenous sectors was then split into productive and unproductive components by analyzing the distribution of government expenditures by function. The functional breakdown and the classification of each function is shown in Table 2.2.[17] The federal government functions are categorized as productive, unproductive, or transfer. Since approximately half of federal government outlays were transfers in the postwar period, the next step was to determine which activities or what proportions of each activity were simply transfer payments to individuals, state and local governments, or foreign governments. Education, health, income security, veterans' benefits, revenue sharing, interest payments, and undistributed receipts are all transfers. Defense, law enforcement and justice, and general government expenditures all consist of purchases of goods and services. The remaining activities are composed of both direct purchases and transfers. For international affairs, it was possible to obtain the proportion between the two by dividing the activity into a foreign aid component and a residual. (For 1967, the benchmark year that is used, the figure was 47 percent transfer payments.) The remaining five functions were split between purchases of goods and services and transfers by computing the percentage figure such that the resulting sum of purchases of goods and services across all federal functions equaled the National Income and Product Accounts total for 1967. The figure was 48 percent transfer payments.

[17] The breakdown of federal government outlays by function is given in the *Economic Report of the President, 1979*, Table B-70, p. 264.

Table 2.2. *Classification of government expenditures into productive and unproductive components*

Government expenditures	Classification[a]
A. Federal[b]	
1. Defense	U
2. International affairs	U (0.53, T (0.47)
3. General science, space, and technology	P (0.52), T (0.48)
4. Natural resources, environment, and energy	P (0.52), T (0.48)
5. Agriculture and rural development	P (0.52), T (0.48)
6. Commerce and transportation	P (0.52), T (0.48)
7. Community and regional development	P (0.52), T (0.48)
8. Education, training, employment, and social services	T
9. Health	T
10. Income security	T
11. Veterans' benefits and services	T
12. Law enforcement and justice	U
13. General government	U
14. Revenue sharing	T
15. Interest payments	T
16. Undistributed offsetting receipts	T
B. State and local[c]	
1. Education	P
2. Health and hospitals	P
3. Sewerage and sanitation	P
4. Welfare	U
5. Police and corrections	U
6. Fire protection	P
7. General government	U
8. Highways	P
9. Natural resources	P
10. Recreation	P
11. Water and air transportation	P
12. Housing and community development	P
13. Public utilities	P
14. Other commercial activity	P

[a] Abbreviations: P, productive activity; U, unproductive activity; T, transfer. Numbers in parentheses indicate percentage breakdown based on 1967 data.
[b] Source for classification: *Economic Report of the President, 1976*, Table B-64, p. 246.
[c] Source for classification: P. Ritz, "New construction and state and local government purchases in the 1967 input–output study," *Survey of Current Business*, Vol. 57, No. 1 (November 1977), 19–27.

Those federal government activities that consist of purchases of goods and services are then classified into a productive or unproductive category. The same criteria are used as for the private sector. Those that provide directly usable services are classified as productive, and those whose main purpose is to secure, maintain, protect, or alter either existing property rights or the rules for determining property rights are classified as unproductive. Thus, defense,[18] international affairs, law enforcement and justice, and general government are all placed in the unproductive category. The remaining activities all provide recognizable use values and are put in the productive category. For state and local government expenditures, only a minute portion consisted of transfers, and these were ignored. Since state and local governments tend to provide directly usable services, most of the activities are classified as productive. The exceptions are welfare expenses, police and corrections, and general government.[19]

Table 2.3 shows unproductive expenditures as a percentage of total government expenditures on goods and services for each of six years. For both the federal and the state and local governments, the proportions were fairly stable over the postwar period. The ratio was much larger for the federal government than for state and local governments because of the very large defense component in the federal budget. (Indeed, in 1967, 80 percent of federal government expenditures on goods and services went to defense.) The major component of state and local government unproductive expenses is so-called general government expenditures. Both the federal component and the state and local component of the government sector (84) were split according to the proportions in Table 2.3 to form a productive government sector (84a) and an unproductive government sector (84b).[20]

The remaining sectors in the input–output table are classified in the following way. The rest-of-the-world sector (85) is a dummy sector consisting of the value added generated in import and export trade. It is classified as unproductive for the same reasons as wholesale and retail trade. Household industry (86) is a dummy sector consisting entirely of wages paid to domestic help. As argued in Section A.1, this

---

[18] Defense spending does yield some productive output in the form of research spin-offs that result in commercially viable applications. Since these expense are likely to be a trivial proportion of total defense spending, they are ignored.

[19] Fire protection is classified as productive even though part of its work is aimed at detecting and eliminating arson.

[20] The value added and employment in sector 84 were first split between the federal government and the state and local government components of final demand according to the relative magnitudes of the purchases of these final-demand components from the original government industry (84).

Table 2.3. *Unproductive expenditures as a percentage of total government expenditures on goods and services*[a]

Year	Federal (%)	State and local[b] (%)
1947	78.8	20.7
1958	94.1	22.0
1963	88.5	22.4
1967	85.8	20.1
1972	84.3	24.5
1976	76.5	26.0

[a] The 1963 data were computed based on the breakdown in federal government activities shown in Table 2.2. Data sources: *Economic Report of the President, 1972*, Table B-64, p. 270, and *Economic Report of the President, 1976*, Table B-67, p. 250. The 1967 and 1972 figures were also based on the Table 2.2 breakdown; the data source was *Economic Report of the President, 1976*, Tables B-64 and B-67. Likewise, the 1976 figures were based on the Table 2.2 breakdown; the data source was *Economic Report of the President, 1979*, Table B-70, p. 264, and Table B-73, p. 268. The breakdown between transfers and expenditures on goods and services was computed for 1967, as shown in Table 2.2, and used for 1963, 1972, and 1976 in addition. For the 1947 and 1958 calculations, the only data available for the composition of federal expenditures were between defense and all other activities, as shown in *Economic Report of the President, 1976*, Table B-1, p. 171. The ratio of unproductive to total expenditures in non-defense federal activities was computed for 1963, 1967, and 1972, and the mean ratio of these three years was used to make the estimates for 1947 and 1958.

[b] The calculation for 1967 was based on the breakdown shown in Table 2.2. For the other five years, the breakdown of total state and local government expenditures between education, highways, and others was used (*Economic Report of the President, 1979*, Table B-75, p. 270) and adjusted using the 1967 ratios of unproductive to total expenditures in each of these three areas.

sector is productive since a useful service is performed.[21] The last sector (87) is equal to the change in the value of inventories held by firms. This change is equivalent to capital gains (or losses) and is therefore a form of surplus income. It is therefore distributed into the property income component of value added across sectors in proportion to gross domestic output.[22]

C.   Classification of unproductive labor by occupation

In the previous section, labor activity is classified as unproductive if the sector in which it was undertaken is unproductive. Yet, as noted above, within many industries that produce productive output, a sizable share of the labor force generates neither value nor surplus value. These employees are involved in circulation activities, such as sales, advertising, public relations, bookkeeping, tax accounting, billing, legal work, management, and administration. Workers employed in productive sectors who are involved in the circulation process are also unproductive.

In order to divide the labor force employed in productive sectors into a productive and unproductive component, it is first necessary to decide which occupations fall into each of the two categories. As with the sectoral classification, a certain degree of arbitrariness is involved in constructing such a classification scheme. However, as with the sector classification scheme, if a category is ambiguous, it is classified in the productive category. This procedure will also lead to an understatement of the extent of unproductive activity.

The categorization is based on the occupational classification schemes provided in the 1950, 1960, 1970, and 1980 U.S. censuses of population. The occupational classifications changed considerably over this 30-year period. However, it is possible to identify almost the same set of unproductive occupations in each of the years. (Most of the changes in classification occurred within the productive set of occupations.) It is also possible to reorganize the occupational schemes of each year to make them largely compatible.

The categorization is shown in Table 2.4. Among professionals, accountants and lawyers are classified as unproductive since their labor activity is primarily devoted to maintaining or changing entitlements

---

[21] This is different from the earlier classification scheme I had proposed [see Wolff (1977a)].

[22] Ideally, it should be distributed across sectors in proportion to the change in the average price of the inventories held by each sector multiplied by the value of the inventories.

Table 2.4. *Classification of productive and unproductive occupations*

Productive	Unproductive
1. Professional and technical (selected)	1. Professional and technical (selected)
a. Architects	a. Accountants and auditors
b. Computer specialists	b. Lawyers and judges
c. Engineers	c. College deans and presidents
d. Farm management advisors	d. Personnel and labor relations workers
e. Foresters and conservationists	e. Religious workers
f. Home management advisors	f. Vocational counselors
g. Librarians, archivists, and curators	g. Public relations personnel and publicity writers
h. Mathematical specialists	
i. Life and physical scientists	
j. Physicians, dentists, nurses, health specialists, and health technicians	
k. Social scientists	
l. Social and recreation workers	
m. Teachers	
n. Engineering, science, and other technicians	
o. Writers, artists, athletes, and entertainers	
p. All other professional, technical, and kindred workers (except unproductive)	
2. Clerical (selected)	2. Clerical (selected)
a. Vehicle dispatchers and starters	a. Bank tellers
b. Expediters and production controllers	b. Billing clerks
c. Library attendants and assistants	c. Bookkeepers
d. Mail carriers and handlers	d. Cashiers
e. Office machine operators (except bookkeeping and billing machine operators)	e. Bill and account collectors
f. Proofreaders	f. Counter clerks
g. Medical secretaries	g. File clerks
h. Statistical clerks	h. Insurance adjusters, examiners, and investigators
i. Teacher aides	i. Messengers and office boys
j. Telegraph and telephone operators	j. Meter readers
	k. Bookkeeping and billing machine operators
	l. Payroll and timekeeping clerks
	m. Postal clerks
	n. Real estate appraisers
	o. Receptionists, secretaries (except medical), stenographers, and typists

(*continued*)

Table 2.4. *(cont.)*

Productive	Unproductive
	p. Shipping and receiving clerks
	q. Stock clerks and storekeepers
	r. Ticket, station, and express agents
	s. Weighers
	t. All other clerical workers (except productive)
3. Craftsmen and kindred workers (all)	3. Managers and administrators except farm
4. Operatives (all)	4. Sales workers (all)
5. Service workers, including firemen and excluding all other protective service workers	5. Protective service workers
	a. Guards and watchmen
6. Nonfarm laborers (all)	b. Marshals and constables
7. Farmers and farm managers (all)	c. Policemen, detectives, sheriffs, and bailiffs
8. Farm laborers and farm foremen (all)	

to property and income. College deans and presidents are administrative workers and therefore unproductive. (In the 1980 census, they were reclassified as administrative workers rather than as professionals.) Personnel and labor relations workers are also judged unproductive since they deal mainly with compensation issues. Religious workers are classified as unproductive since, as argued in Chapter 1, religion is one mechanism for maintaining the political and social status quo. Vocational counselors are unproductive workers since they are involved in job placement. Finally, public relations personnel and publicity writers are involved directly or indirectly in sales promotion and are therefore unproductive.

The remaining professional and technical occupations are categorized as productive labor. This classification is reasonably unambiguous for architects, engineers, foresters, librarians, medical personnel, technicians, athletes, and entertainers since all are directly involved in the production of use values. Computer specialists are classified as productive, though many in this group are involved in designing or writing billing and other basically clerical programs, which is an unproductive activity. Farm and home management advisors can be involved in financial counseling, which is unproductive. Mathematicians, statisticians, and life and physical scientists are involved mainly in research, which is productive, though some of this group, such as actuaries and statisticians, may perform financial services. Social scientists are classified as productive since most are involved in research, though part (if not all) of social science research is concerned with issues of governance and social control. Recreational workers perform a useful function. Social workers do, by and large, perform a useful function, though part of their function is to enforce administrative rules of various governmental agencies. Educators are viewed, by and large, as productive since the transmission of knowledge is essential to the material reproduction of society. However, teachers of unproductive subjects such as law, marketing, business administration, finance, and the like should more legitimately be classified as unproductive (such a detailed breakdown by type of subjects was not available before 1970). Writers and artists are largely productive, though those involved in writing advertising copy or in graphic design in advertising would not be.

Clerical workers are also subdivided into a productive and an unproductive component. Many clerical functions are concerned directly or indirectly with billing, financial collections, financial records processing, and payments. Cashiers, for example, collect money, as do counter clerks. Bank tellers, billing clerks, bookkeepers, bill and account collectors, payroll clerks, postal clerks, shipping and receiving clerks, storekeepers, ticket agents, and weighers all perform these functions. These occupational groups are therefore unproductive. Many other clerical workers perform administrative support functions. (In fact, in the 1980 census, they are classified under this new heading.) This group includes secretaries (except medical), stenographers, and typists; various "information clerks," such as messengers, meter readers, receptionists, and hotel clerks; "records processing occupations," such as file clerks and stock clerks; and adjustors, investigators, and appraisers. These support functions are unproductive since, as will be argued later, administrators perform mainly, if not exclusively, unproductive tasks.

Within the clerical group are also workers who can be classified as "material recording, scheduling, and distributing" clerks. This is a mixed function, involving partly records and invoice processing but partly expediting the material flow of production or the transportation of goods. Since these latter tasks aid in production, this group of occupations is classified as productive. Included in this group are vehicle dispatchers and starters and expediters and production controllers. There are other clerical jobs that are classified as productive because they are involved in transmitting information. These include library attendants and assistants, mail carriers and handlers (excluding, of course, the time spent in delivering bills and advertising flyers), proofreaders, statistical clerks, teacher aides, and telegraph and telephone operators. Office machine operators are also classified as productive, except for bookkeeping and billing machine operators, even though office machine operators are classified in the 1980 census as administrative support functions. The reason is that many of the tasks performed by calculating machine, computer and peripheral equipment, keypunch, and tabulating machine operators may provide information that will expedite material production. Finally, medical secretaries are classified as productive since they schedule patients and often perform low-level health support services. As is evident, an attempt has been made to overstate as much as possible the extent of productive clerical work.

Craftsmen, such as carpenters, mechanics, plumbers, and electricians, are all classified as productive labor since they are directly involved in goods production. Operatives, including truck drivers and machine operators, are classified as productive for the same reason. The same is true for nonfarm unskilled labor such as carpenters' helpers, construction laborers, stock handlers, and lumbermen. Interestingly, these three groups of blue collar workers in manufacturing are officially designated as production workers by the Bureau of Labor Statistics. White collar workers within manufacturing are referred to as nonproduction workers. Thus, even at the official level, there is a recognition of the difference in role played by these two classes of workers.

Service workers, including fire protection workers but excluding other protection workers, are classified as productive labor. This category includes cleaning service workers, such as chambermaids and janitors; food service workers, such as bartenders, busboys, cooks, and dishwashers; health service workers, such as dental assistants and nursing aides; and personal service workers, such as barbers, elevator operators, and ushers. All these workers perform useful services. Also included in service workers are private household workers such as maids and servants. They likewise produce use values such as cleaning and child care. Thus, by the convention established in Section A above, they are classified as productive. However, as noted above, the fact that their services are not exchanged on the market implies that no exchange value or surplus value is generated by their activity.

The remaining group of productive workers consists of those employed in agriculture. These are divided into two subgroups. The first are farmers (both owners and tenants) and farm managers. These are the people who actually run the farms. Though this work is basically administrative in nature, it is the judgment here that the management decisions are largely, if not almost exclusively, concerned directly with production. These include what crops to plant, when to plant and harvest, what equipment and fertilizers to use, and so on. Since these decisions directly affect material production, their labor activity is judged to be productive. The second subgroup consists of the actual farm hands, who perform the basic farm labor.

There are three remaining groups of unproductive labor. The first consists of nonfarm administrators and managers. Though it is possible that part of their time is involved in technical production decisions or capital investment plans, it is the judgment here that the vast majority of their time (or the vast majority of the administrators) is involved with the circulation, allocation, or extraction of surplus value. It should be noted that foremen and supervisors – those that directly monitor the production process – are not included in this category but rather in the various blue collar groups of craft and operative workers that they supervise. Those classified as administrators or managers are concerned with other matters, such as public relations, budgeting, financial decisions, pricing policy, legal problems, sales strategy, hiring and firing, labor relations, wage setting, and employee compensation packages. These activities are thus ultimately geared toward the realization of surplus value and its distribution. In fact, chief executive officers in U.S. corporations tend to have backgrounds and expertise in law, sales, or finance rather than technology, engineering, or production.[23]

The second are sales workers, including auctioneers, demonstrators, peddlers, insurance agents, newsboys, real estate brokers, salesmen, saleswomen, and sales clerks. Their major tasks are to sell goods and services, to collect money and payments, and to guard the merchandise. (In fact, if customers could be trusted to pay for goods that they took, there would be almost no need for sales personnel.) It should be noted that stockhandlers, those who unload the trucks and move the merchandise, are classified in the (nonfarm) labor category. The last group of unproductive workers consists of protection service workers, such as guards, watchmen, and policemen. Their job is to prevent theft (unauthorized transfer of property) and to maintain law, order, and property rights. Since this is ultimately a circulation expense, they are classified as unproductive labor.

[23] Historically, the function of top executives has changed significantly in the United States. At the turn of the century, they were drawn primarily from production and were concerned with the work process, technology, and innovation. By midcentury, many executives came from sales departments and were involved with realization problems. Recently, many have moved up the ranks from financial and legal departments and battle over the division of the social surplus value among the state, financial institutions, and productive sectors. For a discussion of the change in the makeup of corporate executives, see Fleanor et al. (1983), pp. 43–6.

CHAPTER 3

A Marxian accounting framework

The catch in this argument, of course, is the quiet assumption that rules and regulations are all freely chosen through something akin to a market process. In fact, that is far from being the case. All lawsuits are heavily subsidized by the government and are usually desired by only one party to the dispute. Many rules are the work of judges or bureaucrats over whom the general public has little control. Although the public may support the general outlines of a statute, its details and complexities are rarely understood, let alone endorsed, by the average voter. Most of our laws and administrative regulations have been complicated by the efforts of pressure groups and lobbyists. Even legislation widely approved when enacted often proves unexpectedly cumbersome and ineffective, yet efforts at reform quickly die from inertia or from the opposition of vested interests. . . .

In labor law, more than half the work of the National Labor Relations Board is devoted to defining the proper employee unit in which to hold elections and enforcing an intricate body of rules governing the electioneering behavior of unions and employers. Unit determinations often consist of fine-spun applications of vague, even contradictory, principles with no convincing demonstration of how the public interest is served. One can argue that these decisions cause little harm, especially if the size of the election unit is unimportant. But they do cost inordinate amounts of money, time, and energy. At Harvard, for example, a year of effort and over one hundred thousand dollars were consumed by the government and parties trying to decide whether to hold an election among the clerical workers in the entire University or only among those working in the Medical School. Even a rich country cannot afford to spend such sums on issues of this kind. . . .

The net result of these trends is a massive diversion of exceptional talent into pursuits that often add little to the growth of the economy, the pursuit of culture, or the enhancement of the human spirit. I cannot press this point too strongly. As I travel around the country looking at different professions and institutions, I am constantly struck by how complicated many jobs have become, how difficult many institutions are to administer, how pressing are the demands for more creativity and intelligence. However aggressive our schools and colleges are in searching out able youths and giving them a good education, the supply of exceptional people is limited. Yet far too many of these rare individuals are becoming lawyers at a time when the country cries out for more talented business executives, more enlightened public servants, more inventive engineers, [and] more able high-school principals and teachers. (Derek C. Bok, "A flawed system," *Harvard Magazine,* May–June 1983, pp. 40–1.)

To analyze the effects of unproductive activity on the behavior of the economy, it is necessary to establish an accounting framework which

56

incorporates unproductive activity. In this chapter, a Marxian accounting framework is developed that includes both productive and unproductive labor. Particular attention is paid to the measurement of the net product, the total surplus, labor values, and the rate of surplus value.

As noted in Chapter 2, the basic data sources used in this work are input–output tables for the U.S. economy. These require three major transformations. First, input–output tables must be modified to distinguish between productive and unproductive outputs and between productive and unproductive inputs. Second, transaction flows recorded in dollar terms in the standard Leontief framework must be revalued in terms of labor values. Third, new measures of net output and surplus must be developed corresponding to the new accounting framework.[1]

It is perhaps helpful to review the Leontief framework. There are five basic components: (1) a square matrix of interindustry flows, which shows the sales of the output of each sector to each of the others; (2) a matrix of value-added flows, which indicates the income generated in each sector by type of income; (3) a final-demand matrix, showing the sales of the output of each sector to the components of final output, including consumption, investment, government, exports, and imports; (4) an employment vector, indicating total employment of labor in each sector; and (5) a capital vector, which shows the total capital stock owned by each sector. There are two important accounting identities. First, the gross domestic output or gross output (GDO) of each sector is defined as the sum of the total value of interindustry inputs and value added generated in the sector. GDO, in turn, is equal to the total sales of each sector to other industries and to the components of final output. Second, gross national product (GNP) is equal to the total value of final output, which, in turn, is equal to the total value added.

A. Initial modifications

Before the input–output framework can be partitioned into productive and unproductive segments, four modifications are required to transform the Leontief accounting scheme into one conformable with Marxian labor values. The first is the inclusion of depreciation as part of the costs of production. The second is the valuation of imports in terms of its domestic equivalent cost of production. The third involves the division of value added into a necessary and surplus part. The fourth

---

[1] This section is based on Wolff (1977a), though some changes have been made, as will be indicated.

modification entails a similar partition of final output into a necessary and surplus component.

1.   Depreciation

The portion of the fixed capital stock that wears out or otherwise becomes economically useless or obsolete is referred to as *depreciation*. In the standard Leontief framework, depreciation is included as part of the gross profits of an enterprise. GNP includes depreciation, and net national product (NNP) is equal to GNP less depreciation. In a Marxian framework, the costs of production consist of three parts. The first is the direct labor costs. The second is the costs of circulating capital, which are the material inputs completely used up in the production of the final output. Material inputs include both raw materials, such as iron ore in the production of steel, and semifinished products, such as transistors in the production of radios. These inputs are recorded as interindustry flows in a standard Leontief framework. The third is the portion of the fixed capital that is used up in the production of final output. This flow is depreciation. Normally, it is measured as an annual flow, and all plant and equipment that last more than a year are classified as fixed capital, whereas all material inputs that last one year or less fall into the category of circulating capital. The estimation of "true" economic depreciation is a complex task beyond the scope of this work. For the purpose here, capital consumption allowances provided by businesses are used to measure capital stock depreciation.[2] The first modification of the standard Leontief framework is to include an endogenous depreciation row in the interindustry flow table and to subtract depreciation from gross profits in value added.

This modification now entails a corresponding change on the output side since total final output is out of balance with total value added. To restore the balance, it is necessary to include an endogenous depreciation column corresponding to the depreciation row. In a Marxian system, the depreciation of capital goods is valued according to the costs of *replacing* the plant or equipment, not according to original cost.[3] Therefore, the depreciation column should ideally show the in-

---

[2] Since such figures come mainly from corporate income tax returns, they will likely tend, if anything, to overstate the true level of economic depreciation, at least during noninflationary periods. During a high-inflation period, depreciation based on book value (that is, purchase price) may actually understate true economic depreciation.

[3] Marx's discussion of depreciation appears in *Capital*, vol. 1, Chapter 15 (pp. 386–94). He argues, "Be the machine ever so young and full of life, its value is no longer determined by the labour actually materialized in it, but by the labor-time requisite to reproduce either it or the better machine." This statement raises two crucial issues

puts required to reproduce or replace the depreciated capital stock using current technology for the production of the used-up capital goods (or their replacement). Such a task is again beyond this work.[4] Instead, the depreciation column will be formed by assuming that the gross capital formation column of final output is roughly proportional to the replacement investment in every sector. This is equivalent to the assumption that the average cost of replacing one dollar of used capital stock is equal to the average cost of producing one dollar of new capital stock. Though crude, this assumption allows each dollar of depreciated capital stock to be revalued at its current real cost of production.

The depreciation column is then formed by dividing the gross capital formation column by its column sum to obtain the average composition of new capital investment and multiplying the latter by the total dollar value of depreciation. The depreciation column is then subtracted from the gross capital formation column in final demand to yield a net capital formation column. Total final demand then equals total value added and this, in turn, equals NNP.

2.   Imports

The second modification involves the treatment of imports. Since imports are produced abroad, by definition, they have no domestic labor content.[5] How then should they be valued in terms of (domestic) labor values? The basic principle of valuation used is that the value of a commodity is its cost of reproduction or replacement. Thus, in the case of competitive imports – those with close domestic substitutes, such as Japanese steel – their cost of replacement is the domestic cost of manufacturing the domestic substitutes. In labor value terms, they are valued at the labor value of their domestic substitute. As an example, a ton of Japanese steel is valued by the labor required to produce a ton of American steel since this is its cost of replacement. Formally,

---

in the valuation of depreciation. First, how does one reconcile the fact that firms write off equipment at book value (purchase price) with the fact that replacement cost will alter due to price changes and technical change in the production of the capital equipment? Second, how can economic life be measured on a current basis when some machinery may become obsolete in the future not from physical deterioration but from the introduction of improved machinery?

[4] It would require the determination of both the capital goods that are used up in *each* sector and the equipment that constitutes their current replacements.

[5] At least, there is no direct U.S. domestic labor content. Some imports from abroad use inputs produced in the United States in their production and may thus contain indirect U.S. labor content.

then, no modification is required to the input–output flow table. Imports of steel are already recorded in the steel row in a standard input–output table and are treated in exactly the same way as interindustry or final-demand flows of domestically produced steel.

Noncompetitive imports present a different problem. By definition, they are imports of commodities that have no domestic substitutes in the U.S. economy, such as rubber. Their cost of replacement is the domestic cost of producing goods (and services) that must be exchanged in order to acquire these imports. The equivalent domestic labor content of these noncompetitive imports is thus the total labor required to produce an equivalent *dollar value* of exports. Formally, this is accomplished by creating an endogenous export column to correspond to the noncompetitive import row. This is computed by multiplying the original export column by a fraction such that the endogenous export column sums to the total value of noncompetitive imports. The residual then becomes the export column in final output, which I refer to as *net exports*.[6]

3.   Value added and final output

The last two modifications involve value added and final demand. The first step is to measure the costs of reproducing labor power. From Marx: "By labour-power or capacity for labour is to be understood the aggregate of those mental and physical capabilities existing in a human being, which he exercises whenever he produces a use-value of any description" (*Capital,* vol. 1, part II, ch. 6). In modern terminology, labor power, as distinguished from labor, refers to the services provided by labor during the process of production. The cost of reproducing labor power is thus the cost of maintaining the laborer and his family. (The worker's family is included because the calculation must include the cost of providing new laborers to the work force.) Often this is interpreted to mean the *subsistence* wage. The determi-

---

[6] An additional, technical modification is also required. GNP is equal to domestic final demand less imports. The input–output convention is to balance the noncompetitive import row by a negative entry in the row in final output. Since the noncompetitive row is now balanced by an endogenous export column, this negative entry must be set to zero. Total final output is thereby left unchanged and equals NNP. See Wolff (1975) for more details. It is important to note that this is the only place in labor value valuation that market prices – including the exchange rate – enter into the computation of labor values. This has some very important implications concerning unequal exchange and domestic productivity. For example, a change in the terms of trade against the United States will result in a relative transfer of value from the United States to abroad and, also, a relative decline in domestic productivity. This issue is, again, beyond the scope of the present work.

nation of the subsistence level has been the subject of much debate within Marxian circles. Marx himself seems to have explicitly included cultural and historical elements in its determination. Thus, as GNP per capita rises, the subsistence level itself increases (in much the same way as a relative poverty line increases). The issues involved in the calculation of a subsistence level are quite complex and beyond the scope of this work. For the purpose here, it is perhaps convenient to avoid the issue of the subsistence level entirely and focus on the actual costs of reproducing labor power. This will be defined as the mean real standard of living of the labor force at a given point in time.[7] As will be demonstrated in Chapter 6, the mean real standard of living has tended to follow the growth of GNP per capita during the postwar period in the United States. Thus, the costs of reproducing labor power, so defined, do reflect historical developments, at least during this period.

Even with this relatively straightforward definition of the costs of reproducing labor power, there remain several problems in measurement. Mean real labor compensation seems the most direct measure of the costs of reproducing labor power. Employee compensation is the sum of wages, salaries, and tips; fringe benefits such as health insurance, pension contributions, vacation pay, and the like; and the employer contribution to the social security system – the Old Age and Survivor's Insurance (OASI) program. There are three problems with this measure. First, part of the wage and salary income received by workers is transferred to the government in the form of taxes. In most estimates of the rate of surplus value, taxes are treated as part of the surplus [see, for example, Wolff (1975, 1979)]. Yet, as argued in Chapter 2, the state does provide productive and necessary services for the reproduction of the economic system. Some of these services directly benefit the working class, such as sanitation and public transit. Moreover, part of the taxes received by the state are transferred back to individuals in various forms. For the moment, all taxes, with one exception, will be aggregated in a separate row of value added. These taxes include the personal income tax, the corporate income tax, other business taxes, the sales tax, and other indirect business taxes. (In

---

[7] Of course, there is also a large variation in living standards at any point in time. This, in turn, compounds the difficulty of defining a subsistence level or the costs of reproducing labor power. Is the minimum living standard – or, perhaps, the legislated minimum wage – the true subsistence level? Does the cost of reproducing labor power depend on the type of labor power – medical doctors versus unskilled labor, for example? Should these differences be measured by relative wages or by actual costs of production of different skills? These questions, again, go beyond the limits of the present work.

conventional input–output accounting, all indirect business taxes are recorded as a separate row of value added.)

The exception is social security (OASI) taxes. The reason is that contributions into the social security system, though collected nominally as a payroll "tax," function in many ways like pension contributions. Since both pension and social security benefits are necessary for the maintenance of the labor force, albeit when their labor power is no longer used in production, these benefits should be included as part of necessary labor costs.[8] Social security taxes are therefore kept as part of labor compensation. The remaining taxes are recorded as a separate row and, for reasons that will become apparent, divided into two components: (i) a portion paid out of wages and salaries and (ii) a portion paid out of other forms of personal income and out of business profits.

The second problem is that workers may receive other forms of income besides wages and salaries, such as dividends, interest, and government transfers. Property income is excluded from necessary labor costs since it is, by definition, a form of surplus income, not remuneration to labor. That is, even though working class families receive property income, this form of income ultimately comes from returns to capital irrespective of who owns the capital. Conceptually, income must be classified according to its functional source.[9] Government transfers, on the other hand, should be classified according to their function. Social security benefits, as was argued above, are a form of labor compensation and thus a necessary cost of maintaining the labor force. The same is true for unemployment insurance. Government-provided health insurance, such as Medicaid and Medicare, serves a similar function, though it is earmarked for a particular consumption service. Food stamps, Aid to Families with Dependent Children (AFDC), and other forms of welfare are a bit more ambiguous in classification, since they help to support not only the working poor, former members of the labor force, and potential members of the labor force, particularly children but also the ill and disabled, the mentally ill and retarded, prisoners, and other lumpen proletariat who are un-

---

[8] It is also true that the social security benefits an individual worker receives after retirement may bear little relation to the contributions that are made by the worker and the worker's employer. This is also characteristic of many "defined benefit" private pension plans. In both cases, such contributions made into the retirement system constitute an income transfer *within* the working class.

[9] Moreover, quantitatively, property income makes up a very small fraction of the personal income of the working class. The reason is that financial wealth is highly concentrated in the United States, and those families that depend largely on income from property do, indeed, constitute a separate class [see Wolff (1981) and Wolff (1983), for example].

likely to engage in useful labor. Though transfer payments to this last group should be excluded from necessary labor costs, there are no data available to make this adjustment. Moreover, payments to this group are likely to be quite small relative to total welfare expense, and thus, for simplicity, all government transfers to individuals are included in necessary labor costs.

The third measurement problem is that not all the income received by workers is consumed. Many workers save part of their income. The proper measure of the necessary costs of reproducing labor power is consumption expenditures since it is consumption that sustains life, not income. On the surface, this appears as a serious objection to the use of labor remuneration as a measure of variable capital. However, empirically, this is not so for two reasons. First, many working class families will save during their working years and dissave after retirement [see Wolff (1981), for example]. Their net lifetime saving is therefore likely to be small. Second, at any point in time, the working class as a whole is likely to have relatively little net savings since although some are saving, others are dissaving. Moreover, as shown in Ruggles and Ruggles (1982), almost the entire net savings of the household sector in the postwar period has taken the form of equity in owner-occupied housing, life insurance, and pensions. The former is better classified as a consumption expense rather than financial savings, and the latter two forms of saving are types of retirement wealth. Thus, on empirical grounds, it is reasonable to assume that the working class as a whole does not save.

The value-added matrix is provisionally reconstituted into three components (rows): (i) total labor remuneration less personal income taxes on wages and salaries plus government transfers to individuals; (ii) business profits plus personal property income (including proprietor's income, rental income of persons, corporate profits and inventory valuation adjustment, net interest, business transfer payments, and other forms of property income less the difference between subsidies and the current surplus of government enterprise) less income taxes on corporate profits and personal property income; and (iii) personal income taxes, business income taxes, sales, excise, and other indirect business taxes, and all other taxes except social security taxes less government transfers to individuals.

The final-demand matrix is restructured in an analogous fashion to correspond to the three components of value added. It is first necessary to construct a vector of household consumption paid for out of wages and salaries and government transfers. Ideally, the household consumption vector should be split into two parts, one showing the goods and services purchased out of wages and salaries and transfers and the other part showing the goods and services purchased out of property income. Since the major property income recipients are the capitalist class, their consumption patterns would probably differ greatly from that of the working class. Indeed, the differences in consumption would likely reflect a standard Engel curve. However, no data were available on differences in consumption patterns. As a result, the household consumption vector is split proportionally into these two components so that the sum of worker consumption equals the sum of net wage and salary earnings plus transfers. (This follows from the assumption that workers do not save out of wages and salaries and transfers.) The vector of worker consumption is then the estimate of the necessary costs of reproducing the working class.

The residual component of household consumption is included in surplus output. The remaining components of final demand are also included in surplus output, with the exception of government expenditures, since each is paid for out of some component of surplus income. Surplus household consumption is paid for from property income; net investment (that is, net of depreciation) is paid for from retained earnings and borrowings; net inventory change (including the inventory valuation adjustment) must be financed from retained earnings or from borrowing, if positive, or, if negative, it increases the retained earnings of business; and the trade balance (the difference between exogenous exports and imports) must ultimately show up as a change in the portfolio position of firms, particularly financial institutions, and hence as an addition or subtraction to surplus income. For the moment, the government expenditure component of final output is left separate.

B.   Partition into productive and unproductive components

The next stage is to partition the modified input–output framework into productive and unproductive segments according to the classification scheme presented in Chapter 2. The subscript p will be used to refer to productive activities and the subscript u to unproductive activities. Unless otherwise noted, all flows and coefficients are in constant-dollar terms. Let A be a modified interindustry flow matrix.[10] Then A can be

---

[10] As noted in Chapter 2, four other modifications were made to the interindustry matrix. First, the federal government and state and local governments final-demand columns were combined with government industry value added to create an endogenous government sector. This sector was then split into a productive and an unproductive component, and government final demand was recorded as purchases from the endogenous productive and unproductive government sectors. Second, intermediate (in-

partitioned as

$$A = \begin{bmatrix} A_{pp} & A_{pu} \\ A_{up} & A_{uu} \end{bmatrix}$$

where the second subscript designates whether the sector is productive or unproductive and the first subscript indicates whether the input is from a productive or unproductive sector.

The value-added flows can be correspondingly decomposed into productive and unproductive components, where such flows are valued in *current* dollars. Let

$E = (E_p \quad E_u) =$ row vector showing total labor remuneration net of taxes plus government transfers to individuals ("earnings" for short) generated in each productive and unproductive sector[11]

$R = (R_p \quad R_u) =$ row vector of after-tax profits and property income generated in each productive and unproductive sector

$T = (T_p \quad T_u) =$ row vector of taxes generated in each sector less government transfers allocated to sector

For the moment, final output will be portioned in the following fashion. Let

$$D = \begin{bmatrix} D_p \\ D_u \end{bmatrix} =$$ column vector showing worker consumption from productive and unproductive sectors

$$G = \begin{bmatrix} G_p \\ G_u \end{bmatrix} =$$ column vector showing government purchases from productive and unproductive sectors

$$H = \begin{bmatrix} H_p \\ H_u \end{bmatrix} =$$ column vector showing remaining portions of final output purchased from productive and unproductive sectors, including household surplus consumption (SC), net capital formation (CF), net inventory change (IC), and net trade balance (TB) of exogenous exports less competitive imports

dustry) purchases from the amusement sector were reclassified as surplus household consumption. Third, the inventory valuation adjustment was distributed proportionately to gross domestic output across sectors. Fourth, inputed rent to owner-occupied dwellings was excluded from the value added of the real estate sector.

[11] Government transfers to individuals are allocated to sectors proportional to the total taxes collected from or generated in each sector.

Then
$$H = SC + CF + IC + TB$$
Finally, let
$$Y = \begin{bmatrix} Y_p \\ Y_u \end{bmatrix} = \text{column vector showing total final purchases from productive and unproductive sectors}$$

It should be emphasized at the outset that the elements of D_u, H_u, G_u, Y_u, and X_u (see below) *simply represent dollar flows*, not "real" output. They are an accounting convenience that will enable us to transform the input–output framework into a Marxian accounting framework. These elements will also be referred to as "fictitious output."

It then follows that
$$Y = D + H + G$$

The total final product in the conventional framework (CFP) is then given by

$$CFP = \sum Y$$

where CFP corresponds roughly to conventionally measured net national product, except for several accounting modifications to the standard input–output framework.[12] CFP includes both real output Y_p and fictitious output Y_u and is also introduced as an accounting convenience.

By construction, the following accounting identities hold for the base period (0):
$$\sum D_0 = \sum E_0$$
$$\sum H_0 + \sum G_0 = \sum R_0 + \sum T_0$$
$$CFP_0 = \sum Y_0 = \sum (E_0 + R_0 + T_0)$$

Let

$$X = \begin{bmatrix} X_p \\ X_u \end{bmatrix} = \text{column vector showing gross domestic output of productive and unproductive sectors}$$

Then

$$\sum_j (A_{pp} + A_{pu}) + D_p + H_p + G_p = X_p$$
$$\sum_j (A_{up} + A_{uu}) + D_u + H_u + G_u = X_u$$

[12] In particular, CFP differs from the standard net national product in that interindustry purchases from the amusement sector are now classified as final consumption instead of intermediate consumption and imputed rent to owner-occupied houses is excluded from national income.

For reasons that will become apparent in the next section, it is necessary to further decompose D and E. Let D_{pp} be the column vector that shows the purchases from productive sectors by productive workers; D_{pu} the column vector that shows the consumption of productive output by unproductive workers; D_{up} the column vector that shows the purchases from unproductive sectors by productive workers; and D_{uu} the column vector showing the purchases from unproductive sectors by unproductive workers.[13] Then

$$D_p = D_{pp} + D_{pu} \qquad D_u = D_{up} + D_{uu}$$

Since sectors producing productive output employ both productive and unproductive labor, the labor earnings generated in productive sectors can be split into two corresponding components, E_{pp} and E_{up}, where

$$E_p = E_{pp} + E_{up}$$

Then, by construction, for the base period (0),[14]

$$\sum D_{pp0} + \sum D_{up0} = \sum E_{pp0}$$
$$\sum D_{pu} + \sum D_{uu} = \sum E_{up0} + \sum E_{u0}$$

The labor vector can be partitioned in a comfortable fashion. Let

$$L = (L_p \quad L_u) = \text{row vector showing total employment in}$$
$$\text{productive and unproductive sectors}$$

Moreover, the labor vector L_p can be partitioned into two parts: L_{pp}, showing the employment of productive workers in sectors producing productive output, and L_{up}, showing the employment of unproductive labor in sectors producing productive output, where

$$L_p = L_{pp} + L_{up}$$

---

[13] It is assumed that the consumption patterns are the same for productive and unproductive labor. Indeed, there is no reason to suspect that their consumption patterns would differ, except because of differences in income.

[14] There is a troublesome issue of how to divide the government transfer portion of E_p and E_u between productive and unproductive labor compensation. As will be argued, variable capital refers to the necessary cost of maintaining and reproducing the productive members of the work force. For those members of the labor force currently at work, it can be directly determined who are productive workers. For those not currently at work, the issue is complex since, in principle, it is necessary to know who would be (or would have been, in the case of retirees) a productive worker given the *current state of technology* and the *current composition of industry*. (That is, *even if* it could be determined who in this group was a productive worker, this information would not be relevant.) To partition government transfers, it is therefore assumed that potentially productive workers are the same proportion of the nonworking labor class as current productive workers are of the (currently) employed labor force.

Total productive employment is given by

$$N_p = \sum L_{pp}$$

and total unproductive employment by

$$N_u = \sum L_u + \sum L_{up}$$

Total employment is then given by

$$N = N_p + N_u = \sum L$$

The capital stock vector can be likewise partitioned:

$$C = (C_p \quad C_u) = \text{row vector showing capital stock owned}$$
$$\text{by productive and unproductive sectors}^{15}$$

It should be noted that capital goods are produced only by productive sectors and are therefore all productive inputs. The total capital stock K is given by

$$K = \sum C$$

the total productively employed capital stock K_p by

$$K_p = \sum C_p$$

and the total unproductively employed capital stock by

$$K_u = \sum C_u$$

Finally, the following technical coefficients can be formed:

$$a = \begin{pmatrix} a_{pp} & a_{pu} \\ a_{up} & a_{uu} \end{pmatrix} = \text{matrix of interindustry coefficients, where}$$
$$a_{ij} = A_{ij}/X_j$$

$$l = (l_p \quad l_u) = \text{row vector of labor coefficients, where } l_j = L_j/X_j$$

$$c = (c_p \quad c_u) = \text{row vector of capital coefficients, where}$$
$$c_j = C_j/X_j$$

C.   Surplus accounting with unproductive activity

From an accounting point of view, the introduction of unproductive activity mandates some major revisions in the definition and the measurement of product and income. On the product side, it is necessary

---

[15] It should be noted that since depreciation is included as a cost of production, capital stock is valued at the end of the year, net of depreciation.

	Interindustry flows		Final output		
			Worker		Gross
	Machines	Bread	consumption	Investment	output
Machines	3	2	0	8	13
Bread	0	0	10	0	10

Value added Wages	4	6
Profits	6	2

Gross output	13	10

Employment	8	12

Figure 3.1. Two-sector economy: bread and machines. (All figures are in dollars, except employment. CFP = 18 dollars.)

to distinguish between final output and intermediate output and with the latter between necessary and unnecessary inputs. On the income side, it is required to distinguish between income and transfers and with income between necessary and surplus shares. Moreover, in so modifying the conventional income and product accounts, it is still necessary to maintain the basic identity between total income and total (final) product in current dollars since an input–output table is a double-entry bookkeeping system.

A simple numerical example will help illustrate the problem. Suppose there is a two-sector economy, machines and bread (see Figure 3.1). For convenience, all prices are assumed equal to unity. The machine-producing sector uses 3 dollars worth of machinery and 8 workers to produce 12 dollars worth of output. The bread-producing sector uses 2 dollars worth of machinery and 12 workers to produce 10 dollars worth of output. The only intermediate input in this economy is machinery (which for simplicity is treated as an intermediate flow rather than capital stock). Each worker receives the same pay in this economy – half a dollar – and the total wage bill is 4 and 6 dollars in the machine and bread sectors, respectively. The residual in each sector consists of profits – 6 and 2 dollars, respectively. Moreover, all the bread produced is sold to workers for their consumption, and the machinery that is not sold for current (intermediate) use is sold to capitalists for investment. Thus, total wages equals total worker consumption, which equals 10 dollars; total profits equals total investment, which equals 8 dollars; and total income equals the total final product, CFP, which equals 18 dollars.

Suppose both the machine-producing firms and the bread-producing firms have advertising departments. Suppose that in the former, two of the eight workers are employed in the advertising department and one of the three machines is purchased for advertising (a typewriter, for example). Suppose the bread sector is more advertising intensive and that half the machines and half the labor are employed in that department. Since advertising is an unproductive activity, the employment and wages in each sector can be split into a productive and an unproductive component. This is shown in Figure 3.2. In addition, the machines purchased in each sector can be split into productive and unproductive uses. It should be noted that both total income and CFP remain at 18 dollars.

In accounting terms, this is identical to assuming that there exists a separate advertising sector that directly employs eight workers and purchases two machines and sells its services to the machine and bread sectors. This transformation is shown in Figure 3.3. (This is very similar to the way in which the trade sector and the research and development sectors are constructed in standard input–output tables.) The machine sector, whose advertising department is shown as spending 1 dollar on machinery and 1 dollar on wages in Figure 3.2, is now shown as purchasing 2 dollars worth of inputs from the advertising sector. The bread sector, which is shown as spending 1 dollar on machinery and paying 3 dollars in wages for advertising in Figure 3.2, is now shown as spending 4 dollars on advertising services. The wages in the machine sector now amount to 3 dollars and employment to six workers, whereas, coincidentally, wages in the bread sector are also 3 dollars and employment six workers. I have assumed for convenience that the profits in these two sectors are unchanged (though see below). Wages paid out in the advertising sector total 4 dollars and employment eight workers. By assumption, the profits attributed to the advertising sector are zero.

This transformation leaves the basic accounting identities unchanged. Gross output of the machine sector remains at 13 dollars and that of the bread sector at 10 dollars. Total wages and worker consumption still amount to 10 dollars; total profits equal total investment, which remains at 8 dollars. And CFP, which still equals total income, stays at 18 dollars.

Though the formal accounting identities are left unchanged by the

	Interindustry flows		Final output		
	Machines	Bread	Worker consumption	Investment	Gross output
Machines					
a. Productive uses	2	1	0	8	13
b. Unproductive uses	1	1			
Bread	0	0	10	0	10
Value added Wages E_{pp}	3	3			
Wages E_{up}	1	3			
Profits	6	2			
Gross output	13	10			
Employment L_{pp}	6	6			
Employment L_{up}	2	6			

Figure 3.2. Two-sector economy: bread and machines, with resources in advertising department shown separately. (All figures are in dollars, except employment. CFF = 18 dollars.)

transformation shown in Figure 3.3, the separation of unproductive from productive activity now necessitates a significant modification in the basic definition of income and product. The key is provided by Marx, who maintains that unproductive labor creates neither value nor surplus value but merely transfers it (*Capital,* vol. 2, p. 149). Let us look at the income side first. There are two considerations. First, the recorded purchases made by the productive sectors from the unproductive advertising sector must be classified. By definition, they do not form part of the socially necessary costs of making bread or machinery. Moreover, these inputs are not necessary for the maintenance of the work force. As a result, they represent part of the unnecessary or surplus labor time in the economy. This flow, which I have labeled A_{up}, amounts to 6 dollars here (2 + 4) and is treated as part of the surplus income originating in the productive sectors. It should be noted that this part of the surplus income originating in the machine and bread sectors is not retained by the capitalists in these sectors but is *transferred* to the capitalists in the advertising sector in much the same way

| | Interindustry flows | | | Final output | | |
	Machines	Bread	Advertising	Worker consumption	Investment	Gross output
Machines	2	1	2	0	8	13
Bread	0	0	0	10	0	10
Advertising	2	4	0	0	0	6
Value added Wages	3	3	4			
Profits	6	2	0			
Gross output	13	10	6			
Employment	6	6	8			

Figure 3.3. Three-sector economy: bread, machines, and advertising. (All figures are in dollars, except employment. CFP = 18 dollars; TI = TP = 20 dollars; NI = NP = 6 dollars; SI = SP = 14 dollars.)

Interindustry flows

Advertising	2.5	5	0
Profits	5.5	1	1.5
Gross Output	13	10	7.5

Figure 3.4. Modifications to Figure 3.3 entailed by recording of profits in advertising sector. (All figures are in dollars, except employment. CFP = 18 dollars; TI = TP = 20 dollars; NI = NP = 6 dollars; SI = SP = 14 dollars.)

as corporate taxes, through part of a firm's surplus, are transferred to the government. Thus, purchases made from unproductive sectors by productive sectors are merely transfers of surplus from one part of the surplus class to another and, as such, constitute part of surplus income.

Second, the value added recorded in the unproductive sector does not correspond to the creation of any real output and, as such, is merely the other side of the transfer. It is as though part of the profits received by a capitalist is distributed to shareholders in the form of dividends. In this example, the productive capitalists transfer 4 dollars to their unproductive "shareholders." To record this as additional value added would constitute double counting. Therefore, the 4 dollars recorded as wages in the advertising sector (E_u) are voided since it is a portion of the other side of the transfer recorded as A_{up}. Thus, the total income in this modified framework is the sum of wages and profits originating in the *productive sectors only* and the purchases from unproductive sectors.

The exact same argument would apply if there were profits recorded in the unproductive sector. Suppose we arbitrarily assume that a dollar of expenditure on advertising yields 25 cents worth of profit. Thus, of the total profits of 6 dollars in the machine sector shown in Figure 3.2, 50 cents (two-fourths) would originate in the advertising department, as would 1 dollar (four-fourths) of the 2 dollars of profit in the bread sector. There are three resulting adjustments to Figure 3.3, shown in Figure 3.4. First, the profit row would read 5.5 dollars in the machine sector, 1 dollar in the bread sector, and 1.5 dollars in the advertising sector. Second, the gross output of the advertising sector is now 7.5 dollars. Third, the new gross output figure must now be reflected in the interindustry purchases from the advertising sector. In particular, the machine sector now purchases 1.5 dollars worth from advertising and the bread sector 5 dollars worth. It should be apparent that this modification leaves all the accounting identities intact. CFP is still 18 dollars. Moreover, total profits is still equal to 8 dollars. Thus, the presence of surplus income in unproductive sectors does not change the total amount of surplus income, *only its distribution among capitalists*. In addition, and most importantly for the purposes here, the recorded profits in the advertising sector of 1.5 dollars exactly corresponds to the increase in the value of A_{up} from 6 dollars to 7.5 dollars. Thus, as with the wages recorded in unproductive sectors, the profits shown in unproductive sectors simply represent the other side of the transfer A_{up}.

It is now possible to compute the total income (TI) in the economy once the double counting is eliminated. TI is given as the sum of wages and profits originating in the *productive sectors only* plus the purchases made by productive sectors from unproductive sectors ($E_p + R_p + A_{up}$). In this example, TI equals 20 dollars.

There are four considerations on the product side. First, productive output purchased by unproductive sectors and recorded as A_{pu} can no longer be considered as intermediate flows since, by definition, they do not contribute to the production of output. Instead, this output is included as part of the net product. Moreover, since the items contained in A_{pu} do not contribute either directly or indirectly to the maintenance of the work force, such output enters as part of the surplus product of the economy. This part of the surplus output differs from other components in that the activities in which it is used provide no direct use values. However, the products contained in A_{pu} are themselves use values. In this example, typewriters used for advertising are themselves necessary for providing advertising copy. As we shall see in the next section, the resources embodied either directly or indirectly in A_{pu} will themselves be classified as socially unnecessary costs of producing (productive) output.

Second, though not illustrated in this particular example, purchases of unproductive output made by unproductive sectors and recorded as A_{uu} would be omitted from both the interindustry and final output accounts since such a flow would merely record the transfer of surplus from one group of unproductive capitalists to another. For example, if an advertising agency hired a lawyer, the resulting flow would simply be a transfer of surplus income since no new use value is created and would fall outside the production accounts.

Third, though not shown in this example, any purchases from unproductive sectors (Y_u) made by final users would be similarly eliminated from the production accounts. If households pay for legal services, the payments would be considered a transfer of part of their income to that of the surplus class. Indeed, unproductive expenditures made by workers are, in effect, remittances of a portion of the money wages they receive from the capitalist class back to another segment of the capitalist class. Such a flow would entail some corresponding change on the income side. In the case of unproductive expenditures recorded in worker consumption (D_u), it would be necessary to split the wages received by workers into the portions spent on productive and unproductive output. Since the latter portion is not part of the necessary costs of maintaining the labor force, it would be considered part of the surplus income of that sector. In the case of unproductive purchases recorded in surplus final output (H_u) – the hiring of consultants by the defense department, for example – no change would be warranted on the income side since H_u is, in effect, a transfer of surplus income occurring within the surplus class. The flow Y_u is therefore treated in the same manner as A_{uu} and is eliminated from the production accounts. The total net product (TP) is thus given by A_{pu} + Y_p, which equals 20 dollars in this example, the same as TI.[16]

Fourth, the consumption expenditures of unproductive workers are included as part of surplus output. This is implicitly done above by treating the value added generated in the unproductive sector as a transfer of surplus income out of the productive sector. Indeed, the wages paid to unproductive labor are simply a transfer from unproductive capitalists to a new component of the surplus class – unproductive workers. The wages received by unproductive workers are treated in this fashion because these workers do not contribute to the reproduction of use values (and, in particular, to the reproduction of use values consumed by necessary labor). The labor time provided by unproductive workers is thus part of surplus or unnecessary labor time, and their consumption expenditures do not form part of the necessary costs of reproducing the economy. It is much like the consumption of armed forces personnel. Though the vast majority of them may come from the working class, their activity is not a necessary expense. Reproduction of the economy and their consumption is not a necessary expense. Thus, D_{pu} is, in effect, paid for out of the surplus and constitutes part of surplus consumption.[17]

---

[16] Current national accounting practices give a direct analogy. Food purchased for home use is part of the national product. However, the work that is required to transform and cook the food before it is eaten does not enter the national product since this is a process occurring outside the market. This is essentially the way unproductive expenditures in final output are treated.

[17] As in the case of H_u, the expenditures made by unproductive workers on unproductive output (D_{uu}) would be omitted on the product side since it is not part of the net product and on the income side since it represents a further transfer of surplus income to another group of unproductive capitalists.

In the examples shown in Figures 3.3 and 3.4, the total surplus product (SP) is given by $A_{pu} + D_{pu} + CF_p$. In the examples, 40 percent ($\frac{8}{20}$) of the workers are unproductive, so that M_{pu} equals 4 dollars. Thus, SP equals 14 dollars. The remaining portion of the total net product constitutes necessary consumption (NC). In these examples, NC = D_{pp}, which is 6 dollars. On the income side, surplus income (SI) is given by $A_{up} + R_p$ in these two examples. In both cases, SI equals 14 dollars, the same as SP. Finally, the remaining part of total income is called necessary income (NI). In these examples, NI equals E_p, which equals 6 dollars, the same as NC.

The complete accounting scheme: These accounting relations can be formalized as follows. Let us first define the total net product (TP) as the total (productive) output produced in the economy that does not serve as inputs in the production of other (productive) output. Then

$$TP = \sum X_p - \sum A_{pp}$$

or, alternatively,

$$TP = \sum A_{pu} + \sum Y_p$$

TP thus includes not only the final output of productive sectors but also the productive output purchased by unproductive sectors. A second concept of the net product is the total final product (FP). It is defined as

$$FP = \sum Y_p = \sum (D_p + G_p + SC_p + CF_p$$
$$+ IC_p + TB_p) = TP - \sum A_{pu}$$

FP is a better welfare measure than TP and will also prove useful for certain analyses.

On the income side, the concept corresponding to TP is total net income (TI), defined as

$$TI = \sum A_{up} + \sum E_p + \sum R_p + \sum T_p$$

TI is equal to the sum of wages, surplus income, and tax payments originating in the productive sectors plus the expenditures by productive sectors made from unproductive sectors. Moreover, since

$$TI = \sum X_p - \sum A_{pp}$$

then, for the base period *only*,

$$TI_0 = TP_0$$

	Interindustry flows		Final output	
	A_{pp}	A_{pu}	M	Z
Interindustry flows				
	A_{up}	A_{uu}	Y_u	
	E_p	E_u		
Value added	R_p	R_u		
	T_p	T_u		

1. $\text{CFP} = \sum (Z + M) + \sum Y_u = \sum (E_p + R_p + T_p) + \sum (E_u + R_u + T_u)$

2. $\text{TP} = \sum A_{pu} + \sum (Z + M)$

3. $\text{TI} = \sum A_{up} + \sum (E_p + R_p + T_p)$

4. $\text{FP} = \sum (Z + M)$

5. $\text{NC} = \sum M$

6. $\text{SP} = \sum A_{pu} + \sum Z$

7. $\text{SFP} = \sum Z$

Figure 3.5. Construction of measures of product and income from a standard input–output framework.

There is no easily constructed income concept corresponding to FP. These product and income concepts are illustrated in Figure 3.5.

The total net product can now be partitioned into two components: necessary consumption (NC) and surplus product (SP). Following Marx (*Capital*, vol. 1, pp. 212–20), I define necessary consumption as the consumption expenditures of the *productive* labor force. By definition, there are two exclusions from the conventional measure of worker consumption, the vector D. First, fictitious output recorded as M_u is omitted since, by definition, unproductive activities produce no use values. Second, the costs of maintaining and reproducing unproductive labor, recorded as D_{pu}, are also excluded.

This second point may require some clarification. Marx uses the term *necessary costs* in two ways. The first refers to the means of subsistence *necessary* for the reproduction of labor. The second refers to the *socially necessary* costs of producing output, which corresponds to the set of inputs required to produce a unit of output in the most efficient way. The first is entailed by the second since part of the socially necessary costs of producing output are the costs of maintaining the necessary labor input. By definition, the labor power provided by unproductive workers is not essential for the production of any output. Production consists of the work done and the output produced by productive workers. This is the labor power necessary to sustain the operation and reproduction of the economy. The labor time provided by unproductive workers is not part of necessary labor time since the economy could continue to operate and reproduce without it. Thus, the maintenance of unproductive labor is not necessary for the reproduction of the economy and their consumption expenditures, like those of the capitalist class, form part of surplus output. Only the productive consumption of productive workers, D_{pp}, is included as part of necessary consumption.

One further refinement should be added. Not only private consumption but also publicly provided consumption is required to reproduce the labor force. In particular, part of the government's expenditures on education, health, fire protection, roads, and the like contributes directly to the welfare of workers. Thus, in order to correctly estimate the necessary consumption of workers, government expenditures on productive goods and services, G_p, must be distributed among the beneficiaries of the expenditures. Government expenditures also benefit members of the capitalist class in their personal consumption and also benefit business directly, such as the trucking industry through the maintenance of roads. Those government services that benefit business, however, ultimately benefit the final consumers who purchase the output of these businesses, either directly or indirectly, as well as the owners of these businesses. Thus, even this portion of government expenditure could, in principle, be imputed to capitalists and the various classes of workers. Such a task is beyond the scope of this work.[18] The distribution of government benefits to households is, instead, crudely imputed by allocating such benefits proportional to the respective private consumption of productive workers, unproductive workers, and capitalists. Thus, define

---

[18] See Ruggles (1979) for a careful attempt at estimating the distribution of the benefits from government expenditures. Actually, on prima facie grounds, it is evident that the benefits from some government expenditures such as health and education are proportional to the number of people in a particular class. A better imputation might be to distribute G_p proportional to some function of both income and population.

$G_{pp} = dG_p$ = column vector showing portion of productive government expenditures necessary for reproduction of productive labor power

where d is a scalar given by $\sum D_{pp}/(\sum D_{pp} + \sum SC_p)$. Let G_{ps} be the column vector showing the portion of productive government expenditures that benefit the surplus class (including unproductive labor), where

$$G_{ps} \equiv G_p - G_{pp}$$

Then, the vector of necessary consumption, M, is given by

$$M = D_{pp} + G_{pp}$$

and total necessary consumption, NC, by

$$NC = \sum M = \sum (D_{pp} + G_{pp})$$

The vector of surplus final product, Z, is then given by

$$Z = Y_p - M$$

and the total surplus final product, SFP, by

$$SFP = \sum Z = FP - NC$$

The total surplus product, SP, is then given by

$$SP = \sum Z + \sum A_{pu} = TP - NC$$

D.   Measurement of surplus value

Basic Marxian variables can now be constructed in the following manner. Let us first introduce the conventional inverse technical matrix:

$q^* = (I - a)^{-1}$ = square matrix showing total (direct plus indirect) inputs used per unit of final output (fictitious output in case of unproductive sectors)

Both necessary (productive) and unnecessary (unproductive) inputs are included in matrix q^*. To see this, let us partition q^* as follows:

$$q^* = \begin{bmatrix} q_{pp} & q_{pu} \\ q_{up} & q_{uu} \end{bmatrix}$$

Thus, q_{up} shows the purchases made either directly of indirectly from unproductive sectors for the production of productive output; q_{pu} shows the productive inputs used directly or indirectly by unproductive sectors; and q_{uu} shows the unproductive inputs used directly or indirectly by the unproductive sectors. The partition q_{pp} indicates the productive inputs used either directly or indirectly in the production of productive output. Part of the productive inputs picked up in q_{pp} may actually pass through an unproductive sector. This can be seen in the Leontief expansion:

$$q^* = I + \begin{pmatrix} a_{pp} & a_{pu} \\ a_{up} & a_{uu} \end{pmatrix} + \begin{pmatrix} a_{pp} & a_{pu} \\ a_{up} & a_{uu} \end{pmatrix} \begin{pmatrix} a_{pp} & a_{pu} \\ a_{up} & a_{uu} \end{pmatrix} + \cdots$$

Thus,

$$q_{pp} = I + a_{pp} + (a_{pp}^2 + a_{pu}a_{up}) + \cdots$$

The term $a_{pu}a_{up}$ captures the productive inputs to unproductive sectors that, in turn, show up as purchases made by productive sectors. This term, for example, would include paper (a productive input) purchased by banking services (an unproductive sector), which are sold to the steel industry (a productive sector). Such productive inputs are, as a result, not necessary for the production of productive output since the unproductive sectors that purchase them are themselves unnecessary for producing the productive output. Productive inputs that are indirectly "contaminated" in this fashion should therefore be excluded from the necessary costs of producing output. The only socially necessary inputs are thus given by[19]

$$q = (I - a_{pp})^{-1}$$

Let us now introduce the conventional labor absorption vector:

$\lambda^* = lq^* = $ row vector showing productive and unproductive labor time absorbed either directly or indirectly per unit of output (fictitious output in case of unproductive sectors)

---

[19] Actually, even matrix q most likely overstates the socially necessary input requirements. The reason is that sectors that produce productive output also engage in unproductive activities. The labor input in productive sectors is, in fact, segregated into a productive component l_{pp} and an unproductive component l_{up}. In principle, the same separation should be done for intermediate inputs a_{pp} (as well as for the capital stock input C_p). For example, the paper and paper clips used by clerical workers in the automotive sector should be reclassified as unproductive inputs (as well as typewriters, as was done in the example in Section C). However, because of data limitations, this is virtually impossible to do, and all the inputs in a_{pp} (as well as C_p) are considered productive. Though this overstates the amount of productive inputs, the error introduced is probably not excessive since the bulk of material inputs used in manufacturing, processing, transportation, and the like are absorbed directly in production.

Both necessary and unnecessary labor time is included in the computation. This can be made explicit by partitioning λ^* as follows:

$$\lambda^* = (\lambda_p \quad \lambda_u) = (l_p \quad l_u) \begin{bmatrix} q_{pp} & q_{pu} \\ q_{up} & q_{uu} \end{bmatrix}$$

where $l_p = l_{pp} + l_{up}$. Thus, λ_p shows the direct plus indirect labor time, irrespective of whether the labor is productive or unproductive, embodied per unit of (productive) output, and λ_u shows the direct plus indirect labor time, irrespective of whether the labor is employed in productive or unproductive sectors, embodied in fictitious output.

The socially necessary labor time for commodity production can now be defined as the productive labor time required for the production of productive output. This is given by

$$\lambda \equiv l_{pp} q$$

The remaining, or socially unnecessary, labor time for commodity production can be divided into three components. The first of these is λ_{up}, which indicates the unnecessary labor time absorbed in the creation of productive output:

$$\lambda_{up} = l_u q_{up} + l_{pp}(q_{pp} - q^*) + l_{up} q_{pp}$$

The second term on the right is included to capture the productive labor that is indirectly embodied in productive output through purchases of unproductive inputs and the third term is included to capture the unproductive labor directly employed in productive sectors. The second component is λ_{pu}, the labor directly employed in productive sectors that is absorbed in fictitious output:

$$\lambda_{pu} = l_p q_{pu}$$

The third component is λ_{uu}, the labor directly employed in unproductive sectors that is absorbed in fictitious output:

$$\lambda_{uu} = l_u q_{uu}$$

Then

$$\lambda_p = \lambda + \lambda_{up} \qquad \lambda_u = \lambda_{pu} + \lambda_{uu}$$

The *Marxian labor value* of a commodity will refer to λ, which will also be called *total necessary labor requirements* for commodity production. The terms *total labor content, total labor absorbed,* and *total embodied labor* will refer to the vector λ^*.

It is now possible to provide a measure of the value of labor power, which is defined as the necessary costs of reproducing necessary labor power in labor terms. Let

$$m = M/N_p = \text{ the column vector of necessary (private plus public) consumption per productive worker}$$

and

$$w = \sum m = \text{ average Marxian real wage showing the constant dollar value of average consumption per productive worker}$$

The value of labor power, v, is given as the socially necessary labor time required to produce the goods and services consumed per productive worker[20]:

$$v = \lambda m \tag{3.1}$$

where it is implicitly assumed in the calculation of (labor) value that labor is homogenous.

The symbol v was deliberately chosen because v may also be interpreted as the *variable capital* advanced per worker (per year) by the capitalist for reproducing the necessary work force. The total variable capital advanced by the capitalist class, V, is then given by

$$V = N_p v = N_p \lambda m = \lambda M \tag{3.2}$$

Total variable capital V may be viewed as the labor value equivalent of the wages fund advanced by the capitalist class required to support necessary labor time until payment for the product is received by the capitalist. Technically, variable capital is the labor value equivalent of this wages fund advanced for *one turnover period* (the time between the advance of the wages and the receipt of payment for the products). Since no data are currently available on turnover period, it will be assumed throughout that the turnover period for both variable and circulating capital is one year.[21]

---

[20] It should be emphasized again that the value of labor power is taken to be the productive labor content of the actual (average) basket of (productive) goods and services consumed by labor rather than some "subsistence" level, as the concept is sometimes construed. The interpretation here maintains the essential relation between the real wage and the level of surplus at the disposition of the capitalist class as well as avoids difficult problems in measuring a subsistence level of consumption.

[21] Note that if the turnover period is different from one year, the value of labor power still remains λm. However, total variable capital $V = \alpha N \lambda m$, where α is the average turnover period in years. The assumption of an annual turnover rate is fairly well supported by aggregate data. The annual turnover period is fairly well approximated by the inverse of the ratio of the average yearly level of inventory to annual sales. From Table 5.10 of *The National Income and Product Accounts of the United States*,

Total surplus labor time, or *surplus value,* is defined as total labor time less the amount necessary for the maintenance of productive labor power. It is given directly by

$$S = N - V \tag{3.3}$$

There are three components of surplus labor time. The first is the total amount of productive labor time embodied in the surplus final product, SFP. The second is the total labor absorbed in fictitious output, Y_u. The third is the unproductive labor content λ_{up} of the final product Y_p. Thus,

$$S = \lambda Z + \lambda_u Y_u + \lambda_{up} Y_p \tag{3.4}$$

where the first term captures the socially necessary labor time required to produce the surplus product and the last two terms the socially unnecessary labor time absorbed in the final product.[22] The mass of surplus value S generated each year plus total variable capital equals total labor time, N. To see this, note that

$$Y_p = M + Z$$

Hence,

$$
\begin{aligned}
V + S &= \lambda(M + Z) + \lambda_{up} Y_p + \lambda_u Y_u \\
&= (\lambda Y_p + \lambda_{up} Y_p) + \lambda_u Y_u \\
&= \lambda_p Y_p + \lambda_u Y_u \\
&= N
\end{aligned}
$$

1929–76 Statistical Tables, the average annual economywide turnover rate was estimated from seasonally adjusted quarterly data as follows:

1947	0.89
1958	1.04
1963	1.15
1967	1.16
1972	1.19
1976	1.04

Though there were year-to-year fluctuations over these six years, the average annual turnover rate over these six years was 1.08.

[22] It should be noted that the matrix A_{pu} does not directly appear in (3.4) since its labor content is already captured in the surplus through the contributions of λ_u and λ_{up}. It should also be noted that this result differs from that reported in my previous paper (1977a), in which $\lambda_u Y_u$ (the labor embodied in fictitious final output) was excluded from S. In the earlier paper, the component Y_u was treated, as it is here, as fictitious output and the payment for Y_u as a transfer out of surplus. However, the labor component L_u was treated in the earlier paper as if it were a transfer recipient outside of the labor force instead of as surplus labor time as it is here.

The total surplus value generated per productive worker, s, is then given by

$$s = S/N_p$$

From equations (3.1)–(3.3),

$$s = N/N_p - v = N/N_p - \lambda m \tag{3.5}$$

The variable s is then the difference between the ratio N/N_p and the value of labor power. The higher the proportion of unproductive workers in total employment (and, hence, N/N_p), the greater the value of s, ceteris paribus. However, since $S = N_p s$, the lower N_p, the lower total surplus value. Thus, a rise in the ratio of unproductive to productive employment exerts counteracting effects on total surplus value.

The rate of surplus value ϵ is defined as the ratio of total surplus value to total variable capital:

$$\epsilon = S/V = s/v \tag{3.6}$$

From (3.2) and (3.3), we obtain

$$\epsilon = \frac{N}{V} - 1 = \frac{N}{N_p(\lambda m)} - 1 \tag{3.7}$$

Thus, the rate of surplus value equals the ratio of total labor time to the labor time necessary for the reproduction of productive labor less unity. In this case, an increase in the proportion of unproductive labor in total employment will (unambiguously) cause the rate of surplus value to increase.

The last step in the analysis is to relate the rate of surplus value to the *rate of exploitation*. The rate of exploitation, ϵ^*, is defined as the ratio of uncompensated to compensated labor time, *irrespective of whether the labor is employed productively or unproductively*. Under the assumption that the Marxian real wage is the same for both productive and unproductive workers, total compensated labor time, V^*, is given by

$$V^* = N\lambda m \tag{3.8}$$

Thus, total uncompensated labor time, S^*, is given by

$$S^* = N - V^* \tag{3.9}$$

and

$$\epsilon^* \equiv S^*/V^* = 1/\lambda m - 1 \tag{3.10}$$

In an economy with no unproductive labor, the rate of surplus value is identical to the rate of exploitation [cf. equation (3.7)]. In the general case, the relation between the two is given by

$$\epsilon = \frac{1}{1-u}\,(\epsilon^* + 1) - 1 \tag{3.11}$$

where $u \equiv Nu/N$ is the proportion of unproductive labor in total employment. The rate of surplus value can thus increase from two sources. The first is an increase in the ratio of unproductive to productive employment. The second is an increase in the rate of exploitation, which is itself a direct reflection of the class struggle.

CHAPTER 4

A growth model of accumulation and unproductive labor

These points may seem carping or conjectural, but they are not without tangible effects. A nation's values and problems are mirrored in the ways in which it uses its ablest people. In Japan, a country only half our size, 30 percent more engineers graduate each year than in all the United States. But Japan boasts a total of less than 15,000 lawyers, while American universities graduate 35,000 *every year*. It would be hard to claim that these differences have no practical consequences. As the Japanese put it, "Engineers make the pie grow larger; lawyers only decide how to carve it up." . . .

In law, the actors have different names but the plot is much the same. Legal staffs of large corporations have become the most rapidly growing segment of the bar. At the same time, private law firms continue to expand by opening branches in more and more cities. For clients at the lower end of the economic spectrum, larger forms of organization are likewise developing: prepaid group plans, companies offering cut-rate legal services in supermarkets and shopping malls, poverty law offices funded by the federal government.

These new organizations will have effects on what we pay for legal work in this country. To a degree, they may help to lower attorneys' fees by engendering greater competition and economies of scale. Nevertheless, the total bill for legal services in America does not depend nearly so much on the size of attorneys' fees as it does on the *volume of litigation and legal services throughout the society* [emphasis added]. As time goes on, the growth of prepaid plans, legal service corporations, and poverty law offices is likely to focus more organized pressure on the government to find ways of subsidising legal services for the poor and middle class. The mounting oversupply of lawyers promises to push in the same direction. If these pressures are simply allowed to increase access to a very complex and expensive legal system, the total cost of law in our society will continue, as in medicine, to follow a steep, upward trajectory." (Derek C. Bok, "A flawed system," *Harvard Magazine,* May–June 1983, pp. 41, 44.)

To understand the long-term implications of unproductive activity on capital accumulation, productivity growth, and the real wage, it is helpful to develop a long-period growth model based on general trends in critical variables that characterized the postwar American economy. Toward this end, a two-sector growth model is developed with one activity productive and the other unproductive. Because of the nature of the model, it is very difficult to establish short-period dynamics. However, it is possible to establish the limiting values of accumulation, productivity growth, and real wage growth. Such an analysis can help in understanding actual trends in the postwar American economy.

The basic assumption of the model is that unproductive inputs are absorbed in (productive) output as a constant ratio over time. This is assumed to be so for both unproductive inputs directly employed in productive sectors and those directly employed in unproductive sectors. As a result, unproductive inputs become fixed coefficients in the production function of productive sectors. An immediate effect is that unproductive employment will tend to increase over time as a percentage of total employment. This, in turn, will squeeze the portion of surplus value that is reinvested in new capital formation, and the rate of capital accumulation will fall over time. This last effect, together with the increasing share of unproductive labor in total employment, will cause the rate of labor productivity growth and total factor productivity growth to fall and approach zero in the limit. Finally, under the assumption that total worker consumption is a constant fraction of final output, real wage growth will also fall over time and approach zero in the limit.

The presence of unproductive activity diverts to unproductive uses resources that could help produce productive output. This is illustrated by a comparison with the dynamics of a one-sector model without unproductive activity. It is shown that steady-state capital accumulation, productivity growth, and real wage growth are all greater in an economy without unproductive activity than the respective limiting values are in the two-sector case.

A.   Basic assumptions of model

The aim of this chapter is to develop a model that is both analytically tractable and capable of capturing the salient features of the structure of the postwar American economy. In order to achieve the former objective, it is sometimes necessary to make assumptions that distort the factual basis of the model. It is hoped, of course, that even such distortions allow enough of the underlying structure of the economy to be captured so as to permit useful predictions.

Assumption (i): There are two sectors in the economy, one that produces productive output and another that is unproductive. It is assumed that the labor (N_{uu}) and capital (K_u) employed in the unproductive sector bear a fixed ratio to productive output (X_p):

$$N_{uu} = b_1 X_p \tag{4.1}$$

$$K_u = d_2 X_p \tag{4.2}$$

where b_1 and d_2 are positive constants. Over the 1947–76 period, the ratio N_{uu}/X_p actually declined at an annual rate of 0.60 percent. However, this was considerably slower than the rate of decline of N_p/X_p, which averaged 2.92 percent per year. The unproductive capital stock absorbed per unit of (productive) output remained virtually unchanged over the 1947–76 period. The ratio K_u/X_p changed from 0.300 in 1947 to 0.292 in 1976, or by -0.09 percent per year. Moreover, the ratio K_u/N_{uu} changed very little over the period, rising from 10.5 in 1947 (in thousands of 1958 dollars per worker) to 12.2 in 1976, or by 0.50 percent per year.

Assumption (ii): The unproductive labor directly employed in productive sectors (N_{up}) remains a fixed ratio of productive output:

$$N_{up} = b_3 X_p \tag{4.3}$$

where b_3 is a positive constant. There was some reduction in the direct absorption of unproductive labor in the productive sector, with the ratio N_{up}/X_p declining at a rate of 1.60 percent per year.

Assumptions (i) and (ii) now imply that

$$N_u = N_{uu} + N_{up} = d_1 X_p \tag{4.4}$$

where d_1 is a positive constant. In actuality, the ratio N_u/X_p did decline at an annual rate of 0.90 percent per year over the 1947–76 period. However, this was considerably less than the 2.92 percent annual rate of decline of N_p/X_p. The assumption of a fixed absorption of unproductive labor per unit of productive output is thus a simplifying assumption that captures the relative experience of productive and unproductive employment and makes the model tractable.

Assumption (iii): The production function of the productive sector is a Cobb–Douglas function of labor and capital inputs:

$$X_{pt} = c_1 e^{rt} N_{pt}^{\alpha} K_{pt}^{1-\alpha} \tag{4.5}$$

where c_1, r, and α are constants, and $c_1 > 0$, $r > 0$, and $0 < \alpha < 1$. There are quite a few assumptions implicit in this formulation. First, r, the rate of disembodied technical change, is positive and constant over time. Though the rate of total factor productivity (TFP) growth[1]

---

[1] This was estimated by

$$\frac{\dot{\text{TFP}}_{pt}}{\text{TFP}_{pt}} = \frac{\dot{X}_{pt}}{X_{pt}} - \left[\bar{\alpha} \frac{\dot{N}_{pt}}{N_{pt}} + (1 - \bar{\alpha}) \frac{\dot{K}_{pt}}{K_{pt}} \right]$$

where $\bar{\alpha}$ is the average share of labor compensation in value added in the productive sector over the period and a dot over the term indicates the time derivative.

was positive over the 1947–76 period, averaging 1.6 percent per annum, TFP growth did rise slightly from 2.0 percent per year in 1947–58 to 2.2 percent in 1958–67 and then declined to 0.9 percent in 1967–76. However, this recent productivity slowdown in the productive sector may not represent a secular decline but may, instead, be part of a longer productivity cycle. (In fact, evidence from the 1980s indicates that productivity growth, at least in the nonfinancial business sector in the United States, is beginning to increase.) In any case, as long as r remains positive in the long run, the model's predictions should be relatively consistent with observed trends.

Second, the unproductive labor employed in productive sectors, L_{up}, and unproductive inputs in productive sectors, A_{up}, are assumed to have no effect on the level of output, X_{pt}. This follows from the definition of unproductive inputs and labor. Third, the exponents of N_{pt} and K_{pt} are assumed to be constant over time and to sum to unity. This is a technical assumption that allows for analytical simplicity.[2] Fourth, the elasticity of substitution between capital and labor is assumed to be unity. Though it is hard to establish independently that the elasticity is unity, there is evidence of substantial substitution of capital for labor in the U.S. economy. In particular, the ratio K_p/N_p grew from 11.7 in 1947 to 28.4 in 1976, where the unit is thousands of 1958 dollars per worker.

Assumption (iv): It is assumed that there are only two components in the final product (FP), the consumption of both productive and unproductive workers (D_p) and investment ($\dot{K}$):

$$\text{FP}_t = Y_{pt} = D_{pt} + \dot{K}_t \tag{4.6}$$

where $\dot{K} = \text{CF}_p$ (and a dot over a term indicates the time derivative).[3] Moreover, it is assumed that both are a fixed proportion of the final product:

$$D_{pt} = b_4 Y_{pt} \tag{4.7}$$

$$\dot{K}_t = b_5 Y_{pt} \tag{4.8}$$

where b_4 and b_5 are positive constants, and $b_5 = 1 - b_4$. This latter assumption of a constant investment rate is especially crucial for the

---

[2] It should be noted that the parameters α and $1 - \alpha$ cannot be interpreted as class shares (and there is no presumption to doing so here) since part of value added is distributed to unproductive labor, L_{up}. Moreover, the fact that α and $1 - \alpha$ sum to unity implies constant returns to scale with regard to inputs N_{pt} and K_{pt}. In this case, such an implication is relatively harmless, since the level of analysis is the industry, not the firm.

[3] Technically, we should also include public consumption (G_p) in the consumption of workers. This component is ignored to simplify the discussion.

analysis to follow. Aside from cyclical fluctuations, the postwar evidence does indicate a fairly stable investment rate in the economy. The average ratio of gross private domestic fixed investment to GNP in constant dollars was 0.142 in the 1947–58 period, 0.141 in the 1958–67 period, and 0.145 in the 1967–76 period.[4]

Assumption (v): It is also assumed that the productive inputs purchased by unproductive sectors (A_{pu}) are a fixed share of the total net product, TP:

$$A_{put} = b_6 TP_t \tag{4.9}$$

where b_6 is a constant. The ratio A_{pu}/TP actually rose over the postwar period from 0.19 in 1947 to 0.24 in 1976. However, this assumption is not crucial and is introduced simply for algebraic convenience.

From equations (4.6)–(4.9), it follows that the total net product, TP, is divided in fixed shares among worker consumption, investment, and purchases of productive inputs made by unproductive sectors:

$$\text{TP}_t = A_{put} + Y_{pt} = A_{put} + D_{pt} + \dot{K}_t \tag{4.10}$$

Assumption (vi): The next assumption is that the unproductive inputs purchased per unit of productive output, a_{up}, is a fixed coefficient. The postwar evidence does support this assumption, with the value of a_{up} of 0.071 in 1947, 0.085 in 1958, 0.077 in 1967, and 0.079 in 1976.

Remaining assumptions: The next two assumptions are standard for growth models, which permit a solution for the steady-state behavior of the model. The first of these is that the rate of growth of the labor force is exogenously determined and is constant over time at n percent per year. The second of these is that both labor and capital are fully employed at each point in them. Finally, in order to simplify the algebra, it is assumed that

$$A_{pp} = A_{uu} = 0$$

By this, the diagonal of the interindustry flow matrix is set to zero, which is equivalent to measuring the gross output of each sector net of the output reused as inputs by the sector. (For example, the output

---

[4] The source is the *Economic Report of the President, 1979,* Table B.2. Both GNP and investment are in 1972 dollars. Fixed investment is defined as the difference between gross private domestic investment and the change in business inventories and includes both nonresidential and residential investment.

of wheat in agriculture is measured net of the portion used for seed.) This then implies that

$$X_{pt} = TP_t \qquad (4.11)$$

B. Solution of model

From (4.2) and (4.4), it follows that

$$N_p = N - N_u = N - d_1 X_p \qquad (4.12)$$

and

$$K_p = K - K_u = K - d_2 X_p \qquad (4.13)$$

Substituting these into (4.5), we obtain

$$X_{pt} = c_1 e^{rt}(N - d_1 X_p)^\alpha (K - d_2 X_p)^{1-\alpha} \qquad (4.14)$$

where time subscripts are now dropped for convenience. The production function implicitly defined by (4.14) has constant returns to scale in N and K (though it is not Cobb–Douglas). This is evident by noting that for any set of values of X_p, N, and K that solve for (4.14) and any scalar d_0, the set $d_0 X_p$, $d_0 N$, and $d_0 K$ will also solve for (4.14).

We can therefore rewrite (4.14) as

$$X_p = e^{rt}F(N, K) \qquad (4.15)$$

where F is a constant returns to scale (CRTS) production function. It is now possible to solve the system as a Solow growth model in X_p [see Solow (1956)] but with Hicks-neutral technical progress. Define the capital–labor and output–labor ratios as

$$k \equiv K/N \quad \text{and} \quad x \equiv X_p/N$$

Then, from (4.14),

$$x = X_p/N = c_1 e^{rt}(1 - d_1 x)^\alpha (k - d_2 x)^{1-\alpha} \qquad (4.16)$$

Since x is a function simply of k and t, we can rewrite (4.16) as

$$x = f(k, t) = c_1 e^{rt}[1 - d_1 f(k, t)]^\alpha [k - d_2 f(k, t)]^{1-\alpha} \quad (4.17)$$

Three results are immediately apparent from the last equation. First, $f(k, t)$ is bounded from above by $1/d_1$. Second, $f(k, t)$ must lie below k/d_2. Third, since e^{rt} increases without limit over time, x must converge to $1/d_1$ over time or k must approach $d_2 x$ over time or both may happen. It is now necessary to establish the shape of $f(k, t)$.

Lemma 1: The function $f(k, t)$, fulfills the following conditions: (i) $f(0, t) = 0$; (ii) $(\partial f/\partial k)(k, t) > 0$; (iii) $\lim_{k \to \infty}(\partial f/\partial k) = 0$; and (iv) for $k > d_2/d_1$, $(\partial^2 f/\partial k^2)(k, t) < 0$.

Proof: (i) If $k = 0$, then $f(k, t)$ must equal zero also, since $f(k, t)$ is bounded from above by k/d_2.

(ii) Differentiating (4.17), we obtain

$$\frac{\partial f}{\partial k} = c_1 e^{rt}[-\alpha(1 - d_1 f)^{\alpha-1} d_1 \frac{\partial f}{\partial k} (k - d_2 f)^{1-\alpha}$$

$$+ (1 - \alpha)(k - d_2 f)^{-\alpha} \left(1 - d_2 \frac{\partial f}{\partial k}\right) (1 - d_1 f)^{\alpha}]$$

Combining terms and solving for $\partial f/\partial k$, we have

$$\frac{\partial f}{\partial k} = (1 - \alpha)B^{-\alpha}\{1 + c_1 e^{rt}$$

$$\times [\alpha d_1 B^{1-\alpha} + (1 - \alpha)d_2 B^{-\alpha}]\}^{-1} \quad (4.18)$$

where

$$B \equiv \frac{k - d_2 f}{1 - d_1 f}$$

Since $f(k, t) < k/d_2$ and $f(k, t) < 1/d_1$, $B > 0$, and it follows that $\partial f/\partial k > 0$.

(iii) We can now transform (4.18) as follows:

$$\frac{\partial f}{\partial k} = (1 - \alpha)\{B^{\alpha} + c_1 e^{rt}[\alpha d_1 B + (1 - \alpha)d_2]\}^{-1} \quad (4.19)$$

Since f is bounded from above by $1/d_1$, $\lim_{k \to \infty} B = \infty$ and hence $\lim_{k \to \infty} \partial f/\partial k = 0$.

(iv) Differentiating (4.18) with respect to k, we obtain

$$\frac{\partial^2 f}{\partial k^2} = -\frac{(1 - \alpha)B^{-\alpha}}{c^2} \left(\alpha CB^{-1} \frac{\partial B}{\partial k} + \frac{\partial C}{\partial k}\right) \quad (4.20)$$

where

$$C = 1 + c_1 e^{rt}[\alpha d_1 B^{1-\alpha} + (1 - \alpha)d_2 B^{-\alpha}]$$

Since $B > 0$ and $C > 0$, $\partial^2 f/\partial k^2 < 0$ if $\partial B/\partial k > 0$ and $\partial c/\partial k > 0$. Now,

$$\frac{\partial B}{\partial k} = \frac{(1 - d_1 f) + (kd_1 - d_2)\partial f/\partial k}{(1 - d_1 f)^2}$$

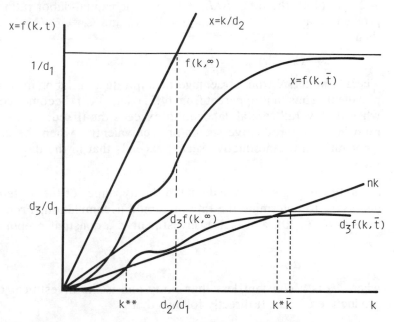

Figure 4.1. Determination of dynamics of two-sector model.

Since k is bounded from above by $1/d_1$, $1 - d_1 f$ is positive. From (ii), $\partial f/\partial k > 0$. Therefore, $\partial B/\partial k > 0$ if $k > d_2/d_1$. Moreover,

$$\frac{\partial C}{\partial k} = c_1 e^{rt}\alpha(1 - \alpha)B^{-\alpha}\frac{\partial B}{\partial k}(d_1 - d_2 B^{-1})$$

Now, the last term $(d_1 - d_2 B^{-1})$ is given by

$$d_1 - d_2 B^{-1} = \frac{d_1 k - d_2}{k - d_2 f}$$

Since f is bounded by k/d_2, $d_1 - d_2 B^{-1} > 0$ if $k > d_2/d_1$. Moreover, if $k > d_2/d_1$, then $\partial B/\partial k > 0$ and hence $\partial C/\partial k > 0$. This completes the proof.

The function $f(k, \bar{t})$ at some time $\bar{t}$ is shown in Figure 4.1. It slopes upward throughout its length and has an asymptote at $1/d_1$. Below $k = d_2/d_1$, there can be several inflection points, but above $k = d_2/d_1$, $f(k, t)$ is strictly concave, with $\partial f/\partial k$ approaching zero in the limit. Finally, $f(k, t)$ is bounded from above by the ray through the origin given by $x = k/d_2$. The point $k = d_2/d_1$ deserves some comment. From

(4.2) and (4.4), the ratio $d_2/d_1 = k_u/N_u$, the capital–labor ratio of unproductive activity. If we let $k_p \equiv K_p/N_p$ and $k_u \equiv K_u/N_u = d_2/d_1$, then

$$k = (1 - u)k_p + uk_u \tag{4.21}$$

where $u \equiv N_u/N$, the percentage of unproductive labor in total employment. Thus, it is apparent from (4.21) that $f(k, t)$ becomes concave when the overall capital–labor ratio exceeds the (fixed) capital–labor ratio in the unproductive sector or, equivalently, when the capital–labor ratio in the productive sector exceeds that in the unproductive sector.

Dynamics of system: To understand the dynamics of the system, it is necessary to determine the rate of capital accumulation. From equations (4.8), (4.10), and (4.11), investment is a constant proportion of X_p:

$$\dot{K} = d_3 X_p \tag{4.22}$$

where d_3 is a constant less than unity and is the investment rate of productive output. It directly follows that

$$k = \frac{\dot{K}}{L} - \frac{K\dot{L}}{L^2} = d_3 f(k, t) - nk \tag{4.23}$$

where n is the exogenously given rate of growth of the labor force (and employment under the assumption of full employment). The curve $d_3 f(k, \bar{t})$ is drawn in Figure 4.1, as well as the line nk. It should be apparent that $d_3 f$ is bounded from above by d_3/d_1. Since $f(k, \bar{t})$ may have one or more inflection points, it is possible that the line nk may cross $d_3 f(k, \bar{t})$ at more than one point. At the points of intersection (k^* and k^{**} are shown in Figure 4.1), the capital–labor ratio k is maintained until the next period. If k equals some value $\bar{k}$ other than k^* or k^{**}, then k will decline at $\bar{t}$ if $d_3 f(\bar{k}, \bar{t}) < n\bar{k}$ and will increase at $\bar{t}$ if $d_3 f(\bar{k}, \bar{t}) > n\bar{k}$.

At the same time, however, $f(k, t)$ is shifting since f is also a function of time. In the limit, as t approaches infinity, $f(k, t)$ will approach the envelope curve given by the two functions $x = 1/d_1$ and $x = k/d_2$ [and shown in bold line as $f(k, \infty)$ in Figure 4.1]:

$$\lim_{t \to \infty} f(k, t) = \begin{cases} k/d_2 & \text{if } k \leq d_2/d_1 \\ 1/d_1 & \text{if } k \geq d_2/d_1 \end{cases} \tag{4.24}$$

This result is evident from (4.17). It is already known that $f(k, t) \leq 1/d_1$ and $f(k, t) \leq k/d_2$. Suppose $f(k, t)$ approaches $\bar{f}$ in the limit as t increases without limit where $\bar{f} < 1/d_1$ and $\bar{f} < k/d_2$. Then, from (4.17),

$f(k, t)$ must approach infinity since e^{rt} increases without limit, which is inconsistent with the assumption.

The limiting function for $d_3 f(k, t)$ directly follows (and is also shown in Figure 4.1):

$$\lim_{t \to \infty} d_3 f(k, t) = \begin{cases} d_3 k/d_2 & \text{if } k \le d_2/d_1 \\ d_3/d_1 & \text{if } k \ge d_2/d_1 \end{cases} \tag{4.25}$$

In the limit, as t approaches infinity, the aggregate capital–labor ratio k will approach a *finite limit* $\bar{k}$ (as shown in Figure 4.1) given by

$$\lim_{t \to \infty} k_t = \bar{k} = d_3/(d_1 n) \tag{4.26}$$

This is a very different result than the standard result that with Hicks-neutral technical progress in a one-sector growth model, the capital–labor ratio will increase without limit [cf. Solow (1956)].[5]

This result leads to the following propositions:

Proposition 1: In the limit, as t approaches infinity, the overall rate of labor productivity growth approaches zero, the rate of growth of productive output approaches n, and the rate of capital accumulation approaches n.

Proof: Define the overall rate of productivity growth g_t as

$$g_t \equiv \dot{X}_{pt}/X_{pt} - n = \dot{x}_t/x_t$$

Since x_t approaches a constant, $1/d_1$, in the limit, $\dot{x}_t$ approaches zero, as does g_t. From this, it directly follows that

$$\lim_{t \to \infty} \dot{X}_{pt}/X_{pt} = n$$

Finally, from (4.26), since $\dot{k}_t/k_t = \dot{K}_t/K_t - \dot{N}_t/N_t = 0$ in the limit,

$$\lim_{t \to \infty} \frac{\dot{K}_t}{K_t} = \frac{\dot{N}_t}{N_t} = n$$

[5] Technically, there are two other possible cases. First, if the ray nk lies above $d_3 k/d_2$, the limiting capital–labor ratio is zero. The reason is that $d_3/d_2 = \dot{K}/K_u \ge \dot{K}/K$. Thus, if $n > \dot{K}/K_u$, this means that the labor force must forever grow faster than the total capital stock and the overall capital–labor ratio must go to zero in the limit. Second, if $n = d_3/d_2$, the same result would occur in the limit. The reason is that the ray nk must forever lie above $d_3 f(k, t)$, and from (4.23), the capital–labor ratio will fall over time and approach zero as t approaches infinity. For simplicity, we shall ignore these "perverse cases" for the remainder of the book. It might also be noted that in the Solow model, there is the additional possibility that with *no* technical change, labor productivity may increase without limit if the savings rate function $d_3 f(k, t)$ always lies above the ray nk. This is not possible in the two-sector model since the savings function $d_3 f(k, t)$ approaches the horizontal asymptote at d_3/d_1.

Proposition 2: In the limit, as t approaches infinity, the rate of growth of the capital stock employed in the unproductive sector and the rate of growth of unproductive employment both approach n; the rate of growth of productivity employed capital stock also approaches n, and the rate of growth of productive employment approaches $n - r/\alpha$. Also, in the limit, $u \equiv N_{ut}/N_t$ approaches unity, whereas $u_K \equiv K_{ut}/K_t$ approaches d_2n/d_3.

Proof: From (4.2) and (4.4), it follows that, at every time t,

$$\frac{\dot{N}_{ut}}{N_{ut}} = \frac{\dot{K}_{ut}}{K_{ut}} = \frac{\dot{X}_{pt}}{X_{pt}} \tag{4.27}$$

From Proposition 1, it directly follows that

$$\lim_{t \to \infty} \frac{\dot{N}_{ut}}{N_{ut}} = \lim_{t \to \infty} \frac{\dot{K}_{ut}}{K_{ut}} = n$$

From (4.4) and since $\lim x_t = 1/d_1$,

$$\lim_{t \to \infty} u_t = \lim_{t \to \infty} \frac{N_{it}}{N_t} = \lim_{t \to \infty} \left(d_1 \frac{x_{pt}}{N_t} \right) = 1$$

From (4.2) and (4.26), it follows that

$$\lim_{t \to \infty} u_{kt} = \lim_{t \to \infty} \frac{K_{ut}}{K_t} = \lim_{t \to \infty} \left(\frac{d_1 n d_2 X_{pt}}{d_3 N_{pt}} \right) = \frac{d_2 n}{d_3} < 1$$

since, by assumption, $d_3 k/d_2 > nk$ (see footnote 5 for more details). By definition,

$$\frac{\dot{K}_t}{K_t} = (1 - u_{K_t}) \frac{\dot{K}_{pt}}{K_{pt}} + u_{K_t} \frac{\dot{K}_{ut}}{K_{ut}}$$

Since $\lim u_{K_t} < 1$, from Proposition 1 and above,

$$\lim \frac{\dot{K}_{pt}}{K_{pt}} = n$$

Finally, from (4.5),

$$\frac{\dot{X}_{pt}}{X_{pt}} = r + \alpha \frac{\dot{N}_{pt}}{N_{pt}} + (1 - \alpha) \frac{\dot{K}_{pt}}{K_{pt}}$$

Hence, from Proposition 1 and above,

$$\lim \frac{\dot{N}_{pt}}{N_{pt}} = n - \frac{r}{\alpha}$$

The limiting growth in productive employment could be either positive or negative.

There are several results that immediately follow from the two propositions. First, if the rate of capital accumulation is greater than the rate of growth of the labor force, as it has been historically in the United States since at least 1870, it must fall over time (though not necessarily continuously). Second, the share of unproductive employment in total employment will increase over time. Third, the overall rate of labor productivity growth, if it is above zero (which has been the case since at least 1870), must fall over time (though not necessarily continuously). Fourth, define the rate of total factor productivity (TFP) growth as

$$\frac{\dot{TFP}_t}{TFP_t} = \frac{\dot{X}_{pt}}{X_{pt}} - \left[\beta_t \frac{\dot{N}_t}{N_t} + (1 - \beta_t) \frac{\dot{K}_t}{K_t} \right]$$

where β_t is the share of wages in total income. For our purposes, it is not necessary to derive β since, in the limit,

$$\lim_{t \to \infty} \frac{\dot{TFp}_t}{TFP_t} = n - [\beta_t n + (1 - \beta_t) n] = 0$$

Thus, if the overall rate of TFP growth is positive, as it has been historically in the United States, it must fall over time. Finally, the real wage, w, is given by

$$w_t \equiv D_{pt}/N_t$$

Since, from (4.7), D_{pt} is a fixed proportion of X_{pt}, in the limit, the rate of growth of w_t must approach zero and, if positive, must fall over time.

Labor values and rate of surplus value: In order to derive the limiting values for the rate of surplus value, it is necessary to obtain limiting expressions for Marxian labor values. Define the standard rate of direct labor productivity growth in the productive sector as

$$g_{pt}^* = \frac{\dot{X}_{pt}}{X_{pt}} - \frac{\dot{N}_{pt}^*}{N_{pt}^*}$$

where

$$N_p^* = N_p + N_{up}$$

and gives total employment in the productive sector.

Lemma 2: In the limit, g_{pt}^* approaches zero.

Proof: Define

$$u^* = \frac{N_{up}}{N_p + N_{up}}$$

Then,

$$\frac{\dot{N}_{pt}^*}{N_{pt}} = (1 - u_t^*)\frac{\dot{N}_{pt}}{N_{pt}} + u_t^*\frac{\dot{N}_{upt}}{N_{upt}}$$

From (4.3) and Proposition 1,

$$\lim \frac{\dot{N}_{upt}}{N_{upt}} = \lim \frac{\dot{X}_{pt}}{X_{pt}} = n$$

where, unless otherwise indicated, $\lim = \lim_{t \to \infty}$. From Proposition 2,

$$\lim \frac{\dot{N}_{pt}}{N_{pt}} = n - \frac{r}{\alpha}$$

Hence,

$$\lim u^* = 1$$

and

$$\lim \frac{\dot{N}_{pt}^*}{N_{pt}^*} = \lim \frac{\dot{N}_{upt}}{N_{upt}} = n$$

Therefore, from Proposition 1,

$$\lim g_{pt}^* = \lim \frac{\dot{X}_{pt}}{X_{pt}} - n = 0$$

The standard technical coefficient matrix at time t is given by

$$a_t = \begin{bmatrix} 0 & a_{put} \\ a_{upt} & 0 \end{bmatrix}$$

Moreover, the vector of labor coefficients l_t is given by

$$l_t = (l_{pt} \; l_{ut})$$

where $l_{pt} = l_{ppt} + l_{upt}$. Therefore, the vector of standard Marxian labor values λ_t^* is given by

$$\lambda_t^* = (\lambda_{pt} \; \lambda_{ut}) = l_t(I - a_t)^{-1}$$

Solving, we obtain

$$\lambda_{pt} = \frac{l_{pt} + l_{ut} a_{upt}}{1 - a_{upt} a_{put}} \tag{4.28}$$

$$\lambda_{ut} = \frac{l_{pt} a_{put} + l_{ut}}{1 - a_{upt} a_{put}} \tag{4.29}$$

where, by the Hawkins–Simon condition, $a_{upt} a_{put} < 1$. Now, by assumption,

$$l_{ut} = \bar{l}_u \qquad a_{put} = \bar{a}_{pu}$$

$$a_{upt} = \bar{a}_{up} \qquad l_{upt} = \bar{l}_{up}$$

where a bar over a term indicates a fixed value. Moreover, from (4.5),

$$l_{ppt} = \frac{N_{pt}}{X_{pt}} = \frac{1}{c_1} e^{-rt} \left(\frac{N_{pt}}{K_{pt}}\right)^{1-\alpha} \tag{4.30}$$

This formula allows us to prove the following:

Lemma 3: In the limit, l_{ppt} approaches zero and l_{pt} approaches a constant.

Proof: From Proposition 2,

$$\lim \frac{\dot{N}_{pt}}{N_{pt}} = n - \frac{r}{\alpha} \qquad \lim \frac{\dot{K}_{pt}}{K_{pt}} = n$$

Therefore, from (4.30) and Proposition 2,

$$\lim l_{ppt} = \lim b_6 e^{-rt} e^{(-r/\alpha)(1-\alpha)t}$$

$$= \lim b_6 e^{-(r/\alpha)t}$$

$$= 0$$

where b_6 is a constant. Therefore,

$$\lim l_{pt} = \lim l_{ppt} + \lim l_{upt}$$

$$= \bar{l}_{up}$$

This leads directly to the following proposition:

Proposition 3: In the limit, λ_{pt} and λ_{ut} both approach constants.

Proof: This follows directly from (4.28), (4.29), Lemma 3, and the fact that l_{ut}, a_{upt}, and a_{put} are fixed coefficients.

Let us define sectoral total labor productivity (TLP) as the inverse of the sectoral labor value. TLP shows the amount of sectoral output produced per unit of direct plus indirect labor requirements. Then, the following corollary follows immediately from Propositon 3:

Corollary 1: In the limit, TLP growth in the productive sector approaches zero.

It is perhaps surprising that even though the direct labor coefficient l_{ppt} vanishes and the unproductive input coefficients a_{upt} and l_{upt} are fixed, TLP growth in the productive sector should approach zero. The reason is that in labor value terms, the inputs a_{up} and l_{up} represent an increasingly greater share of the total costs of producing X_p. Indeed, if labor values are used to measure output prices, the following can be proved:

Corollary 2: In labor value price terms, the share of unproductive input costs in total costs in the productive sector approaches unity in the limit.

Proof: From (4.28) and (4.29), the ratio of the costs of unproductive inputs a_{upt} and l_{upt} to the price of output X_p is given by

$$\theta_t \equiv \frac{l_{upt} + \lambda_{upt}a_{upt}}{\lambda_{pt}} = \frac{l_{upt}}{\lambda_{pt}} + \frac{(l_{pt}\bar{a}_{pt} + \bar{l}_u)\bar{a}_{up}}{l_{pt} + \bar{l}_u\bar{a}_{up}}$$

From Lemma 3,

$$\lim \theta_t = \frac{\bar{l}_{up}(1 - \bar{a}_{up}\bar{a}_{pu}) + \bar{l}_{up}\bar{a}_{pu}\bar{a}_{up} + \bar{l}_u\bar{a}_{up}}{\bar{l}_{up} + \bar{l}_u\bar{a}_{up}}$$

$$= 1$$

It is now possible to determine limiting values for Marxian variables of interest.

Proposition 4: The rate of surplus value ϵ_t and the rate of exploitation ϵ_t^* both increase without limit.

Proof: In this model, variable capital V_t is given by

$$V_t = N_{pt}\lambda_t w_t$$

surplus value by

$$S_t = N_t - V_t$$

and the rate of surplus value by

$$\epsilon_t = \frac{S_t}{V_t} = \frac{N_t}{N_{pt}\lambda_t w_t} - 1 \tag{4.31}$$

Now,

$$\lambda_t = \frac{l_{ppt}}{1 - \bar{a}_{up}\bar{a}_{pu}}$$

From Lemma 3,

$$\lim \lambda_t = 0$$

Hence, since the ratio N_t/N_{pt} increases without limit, λ_t approaches zero, and w_t approaches a positive constant, ϵ_t increases without limit.

From (3.11) and (4.31), the rate of exploitation ϵ^* is given by

$$\epsilon_t^* = \frac{N_t - N_t\lambda_t w_t}{N_t\lambda_t w_t} = \frac{1}{\lambda_t w_t} - 1$$

Since w_t approaches a finite constant and λ_t approaches zero in the limit, the rate of exploitation also increases without limit.

C.　Comparison with one-sector Solow model

In the case of a single-sector economy producing productive output, we can immediately recover the steady-state equilibrium conditions from the standard Solow (1956) model. We shall assume that the production function is Cobb–Douglas with Hicks-neutral technical change [see equation (4.5)] and that investment $\dot{K}_t$ is a constant fraction of output [see equation (4.8)]. In the one-sector case, $d_1 = d_2 = 0$. The steady-state equilibrium results, designated by a superscript e, are

$$\text{(i)} \quad \left(\frac{\dot{K}}{K}\right)^e = \left(\frac{\dot{X}_p}{X_p}\right)^e = n + \frac{r}{\alpha}$$

$$\text{(ii)} \quad g^e = \left(\frac{\dot{X}_p}{X_p}\right)^e - n = \frac{r}{\alpha}$$

$$\text{(iii)} \quad \frac{\dot{\text{TFP}}_t}{\text{TFP}_t} = \frac{\dot{X}_{pt}}{X_{pt}} - \left[\alpha n + (1 - \alpha)\frac{\dot{K}_t}{K_t}\right] = r \quad \text{for all } t$$

(iv) $\left(\dfrac{\dot{w}}{w}\right)^e = \left(\dfrac{\dot{X}_p}{X_p}\right)^e - n = \dfrac{r}{\alpha}$

(v) $\epsilon_t = \epsilon_t^* = \dfrac{X_{pt} - D_{pt}}{D_{pt}} = \dfrac{(1 - b_4)}{b_4}$ a constant for all t

In contrast, in the two-sector case,

(i') $\lim \dfrac{\dot{K}_t}{K_t} = \lim \dfrac{\dot{X}_{pt}}{X_{pt}} = n$

(ii') $\lim g_t = 0$

(iii') $\lim \dfrac{\dot{\text{TFP}}_t}{\text{TFP}_t} = 0$

(iv') $\lim \dfrac{\dot{w}_t}{w_t} = 0$

(v') $\lim \epsilon_t = \lim \epsilon_t^* = \infty$

Thus, the limiting values of output growth, capital accumulation, labor productivity growth, TFP growth, and real wage growth in the two-sector case are all lower than the corresponding steady-state equilibrium values in the one-sector model. In this sense, we can say that unproductive activity depresses output, productivity, and real wage growth. Moreover, both the rate of surplus value and the rate of exploitation increase without limit in the two-sector case but are finite and constant over time in the one-sector case. In this sense, we can say that unproductive activity increases the rate of surplus value and labor exploitation.

D.   Conclusions

Over the past 100 years or so in the United States, the rate of growth of output and the capital stock has generally exceeded that of the labor force, the rate of growth of productivity and the real wage has been generally positive, and unproductive employment has constituted only a fraction of total employment. Based on these historical observations and the results of the analysis, the following predictions can be offered:

(i)   Unproductive employment will increase over time as a fraction of total employment and approach unity in the limit.

(ii)   The rate of growth of total output will decline over time and, in the limit, approach the rate of growth of the labor force.

(iii)   The rate of capital accumulation will decline over time and, in the limit, approach the rate of growth of the labor force.

(iv)   The rate of growth of the capital stock employed in the productive sector will fall over time and approach the rate of growth of the labor force in the limit. Moreover, the ratio of unproductively employed capital stock to the total capital stock will approach a positive constant less than unity.

(v)   The rate of overall labor productivity growth and that of overall TFP growth will decline over time and approach zero in the limit.

(vi)   The rates of simple labor productivity and TLP growth in the productive sector will decline over time and approach zero in the limit.

(vii)   The rate of growth of the real wage will decline over time and approach zero in the limit.

(viii)   The cost of unproductive inputs as a percentage of total costs in the productive sector will rise over time and approach unity in the limit.

A proviso should be added that the results of this model may depend critically on the specification of a CRTS Cobb–Douglas production function for the productive sector. In particular, the CRTS assumption prevents the output of the productive sector from expanding too rapidly over time. In addition, the implicit assumption of a unitary elasticity of substitution between capital and labor (σ) likewise prevents output from expanding too rapidly as capital is substituted for labor in the productive sector. My speculation is that if there were increasing returns to scale with $\sigma = 1$, overall labor productivity may increase without limit. On the other hand, if there were decreasing returns to scale with $\sigma = 1$, overall labor productivity may reach a finite limit in a finite amount of time. Likewise, if there were constant returns to scale, the overall productivity level might increase without limit if $\sigma > 1$ or reach a finite limit in a finite amount of time if $\sigma < 1$.

CHAPTER 5

Rise of unproductive activity in postwar economy

More than half the taxes sent to Washington, Americans feel, are wasted, according to the Gallup Poll.

Democrats, Republicans, men, women, young, old and those of all income levels responded with unusual unanimity to the question, "Of every tax dollar that goes to the Federal Government in Washington, D.C., how many cents of each dollar would you say are wasted?"

Fifty-two cents was their median and most frequent response.

The results were close to those in a poll taken in 1978 that indicated that the American public felt that 48 percent of Federal tax money was wasted.

As in the 1978 survey, the latest poll indicated that the people believed that less money was wasted at the state and local levels than by the Federal Government. At the state level, they think that 29 cents of every tax dollar are wasted, according to the survey. The figure was 32 cents in 1978. At the local level, the figure was 23 cents in the latest poll and 25 cents in 1978. (*New York Times*, December 17, 1979, p. A24. Copyright© 1979 by the New York Times Company. Reprinted by permission.)

In this and the next two chapters, empirical results are presented to document the scope of unproductive activity in the U.S. economy in the postwar period and to demonstrate its effects on capital accumulation and the growth in productivity, the real wage, and per capita consumption. In particular, evidence is gathered that largely confirms the predictions of the two-sector model developed in the previous chapter. In this chapter, findings are presented on the relative growth of unproductive labor in the labor force, as well as on time trends of other unproductive components of the economy. For this purpose, we return to conventional categories of the national income and product accounts. In addition, the composition of the net product in the 1947–76 period is analyzed in this chapter, and particular attention is paid to the inverse relation between the share of unproductive spending in the net product and the share of net investment.

A.   Time trends in unproductive activity by sectoral classification

Table 5.1 presents several measures of the relative share of unproductive activity in total economic activity in the postwar economy using conventional national income and product categories and the sectoral

Table 5.1. *Various measures of relative share of unproductive activity in total activity using conventional categories and sectoral classification scheme (%)*[a]

	1947	1958	1963	1967	1972	1976
1. Employment in unproductive sectors[b] $(\sum L_u/N)$	25.3	34.0	34.2	35.9	37.7	38.1
2. Wages in unproductive sectors $(\sum E_u/\sum E)$	26.8	31.1	30.8	31.2	33.2	32.9
3. Surplus income originating in unproductive sectors $[\sum (R_u + T_u)/\sum (R + T)]$	34.3	36.7	36.8	39.4	45.6	46.8
4. Gross domestic output of unproductive sectors $(\sum X_u/\sum X)$	21.7	25.1	23.7	24.7	26.4	25.0
5. Household consumption of unproductive output $(\sum D_u/\sum D)$	31.8	32.0	32.1	34.2	36.7	35.3
6. Nonhousehold final demand for unproductive output $[\sum (G_u + H_u)/\sum (G + H)]$	32.8	57.4	48.4	45.2	43.2	49.1
7. Total final output of unproductive sectors $(\sum Y_u/CFP)$	32.1	39.6	37.2	37.9	38.6	38.9
8. Unproductive "inputs" purchased by productive sectors $[\sum A_{up}/\sum (A_{pp} + A_{up})]$	11.1	13.0	11.9	12.8	13.9	12.5

[a] All ratios except employment, wages, and surplus income are formed from constant-dollar data. Wage and surplus income ratios are formed from current-dollar data.
[b] Military employment is excluded.

classification scheme for unproductive activity (see Chapter 2). The first row shows the civilian labor employed in unproductive sectors as a proportion of total employment. The numerator, it should be noted, does not include unproductive labor directly employed in productive sectors. This ratio jumped from 0.25 in 1947 to 0.34 in 1958 and then continued to rise, although at a much slower rate, between 1958 and 1976. The conventionally measured wages and salaries paid to workers employed in unproductive sectors as a proportion of total wages and salaries (row 2) increased from 0.27 in 1947 to 0.31 in 1958 and then to 0.33 in 1976. A comparison of row 2 and row 1 indicates that the mean earnings of unproductive workers declined relative to productive workers over this period. The percentage of total surplus income, defined conventionally as the sum of profits, dividends, other property-type income, and taxes, that was generated in unproductive sectors rose from 0.34 in 1947 to 0.37 in 1958 and then to 0.47 in 1976 (row 3).

The proportion of conventionally measured surplus income originating in unproductive sectors was higher than the proportion of unproductive employment, wages, or output in their corresponding totals. In fact, by 1976 almost half of all conventionally measured surplus income was generated in unproductive sectors.

The ratio of conventionally measured unproductive to total output increased from 0.22 in 1947 to 0.25 in 1958 and then leveled off (row 4). The percentage of unproductive output in total output was uniformly lower than the percentage of unproductive employment in total employment and its rate of increase over the 1947–76 time span was also lower. This reflects both the greater labor intensity of unproductive activity and the slower rate of decline of unproductive labor absorption.

Household expenditures on unproductive output as a proportion of total household expenditures registered 0.32 in 1947 and 1958 and then increased to 0.35 by 1976 (row 5). In 1976 over one-third of household expenditures were spent on unproductive output. The unproductive proportion of nonhousehold final output rose sharply from 0.33 in 1947 to 0.57 in 1958 and then declined to 0.49 in 1976 (row 6). This pattern reflects the rapid increase in defense expenditures between 1947 and 1958 and then the growth of state and local government expenditures after 1958, which have a much lower unproductive content than federal expenditures. As a result, the share of unproductive output in total final output (CFP) rose from 0.32 in 1947 to 0.40 in 1958 and then leveled off (row 7). By 1976, almost 40 percent of final demand was expended on unproductive output.

The last row of Table 5.1 shows the ratio of the total value of unproductive inputs purchased by productive sectors to the total value of intermediate inputs used in productive sectors. This ratio was considerably lower than any of the other ratios in Table 5.1. Moreover, this ratio remained virtually constant over the whole 1947–76 period.

By most conventional output measures, unproductive activity as a proportion of total activity showed a sharp rise between 1947 and 1958 and then leveled off between 1958 and 1976. By 1976, depending on the indicator used, somewhere between 30 and 50 percent of all output was unproductive. On the other hand, civilian employment in unproductive sectors rose sharply between 1947 and 1958 and continued to rise after 1958. In 1976, 38 percent of all civilian employment was in unproductive sectors. Moreover, if the armed forces are included as part of the employed labor force, the share of employment in unproductive sectors (including the military) in total employment rose from 27 percent in 1947 to 40 percent in 1976.

Table 5.2 indicates the sources of the growth in both employment

Table 5.2. *Percentage breakdown of employment and gross product originating in unproductive sectors by sector and year* [a]

	1947	1958	1963	1967	1972	1976
A. Employment (civilian only)						
1. Trade (69, 85)	70.3	64.7	61.9	60.8	59.3	58.2
2. Finance (70)	8.2	10.8	11.3	11.7	11.9	11.9
3. Real estate (71)	4.1	3.3	3.1	3.0	3.3	3.4
4. Business services (73)	5.8	7.3	9.4	10.5	10.8	12.4
5. Unproductive government (84b)	11.6	13.9	14.3	14.0	14.6	14.1
Total unproductive	100.0	100.0	100.0	100.0	100.0	100.0
B. Gross product originating (1958 dollars)[b]						
1. Trade (69, 85)	51.0	47.4	48.4	49.1	51.4	52.4
2. Finance (70)	11.8	12.2	12.2	11.8	12.3	12.9
3. Real estate (71)	10.0	10.2	10.9	11.1	10.4	9.9
4. Business services (73)	6.5	7.6	8.6	9.4	9.4	10.1
5. Unproductive government (84b)	20.8	22.7	19.9	18.6	16.4	14.7
Total unproductive	100.0	100.0	100.0	100.0	100.0	100.0

[a] Sector numbers are shown in parentheses. The full names of these sectors are as follows: (1) wholesale, retail, export and import trade; (2) finance and insurance; (3) real estate and rentals; (4) business and professional services; (5) unproductive federal and state and local government activities.
[b] *Source:* Bureau of Economic Analysis, *The National Income and Product Accounts of the United States, 1929–76 Statistical Tables,* September 1981, Tables 6.2 and 6.3.

and conventionally measured gross product originating (GPO) in unproductive sectors.[1] In 1947, 70 percent of all employment in unproductive sectors was concentrated in the trade sector, 12 percent in the government sector, 8 percent in finance and insurance, 6 percent in business and professional services, and 4 percent in real estate (panel A). The share of unproductive sectoral employment in the trade sector declined continuously over the 1947–76 period, reaching 58 percent in 1976. The share of unproductive civilian employment in government rose from 12 to 14 percent between 1947 and 1958 and then leveled off. The proportion of unproductive employment in the finance and insur-

[1] GPO, also called value added in constant prices, is defined as the difference between gross domestic output in constant prices and the deflated value of intermediate inputs. For sector j,

$$\text{GPO}_j = X_j - \sum_i A_{ij}$$

where X and A are in constant dollars. GPO should not be confused with gross domestic output (X).

ance sector increased from 8 to 11 percent from 1947 to 1958 and then increased gradually after 1958, reaching 12 percent in 1976. The biggest change occurred in the business and professional service sector, whose employment share doubled from 6 percent in 1947 to 12 percent in 1976. The share of unproductive employment in real estate remained almost constant over the 1947–76 period. Finally, if the armed forces are included as part of unproductive employment in the government sector, the government's share of unproductive sectoral employment remained almost constant at 20 percent over the 1947–76 period. Thus, the increase in employment in unproductive sectors over the postwar period was primarily a result of the growth in advertising, legal services, other professional and business services, finance and insurance, and unproductive civilian government activities in the postwar economy.

The GPO shares indicate somewhat different time trends (panel B). The trade sector accounted for about a half of total GPO generated in unproductive sectors, and its share remained almost unchanged over the 1947–76 period. The share of unproductive GPO generated in the finance and insurance sector remained almost constant at 12 percent over the entire period, and that of the real estate sector (excluding imputed rent on owner-occupied housing) remained virtually unchanged at 10 percent. The share of unproductive GPO originating in business and professional services showed a marked increased over the period, rising from 6 percent in 1947 to 10 percent in 1976. On the other hand, the proportion of unproductive GPO accounted for by the government sector showed a marked decline, falling from 21 percent in 1947 to 15 percent in 1976. By this conventional output measure, then, the trade, finance and insurance, and real estate sectors grew at virtually the same rate as total unproductive activity, business and professional services considerably more rapidly, and unproductive government services considerably more slowly.

B.   Time trends in unproductive labor by occupational category

The distribution of civilian employment by productive and unproductive occupational groups is shown in Table 5.3 for each of four census years. Employment in unproductive occupations rose from 29.4 percent of total civilian employment in 1950 to 37.6 percent in 1980. In other terms, whereas total employment grew at an average annual rate of 1.7 percent from 1950 to 1980, employment in unproductive occupations grew at an annual rate of 2.6 percent. The relative growth in unproductive occupational employment was spread out fairly evenly

Table 5.3. *Percentage distribution of civilian employment by productive and unproductive occupational groups, 1950–80*[a]

Occupational group	1950[b]	1960[c]	1970[d]	1980[e]
A. Productive				
1. Professional and technical (selected)	7.37	10.01	12.67	13.65
2. Clerical (selected)	1.44	1.70	2.63	1.84
3. Craft (all)	14.01	14.24	13.85	13.07
4. Operative (all)	20.09	19.39	17.54	14.37
5. Service (except protective)	9.45	10.55	11.54	11.63
6. Nonfarm labor (all)	6.16	5.03	4.47	5.62
7. Farmers (all)	7.76	4.08	1.86	1.27
8. Farm labor (all)	4.33	2.34	1.25	0.94
Total productive	70.60	67.35	65.82	62.38
B. Unproductive				
1. Professional and technical (selected)	1.47	1.74	2.24	2.54
2. Clerical (selected)	10.99	13.43	15.31	15.10
3. Managerial and administrative (all)	9.04	8.80	8.32	8.60
4. Sales (all)	7.08	7.56	7.07	9.89
5. Protective services	0.82	1.12	1.25	1.49
Total unproductive	29.40	32.65	34.18	37.62

[a] See Table 2.4 for the classification scheme of productive and unproductive occupations.
[b] *Source:* U.S. Bureau of the Census, *U.S. Census of Population: 1950*, Vol. II, *Characteristics of the Population*, Part I, U.S. Summary. U.S. Government Printing Office, Washington, D.C., 1953, Table 124. The statistics are for the employed labor force, 14 years old and over.
[c] *Source:* U.S. Bureau of the Census, *U.S. Census of Population: 1960, Subject Reports, Occupational Characteristics*, Final Report PC(2)-7A. U.S. Government Printing Office, Washington, D.C., 1963, Table 2. The statistics are for the employed labor force, 14 years old and older.
[d] *Source:* U.S. Bureau of the Census, *U.S. Census of Population: 1970*, Special Reports, Final Report PC(2)-7A, Occupational Characteristics. U.S. Government Printing Office, Washington, D.C., 1973, Table 38. The statistics are for the employed labor force, 16 years old and over.
[e] *Source:* U.S. Bureau of the Census, *U.S. Census of Population: 1980*, Supplementary Report PC 80-51-8, *Detailed Occupation and Years of School Completed by Age, for the Civilian Labor Force by Sex, Race, and Spanish Origin: 1980*. U.S. Government Printing Office, Washington, D.C., March 1983, Table 1. The statistics are for the civilian labor force, 16 years old and over. The 1980 occupational classifications were made compatible with those of previous years.

over the three decades. If armed forces personnel are included as part of both total employment and unproductive employment, the ratio of employment in unproductive occupations to total employment grew from 0.313 in 1950 to 0.389 in 1980.[2] If this trend continues through the present, by 1984, 40 percent of the employed labor force will work in unproductive occupations.

A more detailed breakdown by occupational group reveals some interesting trends. Within productive employment, there were three major shifts. Productive professional and technical workers increased as a share of total civilian employment from 7.4 to 13.7 percent. This was offset by declines in operative and agricultural workers. The share of operatives in total civilian employment fell from 20.1 to 14.4 percent, and farmers and farm labor declined from 12.1 percent of total civilian employment in 1950 to 2.2 percent in 1980. Productive clerical and service workers both increased slightly as a share of total employment, and craft and nonfarm labor both declined slightly in relative terms.

Four of the five unproductive occupational groups grew as a percentage of total employment. Unproductive professional and technical workers increased from 1.5 to 2.5 percent of total civilian employment. Lawyers (including judges) almost tripled in number from 1950 to 1980. Unproductive clerical workers showed the largest increase, from 11.0 to 15.1 percent of total civilian employment. The share of sales workers grew from 7.1 to 9.9 percent, and the share of protective service workers grew from 0.8 to 1.5 percent. The number of protective service workers more than tripled from 1950 to 1980. Managerial and administrative personnel declined slightly as a percentage of total employment.

Table 5.4 shows the occupational breakdown of employment within productive industries only. In 1947, 16.7 percent of those employed in productive sectors worked in unproductive jobs. By 1976, the share had grown to 23.4 percent. In other words, although total employment in productive sectors increased at an annual rate of 0.8 percent between 1947 and 1976, unproductive jobs in productive industries grew by 1.9 percent. Among productive occupations, the biggest gain was again in professional and technical workers and the biggest loss in agricultural employment. Productive service workers increased their share by 4.0 percentage points, whereas the share of operatives declined by 4.1 percentage points and that of nonfarm labor shrank by 2.0 percentage

<hr>

[2] If household workers are classified as unproductive instead of productive workers, the results change rather little since domestic servants represent a small (and declining) part of total employment. With this change in classification, the ratio of unproductive to total employment increased from 0.339 in 1950 to 0.395 in 1980.

Table 5.4. *Percentage distribution of employment by occupational group within productive industries, 1947–76*[a]

Occupational group	1947	1958	1967	1976
A. *Productive*				
1. Professional and technical (selected)	7.12	10.92	12.60	15.27
2. Clerical (selected)	1.44	1.67	2.43	2.33
3. Craft (all)	16.51	17.38	17.70	17.20
4. Operative (all)	24.51	24.44	23.46	20.41
5. Service (except protective)	7.62	9.02	10.08	11.62
6. Nonfarm labor (all)	7.55	6.16	5.05	5.59
7. Farmers (all)	11.91	7.19	3.96	2.46
8. Farm labor (all)	6.62	4.09	2.46	1.73
Total productive	83.27	80.86	77.73	76.61
B. *Unproductive*				
1. Professional and technical (selected)	1.06	1.56	1.94	2.35
2. Clerical (selected)	7.92	9.56	11.55	11.91
3. Managerial and administrative (all)	5.48	5.60	6.13	6.05
4. Sales (all)	1.71	1.68	1.58	1.66
5. Protective services	0.54	0.74	1.11	1.41
Total unproductive	16.73	19.14	22.27	23.39

[a] *Source:* Occupation by industry employment tables, 1947, 1958, 1967, and 1976. See Appendix for details.

points. All but one of the unproductive occupational groups increased as a percentage of total employment in productive sectors. Unproductive clerical workers had the largest increase, with their share rising by 4.0 percentage points. Unproductive professional and technical workers increased their share by 1.3 percentage points, managerial and administrative workers by 0.6 percentage points, and protective service workers by 0.9 percentage points. The share of sales workers showed a very slight decline.

The final breakdown of productive and unproductive employment is shown in Table 5.5. Productive employment is now formally defined as the employment of workers in productive occupations who work in sectors that produce productive output. Unproductive employment is the converse and has three components. The first consists of workers employed in productive sectors but in unproductive occupations; the second consists of employment in unproductive sectors; and the third is armed forces personnel. Between 1947 and 1976, unproductive employment grew from 39.5 percent of total employment to 53.7 percent. In other terms, unproductive employment grew at an annual rate of

Table 5.5. *The final tally: percentage distribution of total (civilian and military) employment among productive and unproductive employments*

Employment distribution	1947	1958	1963	1967	1972	1976
A. *Productive sectors*						
1. Productive occupations	60.51	51.23	50.16	48.36	46.71	46.30
2. Unproductive occupations	12.16	12.13	13.09	13.86	13.79	14.14
B. *Unproductive sectors*						
1. All occupations	24.61	32.64	32.87	33.36	36.61	37.20
C. *Armed forces*	2.71	4.01	3.88	4.43	2.89	2.36
D. *Summary*						
1. Total productive employment[a]	60.51	51.23	50.16	48.36	46.71	46.30
2. Total unproductive employment[b]	39.49	48.77	49.84	51.64	53.29	53.70

[a] Equals row A1.
[b] Equals the sum of rows A2, B1, and C.

2.6 percent over this period, and total employment grew by 1.5 percent. Productive employment grew at an annual rate of 0.6 percent. If the armed forces are excluded, the ratio of unproductive employment to total civilian employment increased from 0.378 in 1947 to 0.526 in 1976.

Most of this increase occurred between the years 1947 and 1958. Over the eleven-year period, the share of unproductive in total employment increased by 9.3 percentage points. From 1958 to 1976, the ratio increased by another 4.9 percentage points. Of the three components of unproductive employment, by far the largest increase was in employment in unproductive sectors. Employment in unproductive occupations in productive sectors increased slightly as a share of total employment, whereas employment in the armed forces tended to behave cyclically over time, depending on pressure from both hot and cold wars.

C.   Cyclical movements in composition of final product

The analysis begins with the distribution of CFP, the conventionally measured final product, in constant dollars over its conventionally defined components during the period 1947–76 (Table 5.6). The first component, D, is household consumption out of labor earnings, and the second component, SC, is household consumption out of property income. Together, they sum to total household consumption. The third

Table 5.6. *Percentage composition of CFP by conventional components in constant dollars*

Component	1947	1958	1963	1967	1972	1976
1. Worker consumption (D)	48.7	50.9	49.2	50.1	58.4	60.0
2. Surplus consumption (SC)	20.3	19.2	19.4	17.0	12.1	13.8
3. Net capital formation (CF)	9.1	4.5	5.5	6.3	7.9	3.7
4. Government (G)	15.9	25.2	23.6	24.2	21.1	21.3
5. Residual (R)	6.0	0.2	2.3	2.4	0.6	1.1
Total (CFP)	100.0	100.0	100.0	100.0	100.0	100.0

component, CF, is total private capital formation net of depreciation. This component does not include government capital formation.[3] The fourth component, G, is the sum of federal and state and local government expenditure. The fifth component, R, is the residual, equaling the sum of the trade balance (TB) and net inventory change (IC).

The share of worker consumption in CFP remained fairly constant between 1947 and 1967 at about 50 percent and then rose to approximately 60 percent in the 1972–6 period. The share of surplus consumption in CFP also remained fairly constant between 1947 and 1967 at around 20 percent, but fell off considerably after 1967. Together, total household consumption as a share of CFP remained fairly constant over the whole 1947–76 period, varying between 70 and 75 percent. Net capital formation as a fraction of CFP fluctuated quite widely over the 29-year span, falling from 9 to 5 percent between 1947 and 1958, rising to 8 percent in 1972, and falling off again to 4 percent in 1976. Finally, government expenditures as a proportion of the total final output rose sharply between 1947 and 1958 from 16 to 25 percent, fell off slightly to 24 percent between 1963 and 1967, and then fell off again to 21 percent after 1967. No clear relations among the components emerge from this breakdown.

The picture is considerably sharper once the unproductive portions of the conventional final output categories are segregated out from the productive portions. In Table 5.7, CFP is divided into the various productive components of final output and Y_u. In this breakdown, the share of worker consumption of productive output, D_p, in CFP remained almost constant between 1947 and 1967 at about 33 percent. In contrast, total worker consumption, D, comprised 50 percent of CFP during this

---

[3] Indeed, because of the conventions of national accounting, there is no separate computation of government capital formation. Rather, it is included in current government expenditure.

Table 5.7. *Percentage composition of CFP by productive and unproductive final demand components in constant dollars*

Component	1947	1958	1963	1967	1972	1976
1. Productive worker consumption (D_p)	33.0	34.4	35.3	32.7	36.6	38.3
2. Productive surplus consumption (SC_p)	14.1	13.3	13.4	11.4	8.0	9.4
3. Productive net capital formation (CF_p)	8.4	4.2	5.1	5.8	7.2	3.4
4. Productive government (G_p)	7.6	9.3	9.9	10.9	10.5	11.7
5. Productive residual (R_p)	4.8	−0.8	1.2	1.3	−0.9	−1.7
6. Unproductive final output (Y_u)	32.1	39.6	37.2	37.9	38.6	38.9
Total (CFP)	100.0	100.0	100.0	100.0	100.0	100.0

period. The percentage point difference is accounted for by worker expenditure on unproductive output, D_u. Productive worker consumption as a share of CFP increased by about 4 percentage points between 1967 and 1972. This was considerably less than the 9 percentage point increase in the share of total worker consumption, D, in CFP. The difference is due to the fact that unproductive expenditures rose from about 32 percent of total worker consumption in the 1947–67 period to 36 percent in the 1972–6 period. On the other hand, productive surplus household consumption, SC_p, fell almost steadily as a share of CFP over the full 29-year time span. As a result, the share of productive household consumption $(D_p + SC_p)$ in CFP remained steady over the 29-year time span at about 47 percent.

The share of productive net capital formation, CF_p, in CFP fluctuated in the same fashion as the share of CF in CFP.[4] Productive government expenditures as a share of CFP showed a gradual increase over the 1947–76 period from 7 to 12 percent. This pattern contrasts sharply to the steep rise in total government expenditure as a percentage of CFP between 1947 and 1958 and its gradual decline thereafter. The patterns differ because unproductive government expenditures comprised about half of total government expenditure for all years except 1958, when the fraction was 0.63. This is reflected in the pattern of the share of unproductive final output, Y_u, in CFP, which increased sharply from 32 percent in 1947 to 40 percent in 1958, fell to 37 percent in 1963, and then gradually increased back to its 1958 level. The sharp

[4] The difference between the net capital formation (CF) figure and the productive net capital formation (CF_p) figure consisted almost entirely of the trade markup.

Table 5.8. *Percentage distribution of TP by component in constant dollars*

Component	1947	1958	1963	1967	1972	1976
1. Productive worker consumption (D_p)	40.0	41.6	39.8	39.5	46.3	48.1
2. Productive surplus consumption (SC_p)	17.1	16.1	16.0	13.8	10.1	11.8
3. Productive net capital formation (CF_p)	10.2	5.0	6.1	7.1	9.1	4.2
4. Productive government (G_p)	9.2	11.3	11.9	13.2	13.2	14.6
5. Productive output consumed in unproductive activity (A_{pu})	17.7	26.9	24.7	25.0	22.5	23.3
6. Productive residual (R_p)	5.8	−0.9	1.5	1.5	−1.2	−2.1
Total (TP)	100.0	100.0	100.0	100.0	100.0	100.0

increase between 1947 and 1958 was due to the large increase in defense spending, and the gradual rise after 1963 was due to the increase in household unproductive spending.

The major result that emerges is that net investment in capital formation moves inversely with unproductive expenditures over time. In the 1947–58 period, when unproductive expenditures as a share of CFP increased sharply, the ratio of net investment to CFP fell sharply. In the 1958–63 period, when the share of unproductive spending fell, the share of net capital formation rose. Between 1963 and 1967 and again between 1967 and 1972, both shares rose slightly by a percentage point, but between 1972 and 1976, when the share of unproductive spending in CFP again rose, the share of capital formation again fell off sharply.

The pattern is even sharper in Table 5.8, which shows the share of the productive components of final demand and of the productive output consumed in unproductive activity, A_{pu}, in TP, the total net product. In the 1947–58 period, when the portion of TP absorbed in unproductive activity jumped by 9 percentage points, the share of capital formation fell by 5 points. Between 1958 and 1963, when the portion of TP absorbed in unproductive activity fell by 2 percentage points, the investment share rose by 1. In the 1963–7 period, the investment share rose despite the fact that the unproductive share was about constant. In the 1967–72 period, when the unproductive share fell by 3 percentage points, the investment share rose by 2. In the last period, the unproductive share rose by 1 percentage point while the investment share fell by 5 points.

These results should caution against the popular but relatively simplistic explanation that government spending tends to "squeeze out" private investment. In Tables 5.7 and 5.8, the relatively steady rise in the share of productive government expenditures in CFP and TP over the 1947–67 period contrasts sharply with the fluctuating share of net capital formation in the two measures of final output. On the other hand, as evident from Table 5.6, the share of total government spending in CFP did tend to move inversely to the share of net capital formation in CFP. The difference in these two sets of results can be explained by the changing proportion of unproductive government spending in total government spending. The negative correlation between the share of unproductive government spending in CFP and the share of net investment in CFP was considerably stronger than that between the shares of total government spending, G, and net investment in CFP. But the strongest negative correlation is found between the share of total unproductive spending in the total net product and the share of net investment.

D.   Growth rate of final output components

Another way of contrasting short-run movements in the various components of final output is by calculating their average annual rate of change. For convenience, the 1947–76 period is divided into three sub-periods, as shown in Table 5.9. The rate of growth of the conventional final product, CFP, increased from 2.9 percent per year in 1947–58 to 4.9 percent per year in 1958–67 and then fell to 1.9 percent per year in 1967–76. Over the whole 29-year time span, its annual rate of growth averaged 3.2 percent. The annual rate of growth of the total net product, TP, was almost identical to that of FP in the first two periods, but in the third period it was lower, at 1.5 percent. Over the full 1947–76 period, it was 3.1 percent, slightly lower than that of CFP. The annual rate of growth of productive worker consumption, D_p, also increased between the first two periods and then declined in the third. However, it grew at a somewhat higher rate than CFP in the first period, at a somewhat lower rate than CFP during the second period, and at almost double the rate of CFP in the third period. Over the full 29-year time span, productive worker consumption grew at an average annual rate of 3.7 percent, 0.5 percentage points higher than that of CFP. Surplus household consumption, SC_p, also grew at a faster rate in the second period than in the other two. However, its rate of growth was consistently less than that of CFP and in the third period was slightly negative. Over the full 1947–76 period, it grew at an average rate of 1.8 percent per annum, more than a full percentage point less than that of CFP.

Table 5.9. *Annual rates of growth of selected components and measures of final output in constant prices (%)*

Component	1947–58	1958–67	1967–76	1947–76
1. Productive worker consumption (D_p)	3.29	4.35	3.69	3.74
2. Productive surplus consumption (SC_p)	2.36	3.24	−0.20	1.84
3. Net capital formation (CF)	−3.44	8.64	−4.00	0.13
4. Productive government (G_p)	4.75	6.68	2.64	4.69
5. Total government (G)	7.13	4.47	0.49	4.25
6. Unproductive final output (Y_u)	4.83	4.39	2.23	3.89
7. Unproductive activity (A_{pu})	6.77	4.10	0.73	4.07
8. CFP	2.91	4.91	1.92	3.22
9. TP	2.93	4.94	1.49	3.11

The most striking pattern is found for net investment in capital formation. It had a negative rate of growth in the first and third periods and a positive rate of growth in the second period that was almost double that of CFP. Over the full 29-year period, it grew at only 0.1 percent per annum, considerably lower than that of CFP. Of course, because of the wide fluctuations in investment over the business cycle, there is some sensitivity of the calculation of the rate of growth of investment to the particular end points selected. However, when adjusted for the troughs and peaks of the business cycle, the change in the average annual rate of growth of net capital formation between the first two periods is roughly comparable.[5]

Productive government expenditure, G_p, was similar in growth pattern to that of productive worker consumption. The rate of growth of productive government expenditure increased from 4.8 percent per

[5] On the basis of cycle peak and trough demarcations of the *Business Conditions Digest* (July, 1980) and data from the *Economic Report of the President, 1979* (Tables B-2, B-14, and B-17), the following average annual rates of growth of net capital formation were calculated:

Peak to peak	1948–57:	−1.70%
Trough to trough	1949–58:	−3.33%
Peak to peak	1957–69:	5.78%
Trough to trough	1958–70:	6.60%

There are no peak-to-peak or trough-to-trough periods close enough to 1967–76 to allow a comparable computation. It should also be noted that the annual rate of growth of gross private domestic capital formation also increased between the 1947–58 period and the 1958–67 period from 2.59 to 5.92 percent and then fell to 2.23 percent in the 1967–76 period. (Source: *Economic Report of the President, 1979*, Table B-2.)

year in 1947–58 to 6.7 percent per year in 1958–67 and then declined to 2.6 percent per year in the third period. However, the annual rate of growth of productive government spending exceeded that of CFP in all three periods. In contrast, the annual rate of growth of total government expenditures, G, showed a steady decline over the three periods. In the first period, its annual rate of growth was 7.1 percent, more than double that of CFP; in the second period, it was 4.5 percent, slightly below that of CFP; and in the third period, it was 0.5 percent, considerably below that of CFP. Even with this conventional category, it is apparent that there is no relation between the rate of change of net capital formation and that of government expenditures.

The remaining two components, unproductive final output (Y_u) and the productive inputs into unproductive activity (A_{pu}), were also characterized by a declining pattern in their annual growth rates over three periods. However, the rate of growth of A_{pu} declined much more sharply than that of Y_u. Moreover, in comparison to the net product, Y_u was the only component that moved countercyclically to net capital formation over the 1947–76 period. In the first period, when the growth rate of Y_u exceeded that of CFP (and also that of TP), the rate of change of net capital formation fell far below that of both CFP and TP. In the second period, when the converse was true, the growth rate of net capital formation far exceeded that of the net product. Finally, in the third period, when the growth rate of Y_u again exceeded that of the net product, the rate of growth of net capital formation again fell far below that of the net product.

E.   Composition of surplus product

The final section of this chapter considers the relation of net capital formation to the other components of the surplus product. As defined in Chapter 3, the surplus product is the difference between the net product and necessary consumption (NC). Moreover, NC is defined as the consumption of productive output by productive labor, where consumption includes an allocated share of productive government expenditure. Thus, NC equals the sum of D_{pp} and G_{pp}. The remaining net product is the surplus product. For the purposes here, the difference between CFP and NC will be used to measure the surplus product and this difference will be referred to as CSP:

$$CSP = CFP - NC$$

Table 5.10 shows the percentage composition of SFP for selected years. In this tabulation, the surplus product is divided into consump-

Table 5.10. *Percentage distribution of CSP by component in constant dollars*

Component	1947	1958	1967	1976
1. Gross productive surplus consumption (including unproductive labor) $(D_{pu} + SC_p + G_{ps})$	40.7	44.9	43.6	47.6
2. Productive net capital formation (CF_p)	11.0	5.3	7.3	4.3
3. Productive residual (R_p)	6.3	−1.0	1.6	−2.2
4. Unproductive final spending (Y_u)	42.1	50.7	47.5	50.3
Total (CSP)	100.0	100.0	100.0	100.0

tion by unproductive labor and the surplus class, capital formation, unproductive spending, and a residual. In this breakdown, the countercyclical relation between capital formation and unproductive final spending appears even sharper. A sharper increase in the share of unproductive expenditure in CSP between 1947 and 1958 corresponded with a sharp fall in the share of capital formation in CSP. Between 1958 and 1967, when the share of unproductive final spending fell by three percentage points, the share of capital formation in CSP increased by two percentage points. Finally, between 1967 and 1976, when the share of Y_u in CSP showed a three percentage point increase, capital formation's share showed a three percentage point decline.

F.   Conclusion

In conclusion, it has been shown that there is a strong inverse relation between changes in net capital formation and changes in unproductive final spending. This relation is apparent when the two components are computed as shares of the net product and when their rates of growth are compared to those of the net product. Moreover, this countercyclical relation appears even more pronounced when each of these two components is treated as a share of the surplus product. It should be emphasized that it has in no way been shown or argued that an increasing share of unproductive final spending *causes* a decrease in the rate of capital accumulation. On the other hand, the popular argument that increasing government expenditure is lowering the rate of capital formation is shown to be unsubstantiated and, indeed, contradicted in tabulations using conventional national accounting categories.

It should be emphasized that these results demonstrate only short-run relations in the components of final output. The net investment concept used here is a measure of the new capital formation that occurs in a given year. The results reported here thus indicate a strong inverse relation between year-to-year fluctuations in the share of investment in the net product and those of the share of unproductive final output in the net product. Moreover, whereas there were sharp year-to-year fluctuations in the share of investment in the total product, secular changes in the investment share were considerably smaller. Indeed, as reported in Chapter 4, the *average* ratio of gross private domestic fixed investment to GNP in constant dollars was 0.142 in 1947–58, 0.141 in 1958–67, and 0.145 in 1967–76. Moreover, the average ratio of net private domestic fixed investment to NNP in constant dollars was 0.055 in 1947–58, 0.051 in 1958–67, and 0.050 in 1967–76.[6] Thus, in the long run, the investment share in GNP and NNP does tend to remain relatively constant over time.[7]

[6] The source for these calculations is the *Economic Report of the President, 1983*, Tables B-2, B-3, and B-16.

[7] It should also be noted that even if the investment share in the net product is constant over time, the rate of growth of the capital stock may change over time. This proposition is proved rigorously under certain conditions in Chapter 4. Moreover, if the investment share in the net product is constant, the rate of growth of the capital stock will converge to the rate of growth of the labor force in the limit.

CHAPTER 6

Absorption of labor and capital and rate of surplus value

Federal officials charged today that a group mostly made up of police officers, firefighters and private security guards set the string of fires three years ago that brought Boston the nationally reported title of "arson capital of the world."

The fires were set, according to United States Attorney William Weld, to scare the public into supporting more positions for the Police and Fire Departments after property tax reductions had reduced their ranks. . . .

The indictment alleges that beginning sometime after July 1981, as the effect of a statewide tax-cutting measure forced layoffs of many police officers and firefighters in Massachusetts, the members of the group set 163 fires in Boston and nine surrounding cities and towns. The outlying fires were set to divert investigators away from Boston, the indictment said.

It also said that defendants who worked for a security company burned a client's building to distract attention from themselves.

The buildings burned included houses, churches, factories, restaurants, a Marine Corps barracks and the Massachusetts Fire Academy. A total of 281 firefighters were injured in the fires.

The fires listed in the indictment grew in frequency and number over the months. They stirred deep public apprehension here, generated local and national news accounts, and two years ago resulted in the Federal investigations that produced the indictments.

The indictments and arrests were announced by an assembly of Federal and state officials that included the District Attorneys of five counties, officials of the Federal Bureau of Investigation and Stephen E. Higgins, director of the Federal Bureau of Alcohol, Tobacco and Firearms.

One district attorney called the case "the most frightening and bizarre criminal conspiracy I have ever seen."

Mr. Higgins held up copies of Boston magazines of the period that he said published cover articles asking the question, "Who's burning Boston?"

"We're here today because we think these charges are a step toward answering that question," Mr. Higgins said.

The indictments allege perjury, obstruction of justice, threatening of witnesses and destruction of evidence, as well as conspiracy. Affidavits presented at a Federal bail hearing this afternoon further allege that one of the defendants threatened to kill the supervisor in the Bureau of Alcohol, Tobacco and Firearms who led the investigations. (Dudley Clandinen, *New York Times*, July 26, 1984, pp. A1, A15. Copyright © 1984 by the New York Times Company. Reprinted by permission.)

Chapter 5 focused on the composition of the final product among end uses. It was found that expenditures made by workers on productive consumption goods increased as a share of the total net product, TP, in constant dollars over the 1947–76 period, whereas surplus household expenditures on productive consumption goods fell as a share of TP. Together, household consumption expenditures remained about constant as a share of the net product over this period. Moreover, productive government expenditures rose as a share of the net product over the period, whereas the share of net investment in TP fell between 1947 and 1958, increased from 1958 through 1972, and fell again between 1972 and 1976. The pattern is very similar for the distribution of the (productive) final product, FP. Consumption expenditures made by workers (D_p) increased from 49 percent of FP in 1947 to 63 percent in 1976, whereas the share of surplus household consumption (SC_p) fell from 21 to 15 percent. Together, household expenditures rose from 69 to 78 percent of the productive final product. Government expenditures (G_p) increased from 11 percent of FP in 1947 to 19 percent in 1976, whereas net investment fell from 12 percent in 1947 to 7 percent in 1958, increased to 12 percent in 1972, and then fell to 5 percent in 1976.

This chapter considers the input side – in particular, the absorption of resources in the components of final output. Calculations are made of the labor and the capital employed both directly and indirectly in the production of the various components of final output. If the rate of change of labor absorption were the same in each component of final output, the change in the allocation of labor would mirror that of the real components.[1] However, since the rates of change of labor absorption differ for different components, the allocation of labor will have a different pattern over time from the distribution of the final product. For analogous reasons, if the rate change of capital absorption differs across sectors, the allocation of the capital stock will have a different pattern from that of the final product.

This method of analysis highlights the shift of resources away from useful employments to unproductive dispositions. Resources that could otherwise support new capital formation, household consumption, and productive government services are instead diverted into the wasteful forces of competition and the protection of property. The magnitudes are particularly striking, and the results will therefore be gradually developed.

Section A will report calculations of the direct plus indirect allocation of labor to the various end uses of the final product. For this purpose,

[1] Indeed, if the labor absorbed per unit of output were equal for each component, the percentage allocation of labor would be identical to that of the final product.

I shall abandon the conventional breakdown of final output in favor of the distribution of the productive final product, FP, over its parts. In Section B, the rates of growth of both the average labor content and the total labor content of the various final demand components will be investigated. These computations will show the relative growth in both productive and unproductive labor absorption. These computations lead directly to an estimate of the rate of surplus value, which is provided in Section C. In addition, computations will be performed of the relative absorption of labor value by the various components of the surplus product. Finally, in Section D, analogous computations will be performed to show the allocation of the capital stock to various end uses.

Tables will document the major shift in resources from productive to unproductive usage that occurred in the U.S. economy during the postwar period. This shift is more striking for employment than for the capital stock (which is to be expected from the model developed in Chapter 4) and more pronounced for employment than for the final product because of relative movements in labor absorption. Indeed, it will be shown that almost the entire net increase in employment and much of the increase in the capital stock since 1947 has been absorbed in unproductive uses. The welfare implications of these shifts will be considered in the next chapter.

A.   Absorption of labor in final output

The analysis begins with the absorption of labor in the (productive) components of the final product, FP, shown in Table 6.1. Only civilian employment is included in the tables of Chapters 6 and 7. Labor absorption is estimated as the product of the vector of labor values, λ_p, and the column vector of the final demand component. The first row of Table 6.1 shows the total labor embodied either directly or indirectly in worker consumption D_p as a percentage of total employment. This fraction fell from 38 percent in 1947 to 31 percent in 1967 and then increased to 37 percent in 1976. In contrast, the share of real worker consumption D_p in the final product FP rose from 49 percent in 1947 to 53 percent in 1967 and then increased more sharply to 63 percent in 1976. The difference in results suggests a higher than average rate of productivity growth in the production of consumption goods, as will be seen below. The labor absorbed in surplus household consumption fell from 16 percent of total labor value in 1947 to 9 percent in 1976. The share of surplus consumption, SC_p, in FP also fell over the period, though not as sharply. Together, the share of labor allocated to total

Table 6.1. *Percentage allocation of labor to productive final demand components*

Component	1947	1958	1963	1967	1972	1976
1. Productive worker consumption ($\lambda_p D_p$)	38.3	34.5	32.5	31.4	36.1	36.6
2. Productive surplus consumption ($\lambda_p SC_p$)	16.1	13.3	13.2	11.1	8.1	9.1
3. Productive net capital formation ($\lambda_p CF_p$)	7.0	3.7	4.2	4.7	5.9	2.7
4. Productive government ($\lambda_p G_p$)	7.8	10.7	12.6	14.3	13.0	15.8
5. Productive residual ($\lambda_p R_p$)	3.9	−0.3	1.1	1.1	−0.5	−1.3
6. Unproductively employed labor ($\lambda_u Y_u$ only)	26.9	38.2	36.5	37.5	37.5	37.1
Total ($\lambda^* Y = N$)	100.0	100.0	100.0	100.0	100.0	100.0

household consumption fell from 54 percent in 1947 to 43 percent in 1967 and then increased to 46 percent in 1976. The proportion of total labor embodied in net investment fell between 1947 and 1958, rose from 1958 to 1972, and then fell again in 1976. This pattern paralleled the change in the share of net investment in the final product. The share of labor absorbed in productive government expenditure increased almost continuously over the 29-year time span. Between 1947 and 1976, the labor share doubled from 8 to 16 percent, whereas its real share increased from 11 to 18 percent. Finally, the share of labor absorbed either directly or indirectly in fictitious output, Y_u, increased from 27 percent in 1947 to 38 percent in 1958 and then remained almost unchanged between 1958 and 1976.

The proportion of labor used unproductively is understated in Table 6.1 because λ_p, the labor value vector for productive output, also includes unproductive labor. As shown in Chapter 3, it is possible to split the unproductive labor embodied in λ_p from its productive labor content. The unproductive portion of λ_p is given by λ_{up} and its productive portion by λ. The total unproductive labor content of final output thus consists of the labor embodied in fictitious output, $\lambda_u Y_u$ (irrespective of whether it is employed in a productive or an unproductive sector) and the unproductively used labor embodied in productive final output, $\lambda_{up} Y_p$.

Table 6.2 shows the total unproductive labor content of selected components of final output as a share of its total labor content. The last line shows the overall proportion of labor that is unproductively employed. In 1947, 47 percent of the total labor employed was directly

Table 6.2. *Unproductive labor content of selected components of final output as a share of its total labor content (%)*

Component	1947	1958	1963	1967	1972	1976
1. Household consumption[a]	44.3	52.9	53.6	57.8	58.4	58.8
2. Net capital formation[b]	35.1	41.5	40.0	44.2	44.2	44.9
3. Government[c]	68.4	78.0	74.5	67.7	67.5	63.3
4. Final product[d]	46.7	59.4	58.6	58.6	60.4	61.0

[a] Defined as $[\lambda_{up}(D_p + SC_p) + \lambda_u(D_u + SC_u)]/\lambda^*(D + SC)$.
[b] Defined as $(\lambda_{up}CF_p + \lambda_u CF_u)/\lambda^*CF$.
[c] Defined as $(\lambda_{up}G_p + \lambda_u G_u)/\lambda^*G$.
[d] Defined as $(\lambda_{up}Y_p + \lambda_u Y_u)/\lambda^*Y$.

or indirectly unproductive, and by 1958, the figure had risen by 13 percentage points to 59 percent. After 1958, there was a gradual increase and, by 1976, 61 percent of the total labor employed were absorbed in some unproductive capacity. The relative unproductive labor content of household consumption also increased sharply between 1947 and 1958 and then gradually over the next 18 years. Its unproductive labor content was somewhat lower than that of the total product. A similar pattern held for the relative unproductive labor content of investment, which rose sharply between 1947 and 1958 and then more slowly thereafter, though its relative unproductive content was considerably lower than that of the total product. In contrast, the relative unproductive labor content of government expenditures jumped by 10 percentage points between 1947 and 1958 and then declined by 15 percentage points between 1958 and 1976. In 1947, the relative unproductive labor content of government expenditures was considerably higher than that of the final product. However, in 1976, the government sector absorbed almost the same relative proportion of unproductive labor as the total final product. This reduction in the unproductive labor content of total government spending was due to the more rapid growth in state and local government expenditures, which have a relatively low unproductive labor content, than in federal expenditures over the period.

Table 6.3 presents the final breakdown in the allocation of employment between productive and unproductive uses. The unproductively employed portion of the labor force rose from 47 percent of total employment in 1947 to 61 percent in 1976. The biggest increase occurred between 1947 and 1958, and thereafter the fraction rose more slowly. In 1947, the productive labor time absorbed in household consumption

Table 6.3. *Percentage allocation of productively and unproductively employed labor to components of final demand*

Component	1947	1958	1963	1967	1972	1976
1. Productive worker consumption (λD_p)	29.1	23.6	22.2	20.2	23.1	22.7
2. Productive surplus consumption (λSC_p)	12.2	9.0	9.0	7.1	5.1	5.6
3. Productive net capital formation (λCF_p)	5.0	2.3	2.8	2.9	3.6	1.7
4. Productive government (λG_p)	4.2	5.7	6.7	9.0	8.1	9.8
5. Productive residual (λR_p)	2.8	−0.1	0.8	0.7	−0.3	−0.7
6. Unproductive labor content of productive final output ($\lambda_{up} Y_p$)	19.8	21.2	22.1	22.6	22.9	23.9
7. Remaining unproductively employed labor ($\lambda_u Y_u$)	26.9	38.2	36.5	37.5	37.5	37.1
Total ($\lambda^* Y = N$)	100.0	100.0	100.0	100.0	100.0	100.0
Addendum:						
6. Unproductive labor content of productive final output ($\lambda_{up} Y_p$)	19.8	21.2	22.1	22.6	22.9	23.9
(a) $l_u q_{up} Y_p$		6.2	7.8	8.0	8.4	8.8	9.3
(b) $l_{pp}(q_{pp} - q_{pp}^*) Y_p$		2.1	2.9	2.5	2.4	2.0	2.1
(c) $l_{up} q_{pp} Y_p$		11.5	10.6	11.7	11.8	12.1	12.6

comprised 41 percent of total labor time, whereas in 1976, the corresponding fraction was 28 percent. The productive labor time embodied in new capital formation fell from 5 percent in 1947 to 2 percent in 1976. Finally, the productive labor time absorbed in government activity rose from 4 percent in 1947 to 10 percent in 1976. In contrast, the share of real household consumption in FP increased from 69 percent in 1947 to 78 percent in 1976, the share of net investment in FP fell from 12 to 5 percent, and the share of real government expenditures in FP rose from 11 to 19 percent.

A breakdown of the allocation of unproductive labor time is provided in lines 6 and 7 and the addendum of Table 6.3. Unproductive labor time absorbed in productive final output rose from 20 percent of total labor time in 1947 to 24 percent in 1976. This portion of unproductive labor time can be subdivided into three components. The first of these consists of labor employed in unproductive sectors that is indirectly embodied in productive final output ($l_u q_{up}$). It accounted for 6 percent of total labor time in 1947 and 9 percent in 1976. The second consists of productive labor working in productive sectors whose labor is embodied in productive output but indirectly routed through unproductive inputs $[l_{pp}(q_{pp} - q_{pp}^*)]$. This portion accounted for 2 percent of total labor time in both 1947 and 1976. The third portion consists of labor employed in productive sectors but in unproductive occupations absorbed in a productive final product ($l_{up}q_{pp}$). This portion represented 12 percent of total labor time in 1947 and 13 percent in 1976. The remaining unproductively employed labor (line 7) rose from 27 percent of total labor time in 1947 to 37 percent in 1976.

B.   Productivity growth, unproductive labor absorption, and labor content of final output

The total amount of labor absorbed in a component of final output is the product of two factors: the magnitude of the component in real terms and the average labor content of the component. The latter, in turn, reflects changes in the amount of labor absorbed per unit of output of the sectors that contribute either directly or indirectly to this component of final output. The total labor absorbed per unit of output of sector i, TLA_i, is directly given by

$$TLA_i = \lambda_{pi}$$

As should be apparent, this concept applies only to productive output since fictitious output has no unit of measurement. In Chapter 1, I introduced the conventional concept *total labor productivity*, TLP, defined as the inverse of the direct plus indirect labor requirements per unit of output:

$$TLP_i = 1/\lambda_{pi}$$

where no distinction was drawn between productive and unproductive labor time. It is now apparent that such a concept is not suitable since unproductive labor time, by definition, is not a requirement for production. However, as an alternative, it is possible to introduce the notion of the rate of displacement of the total labor absorbed per unit of output. This can be formally defined as

$$TLD_i = -\frac{\dot{TLA}}{TLA_i} = -\frac{\dot{\lambda}_{pi}}{\lambda_{pi}}$$

where, as before, a dot over a term indicates the term derivative.

The TLA of a sector can be divided into two parts, as shown in Chapter 3:

$$TLA_i = \lambda_{pi} = \lambda_i + \lambda_{upi}$$

The first part reflects the actual (productive) labor requirements per unit of output and leads directly to a concept of labor productivity. Let us formally define this as

$$LP_i = 1/\lambda_i$$

where LP_i is the inverse of the direct plus indirect (productive) labor requirements per unit of output. The rate of labor productivity growth, LPG, is then given by

$$LPG_i = -\frac{\dot{\lambda}_i}{\lambda_i}$$

The second part shows the unproductive labor time absorbed per unit of output:

$$ULA_i = \lambda_{upi}$$

The rate of displacement of unproductive labor absorbed per unit of output is directly given by

$$ULD_i = -\frac{\dot{ULA}_i}{ULA_i} = -\frac{\dot{\lambda}_{upi}}{\lambda_{upi}}$$

It is also possible to measure corresponding concepts for components of the final output. For example, the TLA of household consumption is given by

$$TLA_D = \lambda_p D_p / \sum D_p$$

where it should be recalled that all flows are in constant-dollar terms. Likewise,

$$LP_D = \sum D_p / \lambda D_p$$

and

$$ULA_D = \lambda_{up} D_p / \sum D_p$$

Finally, the unproductive labor absorbed per unit of final output consists of two parts. The first is the unproductive labor absorbed directly in the final product, FP:

$$ULA_1 = \lambda_{up} Y_p / \sum Y_p = \lambda_{up} Y_p / FP$$

The second is the unproductive labor absorbed in fictitious output Y_u and thus directly in the final product:

$$ULA_2 = \lambda_u Y_u / FP$$

Table 6.4. *Annual rates of PLG, ULD, and TLD for selected components of final output (%)*

Component	1947–58	1958–67	1967–76	1947–76
1. LPG of household consumption $[\sum (D_p + SC_p)/\lambda(D_p + SC_p)]$	4.24	4.22	0.59	3.10
2. LPG of net capital formation $(\sum CF_p/\lambda CF_p)$	2.48	4.55	0.02	2.36
3. LPG of government output $(\sum G_p/\lambda G_p)$	1.02	−0.21	−0.01	0.32
4. LPG of total final product $(FP/\lambda Y_p)$	3.41	3.57	0.19	2.46
5. ULD_1 of total final product $(FP/\lambda_{up} Y_p)$	0.32	2.68	−0.67	0.75
6. ULD_2 of total final product $(FP/\lambda_u Y_u)$	−2.25	3.54	0.05	0.28
7. TULD of total final product $[FP/(\lambda_u Y_u + \lambda_{up} Y_p)]$	−1.24	3.27	−0.24	0.47
8. TLD of total final product $(FP/\lambda^* Y = FP/N)$	0.94	3.34	−0.08	1.39

The total unproductive labor absorbed per unit of final output is thus given by

$$TULA = ULA_1 + ULA_2 = (\lambda_{up} Y_p + \lambda_u Y_u)/FP$$

Table 6.4 shows the annual rates of productivity growth and unproductive labor displacement for selected components of final output. Over the entire 1947–76 period, labor productivity growth, LPG, for the total (productive) final output averaged 3.4 percent per year (line 4). LPG increased slightly between the 1947–58 and 1958–67 periods, averaging 3.5 percent per year, and then fell to 0.2 percent per year in 1967–76. The pattern was somewhat similar for LPG in the production of household consumption goods. It remained almost unchanged between the 1947–58 and 1958–67 periods and then fell sharply in the 1967–76 period. Over the entire 1947–76 period, it averaged 3.1 percent per year, 0.6 percentage points higher than overall LPG. The rate of labor productivity growth in investment goods was slightly lower than that of total final output over the 1947–76 period. However, it increased sharply between the first and second period and then declined to zero in the third period. LPG for government final output averaged 1.0 percent in the 1947–58 period and then turned negative in the next two periods. Over the entire 1947–76 period, it averaged 0.3 percent per annum.

The rate of displacement of the unproductive labor directly absorbed in final output, ULD_1, was considerably lower than overall LPG (see line 5). It averaged 0.8 percent per year from 1947 to 1976, compared to an overall labor productivity growth rate of 2.5 percent per year. This indicates that the productive labor embodied per unit of (productive) output was displaced at a much faster rate than the unproductive labor directly absorbed in productive output. The discrepancy was particularly marked in the 1947–58 period, when the unproductive labor directly absorbed per unit of productive output remained virtually constant. In the 1958–67 period, unproductive labor was displaced at an annual rate of 2.7 percent per unit of productive output, compared to an annual rate of LPG of 3.6 percent. In the 1967–76 period, the unproductive labor directly absorbed per unit of productive output actually increased.

The unproductive labor indirectly absorbed per unit of final output (line 6) actually increased over the 1947–58 period. During the next two periods, the annual rate of ULD_2 was about equal to overall LPG. Over the whole 1947–76 period, ULD_2 averaged a mere 0.3 percent per year, a tenth of overall LPG.

Line 7 shows the overall rate of displacement of unproductive labor per unit of (productive) output, TULD. In the 1947–58 and 1967–76 periods, the total unproductive labor absorbed per unit of productive output actually increased, and in the first period it rose at over 1 percent per year. In the 1958–67 period, unproductive labor per unit of productive output was displaced at an annual rate of 3.3 percent per year, which was only slightly below the overall rate of productivity growth. Over the entire 1947–76 time period, the total unproductive labor absorbed per unit of output was displaced at an annual rate of 0.5 percent, which was about a fifth of overall labor productivity growth.

The last line shows the overall rate of displacement of the total labor absorbed per unit of final output, TLD. It is approximately a weighted average of overall labor productivity growth, LPG (line 4), and the rate of displacement of unproductive labor, TULD (line 7). Over the entire 1947–76 period, the rate of TLD averaged 1.4 percent, about half that of overall labor productivity growth and about three times that of TULD. In the 1947–58 period, TLD fell short of overall LPG by almost 2.5 percentage points due to the actual increase in unproductive labor absorbed per unit of output. In the 1958–67 period, both LPG and TLD were high, with the former exceeding the latter by only 0.2 percentage points. In the 1967–76 period, both were low, with LPG exceeding TLD by 0.3 percentage points per year.

The differential rate of productivity growth and labor absorption together with the differential rate of growth in the real levels of the final demand components determine the rate at which the total labor allo-

Table 6.5. *Annual rate of growth of productive, unproductive, and total labor content of selected components of final output (%)*

Component	1947–58	1958–67	1967–76	1947–76
1. Productive labor content of worker consumption (λD_p)	−0.97	0.08	3.13	0.63
2. Productive labor content of surplus consumption (λSC_p)	−1.82	−0.85	−0.87	−1.22
3. Productive labor content of net capital formation (λCF_p)	−5.90	4.11	−4.28	−2.29
4. Productive labor content of government (λG_p)	3.72	6.88	2.66	4.37
5. Productive labor content of final demand (λY_p)	−1.56	1.65	1.54	0.40
6. Total unproductive labor content of final demand ($\lambda_u Y_u + \lambda_{up} Y_p$)	3.09	1.96	1.97	2.39
7. Total employment ($\lambda^* Y = N$)	0.91	1.84	1.81	1.47

cated to the different components grow. These are reported in Table 6.5 where, as in Table 6.3, the allocation of labor is classified according to whether it is productively or unproductively employed. Over the full 1947–76 time span, total (civilian) employment increased at an annual rate of 1.5 percent (line 9). Compared to this, the productive labor content of (productive) worker consumption grew much slower, at a rate of 0.6 percent per year. Indeed, over the 1947–67 period, this portion of total employment actually declined in absolute terms, though in the 1967–76 period, it did increase at a fairly high rate. The slower rate of growth of this portion of employment relative to total employment contrasts with the faster rate of growth of productive worker consumption, D_p, relative to the total final product over the 1947–76 period. The difference is due to the fact that LPG in worker consumption was considerably greater than overall TLD.

The productive labor embodied in productive surplus consumption fell rather considerably over the 29-year stretch. Indeed, it fell in each subperiod. Putting the first two components together, we find that the total productive labor embodied in productive household consumption increased at an annual rate of only 0.2 percent. This was considerably below the overall rate of increase of employment despite the fact that productive household consumption in real terms grew at a slightly higher rate than the total final product.

The productive labor allocated to productive government expenditures increased at an average annual rate of 4.4 percent over the full

29-year time span. This was almost triple the rate of growth of total employment. Indeed, in each of the three subperiods, this portion of the labor force increased at a considerably faster pace than overall employment, and between 1947 and 1958, it increased at a rate four times that of employment.

In sum, the productive labor content of final output increased at an annual rate of 0.4 percent from 1947 to 1976, which was considerably lower than the growth rate in total employment. Between 1947 and 1967, there was actually an absolute decline in the productive labor allocated to (productive) final output. Between 1967 and 1976, it grew at a rate slightly below that of total employment. In contrast, total unproductive labor time increased at 2.4 percent per year from 1947 to 1976, which was about a percentage point higher than the growth in total employment. Between 1947 and 1958, this part of employment increased over three times faster than total employment, and from 1958 to 1976, it increased slightly faster.

In summary, there was actually an *absolute decline* of productive labor time absorbed in final output in the 1947–58 period. In the 1958–67 period, there was some recovery, but still the total productive labor embodied in final output was less in 1967 than in 1947. Thus, between 1947 and 1967, the total net increase in labor time was absorbed directly or indirectly as unproductive labor time. It was not until the 1967–76 period that there was a significant reversal in this trend. But more about this in Chapter 7.

C.   Rate of surplus value and absorption of surplus labor time

As discussed in Chapter 3, variable capital or *necessary labor time* is defined as the amount of labor time that is necessary for the reproduction of the necessary or productive labor force. It is given by

$$V = N_p \lambda m$$

where m is the column vector of (productive) private and public consumption. The remaining labor time is surplus labor time:

$$S = N - V$$

Table 6.6 shows the ratio of surplus labor time to total labor time. This ratio is derived in five steps. First, the conventional final product, CFP, is divided into two parts: conventional worker consumption (D) and conventional surplus product ($Y - D$). Total labor value is correspondingly divided into the total labor content (productive and unproductive) of conventional worker consumption (λ^*D) and the total

Table 6.6. *Derivation of ratio of surplus labor time to total labor time*

Measure	1947	1958	1963	1967	1972	1976
1. $(N - \lambda^*D)/N$	0.477	0.496	0.519	0.518	0.441	0.443
2. $[N - \lambda^*(D + G_d)]/N$	0.383	0.307	0.332	0.310	0.235	0.227
3. $(N - \lambda_p Nm)/N$	0.562	0.577	0.586	0.581	0.533	0.507
4. $S^*/N = (N - \lambda Nm)/N$	0.679	0.722	0.731	0.731	0.703	0.694
5. $S/N = (N - \lambda N_p m)/N$	0.802	0.833	0.860	0.866	0.857	0.855

labor content of the conventional surplus product $(N - \lambda^*D)$. The latter is the conventional estimate of surplus value when no distinction is drawn between productive and unproductive activity and the government product is treated as part of the surplus product [see Morishima (1973) or Wolff (1979), for example]. The ratio of this conventional estimate of surplus value to total labor value is shown in line 1. It increased from 0.48 in 1947 to 0.52 in 1967 and then fell sharply to 0.44 in 1972 and remained at this figure in 1976.

The second step is to treat conventional government output as (conventional) public consumption and allocate a portion of this to worker consumption (and the residual to surplus household consumption). This is computed as

$$G_d = \frac{\sum D}{\sum (D + SC)} G$$

The vector G_d is then subtracted from the conventional surplus product and added as part of necessary consumption to obtain an estimate of the private and public costs of reproducing the labor force. The ratio of the resulting estimate of surplus labor time to total labor time is shown in line 2. The line 2 ratios are considerably below those in line 1. In 1947, the difference was 9 percentage points, and in 1976, the difference was 22 percentage points, reflecting the relative growth in government services. Moreover, the line 2 ratio declined almost continuously over the 1947–76 period, from a high of 0.38 in 1947 to a low of 0.23 in 1976.

The third step is to strip away the unproductive portion of worker consumption (both private and public) from the necessary costs of reproducing the labor force and add the labor content of this to surplus labor time. This is done in line 3, where it should be recalled that

$$m = (D_{pp} + G_{pp})/N_p$$

The ratio of this new (augmented) estimate of surplus labor time to total labor time rose moderately from 0.56 in 1947 to 0.58 in 1967 and then fell off sharply to 0.53 in 1972 and again to 0.51 in 1976. This ratio was considerably higher than the line 2 ratio, and this difference widened over the period from 18 percentage points in 1947 to 28 percentage points in 1976. This trend reflected the increasing absorption of unproductive labor time in fictitious final output.

The fourth step is to separate from productive labor time the unproductive labor time directly embodied in (productive) worker consumption ($\lambda_{up}m$) and add this to surplus labor time. The resulting division is between what has previously been called compensated labor time V^* and uncompensated labor time S^* [see equations (3.8) and (3.9)]. The ratio S^*/N, shown in line 4, rose from 0.68 in 1947 to 0.73 in 1967 and then fell to 0.69 in 1976. Unlike the ratio in line 3, which fell over the full 1947–76 period, this ratio increased slightly. The difference was due to the increasing absorption of unproductive labor time directly in worker consumption. Indeed, the difference between the two ratios increased from 12 percentage points in 1947 to 19 percentage points in 1976.

Line 5 shows the ratio of actual surplus labor time to total labor time. It differs from the previous line in that the consumption of unproductive workers ($N_u m$) is now excluded from necessary consumption and its labor content added to surplus labor time. The ratio of S/N increased from 0.80 in 1947 to 0.87 in 1967 and then declined slightly to 0.86 in 1976. Over the full 1947–76 period, the ratio of surplus value to total labor value increased by 5 percentage points. This contrasts with the ratio S^*/N, which increased by only 1 percentage point over the period. The difference is due to the increasing share of unproductive workers in total employment:

$$S/N - S^*/N = u\lambda m = uv$$

where, it should be recalled, $u = N_u/N$. The factor uv increased from 12 percentage points in 1947 to 16 percentage points in 1976, which accounted for the more rapid rise of S/N. Moreover, the time trend of S/N contrasts sharply with that of the ratio of the traditional measure of surplus value to total labor value, which fell by 3 percentage points over the 1947–76 period. The difference between S/N and the ratio shown in the first line increased from 33 percentage points in 1947 to 41 percentage points in 1976, for a change of 8.7 percentage points over the full period. Of these 8.7 percentage points, a *negative* 12.2 percentage points was due to the relative increase of publicly provided consumption in worker consumption; 10.1 percentage points was due to the increasing labor content of fictitious output; 7.0 percentage points was due to the increasing unproductive labor content of (productive) worker consumption; and 3.8 percentage points was due to the increasing share of unproductive workers in total employment.

Finally, the trend in the ratio of S/N also contrasts with the time trend in the ratio of the surplus final product, SFP, to the final product, FP. The ratio SFP to FP actually declined from 0.651 in 1947 to 0.629 in 1976, or by 2 percentage points. The ratio S/N increased by 5 percentage points. The difference in time trends reflects the greater rate of LPG in necessary consumption than overall TLD. Moreover, the greater magnitude of S/N than of SFP/FP reflects the greater amount of labor time absorbed in the surplus product than in the goods that compose necessary consumption.

In gross terms, however, the results indicate that since 1947, four out of five workers in the U.S. economy directly or indirectly contributed to the production of surplus output of one form or another. Conversely, this implies that only one hour out of every five worked by productive labor was necessary to sustain and expand its numbers. This suggests an economy that is tremendously productive in that each (necessary) worker can produce enough to maintain himself plus four other workers! In principle, then, four-fifths of the employed labor force could retire and still be supported at the average consumption level. On the other hand, this result also suggests that the economy may waste a tremendous amount of resources in useless goods and services.[2]

Table 6.7 shows how the total surplus value generated in each of the six years is divided among four components: (i) new investment, (ii) private and public (productive) consumption of unproductive workers and the surplus class, (iii) unproductive labor time embodied in the final output, and (iv) the residual. The largest proportion of surplus value was absorbed as unproductive labor time. Its share increased sharply from 58 percent in 1947 to 71 percent in 1958 and then remained fairly steady in the remaining years. The other large component was

---

[2] Even these estimates of the ratio of surplus to total labor time may be understated because productive workers have been defined as those working in productive occupations within productive sectors. This definition therefore includes some labor time that is indirectly embodied in unproductive output. This is the appropriate definition of productive labor if TP is the measure of the final product. If FP is used to measure the final product, workers employed in productive occupations within productive sectors whose labor is indirectly embodied in unproductive output should also be classified as unproductive workers. Their consumption should likewise be excluded from necessary consumption. The resulting ratio of surplus labor time to total labor time is 0.83 in 1947 and 0.88 in 1976. For convenience and consistency with the previous chapters, I shall continue to use the definition of productive labor developed in Chapter 2.

Table 6.7. *Absorption of surplus value by final demand component (%)*

Component	1947	1958	1963	1967	1972	1976
1. Productive net capital formation (λCF_p)	6.2	2.8	3.2	3.3	4.2	1.9
2. Surplus household consumption[a] $[\lambda(SC_p + D_{pu} + G_{ps})]$	32.0	26.1	27.7	26.5	25.6	27.6
3. Unproductive component $(\lambda_{up}Y_p + \lambda_u Y_u)$	58.3	71.3	68.2	69.4	70.5	71.3
4. Residual (λR_p)	3.5	-0.2	0.9	0.9	-0.3	-0.9
Total surplus value (S)	100.0	100.0	100.0	100.0	100.0	100.0

[a] Includes consumption of unproductive labor.

surplus household consumption, which absorbed 32 percent of surplus value in 1947 and then 26–28 percent in the remaining years. Aside from the residual, new investment absorbed the smallest amount of surplus value. Moreover, there was a sharp decline in the proportion of surplus value absorbed in new investment from 6 percent in 1947 to 3 percent in 1958. Its share increased to 4 percent in 1972 and then dropped to 2 percent in 1976. Indeed, its share of surplus value moved more or less inversely to the share of unproductive labor time in surplus value (see the corresponding discussion of the inverse relation of net investment and fictitious output in Chapter 5). However, from 1958 onward, about 70 percent of surplus labor time was used unproductively, about 25 percent went to support the consumption of the surplus classes, and less than 5 percent remained to support new net capital formation.

D.   Allocation of capital stock

In analogous fashion, it is possible to analyze the direct and indirect allocation of the other major resource, capital stock, to the components of final demand.

Let us define the total (direct plus indirect) capital required per unit of final output as

$$\gamma^* = cq^*$$

where c is the vector of direct capital coefficients. The vector γ^* can be partitioned as

$$\gamma^* = (\gamma_p \quad \gamma_u) = (c_p \quad c_u)\begin{bmatrix} q_{pp} & q_{pu} \\ q_{up} & q_{uu} \end{bmatrix}$$

Table 6.8. *Percentage distribution of total capital stock between productive and unproductive sectors*

Classification	1947	1958	1963	1967	1972	1976
1. Productive capital stock (K_p)	73.1	71.5	72.1	72.6	72.8	74.4
2. Unproductive capital stock (K_u)	26.9	28.5	27.9	27.4	27.2	25.6
Total capital stock (K)	100.0	100.0	100.0	100.0	100.0	100.0

where γ_p shows the total capital requirements per unit of productive output and γ_u the total capital absorbed per unit of fictitious output.

Productive capital requirements can be defined as the capital stock employed in productive sectors necessary for the production of productive output. Its coefficients are given by

$$\gamma = c_p q_{pp}$$

Finally, the total capital requirements per unit of productive output can be separated into a productive and unproductive part as

$$\gamma_{up} = \lambda_p - \gamma$$

where γ_{up} shows the capital employed either directly or indirectly in unproductive sectors that is embodied in productive final output. The component γ will be referred to as *productively employed capital stock* and the components γ_{up} and γ_u as *unproductively employed capital stock*.

Table 6.8 shows the percentage of the total capital stock owned by productive and unproductive sectors. The percentage of the total capital stock owned by productive sectors fell from 73.1 percent in 1947 to 71.5 percent in 1958 and then increased gradually to 74.4 percent in 1976. The decline between 1947 and 1958 corresponded to the sharp rise in unproductive employment relative to total employment (cf. Table 5.5). Between 1947 and 1958, K_u grew at an annual rate of 3.6 percent whereas K_p grew at a rate of 2.9 percent. In the remaining 18 years, when unproductive employment grew more slowly relative to total employment, K_p increased at an annual rate of 4.1 percent whereas K_u rose at a rate of only 3.2 percent per year.

The results of Tables 6.8 and 5.5 indicate that the capital–labor ratio of the productive sector, $K_p/(N_p + N_{up})$ in terms of thousands of 1958 dollars per worker, rose from 9.7 in 1947 to 13.6 in 1958 and to 21.8 in 1976, whereas the capital–labor ratio of the unproductive sector, K_u/N_{uu}, in the same units, was 10.5 in 1947, 10.5 in 1958, and 12.2 in 1976. Moreover, the capital–output ratio, in 1958 dollars, in the pro-

Table 6.9. *Percentage allocation of productively and unproductively employed capital stock by final demand component*

Component	1947	1958	1963	1967	1972	1976
1. Productive worker consumption (γD_p)	24.4	28.3	28.5	27.8	31.9	33.4
2. Productive surplus consumption (γSC_p)	10.4	11.0	9.9	9.7	7.0	8.2
3. Productive net capital formation (γCF_p)	3.2	2.0	2.2	2.5	3.2	1.6
4. Productive government (γG_p)	21.7	14.8	17.1	17.9	19.0	19.2
5. Productive residual (γR_p)	3.0	−0.8	0.3	0.4	−1.0	−1.6
6. Unproductively employed capital content of productive final demand $(\gamma_{up} Y_p)$	9.2	10.3	9.8	9.8	9.3	9.5
7. Remaining unproductively employed capital $(\lambda_u Y_u)$	28.1	34.5	32.2	31.9	30.6	29.7
8. Total capital stock $(\gamma^* Y = K)$	100.0	100.0	100.0	100.0	100.0	100.0

ductive sector, K_p/X_p, rose moderately from 2.5 in 1958 to 2.8 in 1976. These results are all reasonably consistent with the growth model of accumulation and unproductive labor developed in Chapter 4.

Moreover, the model predicts that the ratio of unproductively employed capital stock to total capital stock, K_u/K, converges to $d_2 n/d_3$, where d_2 is the ratio K_u/X_p, n is the annual rate of growth of the labor force, and d_3 is the ratio of investment to X_p. The ratio K_u/X_p was virtually unchanged over the 1947–76 period at 0.296. The average annual rate of growth of employment was 1.48 percent over the whole period. Finally, the average ratio of net investment CF_p to X_p over the 1947–76 period was 0.029 with these figures, the limit of K_u/K is 14.8 percent. The model would therefore predict that the growth rate of productively employed capital stock, K_p, would continue to exceed that of K_u for the foreseeable future.

Table 6.9 shows the absorption of the capital stock by both final use and sector of origin. The time trend in the relative capital content of the various components of final output reflects both their relative real share in final output and their relative capital intensity of production. The productively employed capital embodied in productive worker consumption increased as a share of the total capital stock between 1947 and 1976, as did its real share of the final product. The productively employed capital embodied in both surplus household consumption and new capital formation declined as a percentage of total capital stock, as did their respective real shares in the final product. The productively employed capital content of government expenditure showed a sharp decline between 1947 and 1958, whereas its real share

Table 6.10. *Annual rate of growth of total capital content by final
demand component and by type of capital (%)*

Component	1947–58	1958–67	1967–76	1947–76
1. Productive worker consumption (γD_p)	4.45	3.66	5.86	4.64
2. Productive surplus consumption (γSC_p)	3.55	2.50	1.96	2.73
3. Productive net capital formation (γCF_p)	−1.33	6.64	−0.83	1.30
4. Productive government (γG_p)	−0.37	5.98	4.58	3.14
5. Unproductive component ($\gamma_{up} Y_p + \gamma_u Y_u$)	4.67	3.04	3.18	3.74
6. Total capital stock ($\gamma^* Y = K$)	3.10	3.85	3.85	3.56

in FP increased.[3] After 1958, the productively employed capital content
of government spending increased gradually, following the movement
of its real share. The unproductively employed capital content of (productive) final output remained almost constant as a percentage of the
total capital stock in the 1947–76 period. Finally, the remaining unproductively used capital increased sharply as a share of total capital
between 1947 and 1958 and then declined gradually from 1958 to 1976.
As a result, the total unproductively used capital stock increased from
37 percent of the total capital stock in 1947 to 45 percent in 1958 and
then fell to 39 percent in 1976.

Table 6.10 presents the same set of results in terms of the annual
rate of growth of the total capital embodied in selected final demand
components. Over the full 1947–76 period, the total capital stock grew
at an average annual rate of 3.6 percent. The productively employed
capital stock embodied in total household consumption grew at an annual rate of 4.2 percent and that absorbed in productive government
expenditures at an annual rate of 3.1 percent. That part of the productively employed capital stock allocated to the production of new
investment goods grew at an annual rate of 1.3 percent. Finally, the

[3] There is a potential source of bias in the estimates of the capital stock embodied in
productive government expenditure G_p and unproductive government expenditure G_u.
As discussed in the Appendix, the total federal government capital stock was split
between productive government and unproductive government activities in proportion
to its *current* spending on productive and unproductive services (see Chapter 2). Thus,
a large increase in relative defense expenditures by the federal government between
two years, as occurred between 1947 and 1958, might very well result in an overstate-
ment of the increase in unproductive government capital stock and an understatement
of the increase in productive government capital stock. Therefore, γG_p was probably
somewhat lower and $\gamma_u Y_u$ somewhat higher than reported for 1947 since defense spending was relatively low that year and γG_p higher and $\gamma_u Y_u$ lower than reported in 1958
since defense spending was very high.

rate of growth of the unproductively used capital stock grew at 3.7 percent per year, slightly higher than the total capital stock, whereas the productively used capital stock increased at 3.5 percent per year.

In summary, then, there was only a minor shift in the relative allocation of the capital stock to unproductive uses over the 1947–76 period. This contrasts strikingly with the allocation of labor time. However, from a resource point of view, the unproductive employment of the capital stock was still high. More than one-fourth of the capital stock was directly employed in unproductive activities, and more than one-third was so employed either directly or indirectly. As in the case of the labor force, this too represents a huge waste of resources that could otherwise have been used to provide consumption benefits to families and individuals or new investment. Indeed, given the small fraction of the capital stock devoted either directly or indirectly to the production of new capital goods and given its low rate of growth over the period, even a modest shift of resources away from unproductive uses could have significantly increased the rate of new capital formation.

CHAPTER 7

Absorption of new resources and growth in real income

The cost of winning a seat in the House of Representatives rose again in 1984, but only by about half as much as it has in recent elections, according to an analysis of compaign spending reports.

This year's winners will have spent an average of about $325,000 when all reports are filed, up about 23 percent from the average spending in 1982, according to an analysis done for The New York Times by Sunshine News Services, a company that studies compaign spending. The 1982 averages were 47 percent above those of 1980, which were 40 percent above 1978's.

Political analysis offered several explanations for the slowdown of campaign inflation, an effect that was not found in this year's very expensive Senate races. They cited the small number of serious challengers to incumbents, the decline in the overall rate of inflation and the fact that there had been fewer technological advances in campaigning, which drive up costs, than there had been in recent elections. . . .

One reason for the slowdown of inflation in House election spending, suggested Eddie Mahe, a leading Republican political consultant, "is the decline in the overall rate of inflation," a view that was shared by Peter Fenn, a Democratic consultant who works with House candidates.

Between 1980 and 1982, when the average amount spent on winning a House seat went from $179,140 to $263,290, a 47 percent increase, the estimated inflation for the entire economy was 16 percent.

For the period 1982 to 1984 the inflation rate for campaign spending was 23 percent, much larger than the overall inflation rate of 8 percent, according to an analysis by Robert Gough, senior vice president of Data Resources, Inc., an economic consulting company in Lexington, Mass. Looked at in constant dollars based on 1976, when Federal records of this sort were first available, the cost of an average House seat has gone from $87,356 then to $192,733 in 1984.

Another theory was offered by Gary C. Jacobson, professor of political science at the University of California at San Diego. He said spending in House races has increased when strong challengers have taken on House incumbents, and in 1984 "neither party fielded a lot of strong challengers."

For example, Mr. Jacobson said, 43 percent of the Democrats running against incumbent Republicans in 1982 had held elective office before, but this year only 18 percent were prior officeholders, Mr. Mahe agreed. "We did burn up a bunch of really fine candidates in 1982," he said. He characterized this year's candidates as "less qualified, less able, less everything."

Money talked in the close races. In all but one or two of the 30 races decided by five points or less, the winner reported spending more money than the loser. Of the 13 Republicans who defeated Democratic incumbents, 10 overcame the fund raising advantage generally held by incumbents and outspent them, according to the pre-election totals. The three Democrats who defeated incumbent Republicans, however, reported lower spending totals than their opponents. Republican challengers who won averaged $396,394; the three Democrats averaged $163,905.

A reduced pace of technological advance in politics may also have affected the rate of political inflation. Martin Franks, executive director of the Democratic Congressional Campaign Committee, said, "Prior to 1982 some of the increase came from people making the adjustment to technology, the sound-truck to targeted direct mail, if you will." Once those adjustments were made, he said, the next level of increases was smaller.

Joe Gaylord, executive director of the National Republican Congressional Committee, saw another reason for the sharp increases in earlier campaigns. "The awareness that incumbents could be defeated was strong in 1980 and 1982," he said, and that led incumbents to increase their spending levels to defend their seats.

In 1980 victorious Democratic incumbents spent an average of $141,097 each and victorious Republican incumbents spent $174,192. In 1982 victorious Democratic incumbents spent an average of $246,584, a 75 percent increase over 1980. Victorious Republican incumbents spent an average of $247,037, a 42 percent increase.

Victorious Democratic incumbents this year are likely to have spent about $308,000, a 25 percent increase over 1982, while victorious Republican incumbents will have spent about $327,280, a 32 percent increase.

Finally, several of the analysts suggested that the outlays in the last election meant that campaign spending may, for a time, be near a practical ceiling.

"There's never a lid," Mr. Mahe said, "but there is some kind of an optimum size budget. You're starting to get in the range of what a campaign can reasonably spend."

"You can just kind of do so much," Mr. Fenn said. "If you spend $250,000 in a contested race, unless you're in a very hot media market, that's probably enough."

Of course, an opponent is not a requirement for spending campaign money. The 68 House members who did not have major party opposition on Nov. 6 reported spending an average of $161,678 in their pre-election filings. In 1982 the 56 candidates without major party opposition spent 159,686 each. (Adam Clymer, *New York Times*, December 4, 1984. Copyright © by the New York Times Company. Reprinted by permission.)

In Chapter 5, it was shown that (productive) household consumption remained constant as a share of the total net product, TP, over the 1947–76 period and increased as a share of the final product, FP. The share of (productive) government expenditures in both TP and FP rose over the period, whereas net investment fell as a share of both. In contrast, it was reported in the previous chapter that the amount of productive labor time allocated either directly or indirectly to (productive) household consumption fell sharply between 1947 and 1958 as a share of total labor time and then declined more moderately between

1958 and 1976, whereas the fraction of labor absorbed either directly or indirectly in unproductive pursuits increased sharply between 1947 and 1958 and then rose slowly throughout the remainder of the period. In addition, the productive labor content of new investment fell as a proportion of total labor over the entire period, whereas that proportion allocated to (productive) government expenditures increased.

The movements in the real shares differed from those in the labor shares because of differential movements in labor absorption among the various components. If the rate of displacement of the total absorbed per unit of output were equal in the production of the various components of the final product, the movement in the total labor content of the components would mirror that in the composition of output. However, uneven movements in labor absorption among the various components will create disproportionate movements on the two sides. In Chapter 6, movements in TLD and LPG were reported for the various components of final demand. Over the 1947–76 period, household consumption experienced above-average productivity gains and capital formation average productivity growth, whereas the government sector showed minimal advances (cf. Table 6.4).

This chapter is concerned with a related issue, which is how the newly added resources in each period were allocated among competing uses. The chapter investigates how the labor added in each period is divided among the constituent parts of the final output. Two factors play a role in the absorption of newly added labor time. The first is the growth in the real shares of the final product and the second is the differential rates of labor absorption associated with each component. The absorption of the additional capital stock provided in each period among competing end uses is also analyzed in this chapter. The analysis of the allocation of newly added resources in each period highlights more dramatically the absorption of resources in unproductive uses during the postwar period. In addition, welfare implications will be drawn from differential productivity movements and the allocation of resources over the period.

In Section A of this chapter, differential movements in labor absorption and labor productivity growth reported in Chapter 6 will be briefly reviewed. In Section B, the distribution of the newly added surplus labor time in each period is broken down by component of the surplus product. These changes are then decomposed into two effects: one from the change in real shares and the other from differential movements in labor absorption. In Section C, the change in the variable capital in each period is decomposed into three effects: the first from changes in productivity levels, the second from changes in the real wage, and the third from changes in employment. In Section D, the distribution of the total additional labor time in each period is broken down by end use, and in Section E, the distribution of the newly added capital stock is also broken down by end use. In the last part, the allocation of labor and capital is related to the rate of growth of the real wage and other measures of per capita welfare.

A.   Relative movements in labor absorption

In Chapter 6, two different concepts of labor absorption were developed. The first is the rate of total labor displacement, TLD, which indicates how the total labor absorbed per unit of (productive) output changes over time. The second is (productive) labor productivity growth, LPG, which indicates how the socially necessary labor requirements per unit of final output change over time. The nonessential, or socially unnecessary, labor content of each component of output is precisely the unproductive labor absorbed in its production. This portion is treated separately in the labor allocation accounts. Since, by definition, only productive labor is required for production and only productive output represents real output, the only proper concept of productivity is LPG for the productive components of the final product. TLD in the production of productive output reflects both LPG and the change in the absorption (actually, the displacement) of unproductive labor per unit of productive output (ULA). Moreover, neither TLP nor ULA can be technically measured for unproductive output Y_u since it does not constitute real output. Instead, the labor absorbed in Y_u is technically charged against productive final output, Y_p, and the ratio of $\sum Y_p$ to the labor absorbed in Y_u can also be measured as ULA. As a result, the ratio of total (productive) output, $\sum Y_p$, to the total labor input, N, is measured by TLA, the total labor absorbed per unit of output.

As shown in Table 6.4, overall LPG averaged 2.5 percent per year from 1947 to 1976. LPG was highest for household consumption, at 3.1 percent per year, about average for the production of new investment goods, at 2.4 percent per year, and very low for government, at 0.3 percent per year. Overall LPG averaged 3.4 percent per year over the 1947–58 period, increased to 3.6 percent in the 1958–67 period, and then fell precipitously to 0.2 percent in the 1967–76 period. The mid-1960s mark the beginning of the productivity slowdown, and almost all conventional measures of productivity growth show a sharp decline after 1965 or so. The three components of the productive final product experienced very different patterns in productivity growth over the three periods. LPG in household consumption remained constant between the first two periods and then showed a very sharp decline in the third. LPG in the production of investment goods jumped by over two percentage points between the 1947–58 and 1958–67 periods and then declined to zero in the third period. Finally, LPG for the government sector declined from 1.0 percent per year in 1947–58 to a negative value in the 1958–67 period and then increased slightly to zero percent in the third period.

The rate of displacement of unproductive labor absorbed directly in Y_p, ULD_1, averaged 0.8 percent per year over the 1947–76 period, considerably below that of LPG. The rate of displacement of the unproductive labor absorbed in fictitious output, Y_u, and hence indirectly in Y_p, ULD_2 averaged 0.3 percent per year over the whole period, also considerably below the rate of growth of overall LPG over the period. Together, TULD averaged 0.5 percent per year between 1947 and 1976. TULD was actually negative in the 1947–58 and the 1967–76 periods, indicating that additional unproductive labor was absorbed per unit of productive output. In the 1958–67 period, TULD was 3.3 percent per year, almost equal to that of overall LPG in the period. Finally, TLD for total productive output averaged 1.4 percent per year over the entire 1947–76 period, almost a full percentage point below that of overall LPG. The annual rate of TLD increased from 0.9 percent in 1947–58 to 3.3 percent in 1958–67 and then declined to zero in the 1967–76 period. Except for the 1958–67 period, TLD was considerably below that of LPG.[1]

B.   Distribution of newly added surplus labor time

The relative movements in labor absorption among the various components of final output directly affect the absorption of newly added

---

[1] Nothing has been said here about the *reasons* for the differences in rates of labor absorption across components or over time. Such a discussion would carry us too far afield since we are interested not in *causes* but in *effects* of differential movements in labor absorption. However, for LPG at least, it is possible to relate the differences in productivity movements to differences in rates of capital accumulation for the various components of final output. In this regard, the ratio of the total productive labor content to the total productive capital content increased at an average annual rate over the full 1947–76 period of 4.00 percent for productive household consumption, 3.59 percent for productive investment, and − 1.24 percent for productive government expenditures. The rank order is identical to that of LPG by final-demand component. Moreover, the ratio of the total productive labor content to the total productive capital content of total productive final output increased at an average annual rate of 3.06 pecent over the entire period.

resources in the economy. These effects will be documented in four stages: (1) the absorption of newly added surplus value, (2) the absorption of newly added variable capital, (3) the absorption of newly added labor value, and (4) the absorption of newly added capital stock.

Let us first define total (productive) surplus household consumption, TSC, as

$$\text{TSC} = C_p + M_{pu} + G_{ps} \tag{7.1}$$

where TSC includes (private) surplus household consumption, (private) consumption of unproductive workers, and the consumption of publicly provided services attributed to these two groups. The total (productive) surplus final product, SFP, is then given in vector form by

$$Z = \text{TSC} + \text{CF}_p + R_p \tag{7.2}$$

where CF_p and R_p are, respectively, productive net capital formation and the productive portion of the residual. The total surplus value at time t, S^t, is then given by

$$S^t = \lambda^t Z^t + \lambda_{up}^t Y_p^t + \lambda_u^t Y_u^t \tag{7.3}$$

where the superscript t refers to time. Alternatively, the total surplus value at time t can be expressed as

$$S^t = S_C^t + S_I^t + S_U^t + S_R^t \tag{7.4}$$

where

$$S_C^t = \lambda^t \text{TSC}^t$$

is the total surplus value absorbed in total surplus consumption,

$$S_I^t = \lambda^t \text{CF}_p^t$$

is the total surplus value absorbed in net capital formation,

$$S_U^t = \lambda_{up}^t Y_p^t + \lambda_u^t Y_u^t$$

is the total surplus value absorbed either directly or indirectly in the unproductive portion of the product, and

$$S_R^t = \lambda^t R_p^t$$

is the surplus value absorbed in the trade balance and net inventory change.

As a first step in the analysis, Table 7.1 shows how the net increase in surplus value in each period was distributed over the four components of surplus value. Of the net increase in surplus labor time of 8.0 million person-years in the 1947–58 period, 0.3 million person-years,

Table 7.1. *Percentage distribution of newly created surplus value over components of surplus product*

Component	1947–58	1958–67	1967–76	1947–76
1. Total surplus consumption $[(S_C^2 - S_C^1)/(S^2 - S^1)]$	0.033	0.200	0.343	0.205
2. Net capital formation $[(S_I^2 - S_I^1)/(S^2 - S^1)]$	−0.169	0.062	−0.065	−0.047
3. Unproductive activity $[(S_U^2 - S_U^1)/(S^2 - S^1)]$	1.346	0.678	0.838	0.919
4. Residual $[(S_R^2 - S_R^1)/(S^2 - S^1)]$	−0.211	0.060	−0.116	−0.077
Total	1.000	1.000	1.000	1.000

or 3 percent, went toward increasing total surplus household consumption. On the other hand, there was actually a net decline in the amount of surplus value allocated to new investment of 1.4 million person-years, or − 17 percent, of the net increase in surplus value and also a large decline in the amount absorbed in the residual.[2] The bulk of the increased surplus value was absorbed either directly or indirectly in increased unproductive activity. In fact, the increase in surplus labor time routed to unproductive output actually *exceeded* the net increase in total surplus labor time by 35 percent. The reason is that surplus value was freed up in investment and the trade balance.

In the next period, 68 percent of the newly added surplus value was absorbed in increased unproductive activity. A fifth went toward increased surplus household consumption, and 12 percent went toward increased investment and the change in the residual. In the 1967–76 period, the bulk of increased surplus labor time again went toward increased unproductive activity. A large portion also helped fuel increased surplus household consumption, whereas net declines were again recorded in investment and in the residual.

Over the full 1947–76 time span, surplus labor time increased by 29.1 million person-years. Of this amount, 6.0 million person-years, or 21 percent, was absorbed in increased surplus household consumption; unproductive activity gained 26.7 million person-years, or 92 percent, of the total; and net capital formation actually lost 1.4 million person-years. Thus, from the standpoint of the allocation of surplus labor time,

[2] The large decline in the surplus value absorbed in the residual is attributable to the large balance of trade surplus in 1947 and a small deficit in 1958.

the postwar period was one in which the vast majority of increased labor resources was absorbed in unproductive endeavors. A moderate amount went toward increasing household consumption, but there was actually a net release of labor time allocated for new investment.

The allocation of newly added labor time depends on two factors: (1) the change in real activity levels and (2) relative movements in the rate of labor displacement or of labor productivity growth.

A simple decomposition can show how the two are related. Define

$$\Delta\lambda \equiv \lambda^2 - \lambda^1$$

$$\Delta TSC \equiv TSC^2 - TSC^1$$

Then[3]

$$\Delta S_C \equiv S_C^2 - S_C^1 = (\Delta\lambda)TSC^1 + \lambda^2 \Delta TSC \tag{7.5}$$

The first term on the right side shows the change in the total productive labor required to produce the same real level of surplus household consumption of period 1 with period 2 technology. The first term is therefore referred to as the *productivity effect*, and it is usually negative. The second term shows the amount of additional labor time required to provide for the net change in real surplus household consumption from period 1 to period 2 with period 2 technology. This term is called the *real product effect* and is positive as long as there is a positive change in surplus household consumption and conversely.

In similar fashion, the change in surplus time absorbed in net investment can be decomposed as follows:

$$\Delta S_I = (\Delta\lambda)CF_p^1 + \lambda^2 \Delta CF_p \tag{7.6}$$

The change in the surplus value absorbed unproductively requires a somewhat different decomposition since there is no real product effect directly corresponding to the unproductive labor absorbed in fictitious output. For this purpose, we can use

$$S_U = TULA \cdot FP$$

and, hence

$$\Delta S_U = (\Delta TULA)FP^1 + TULA^2 (\Delta FP) \tag{7.7}$$

---

[3] The decomposition is very close in form to the differential of the product of two variables:

$$dS_C = (d\lambda)TSC + \lambda \, dTSC$$

where d is the differential operator.

where the first term indicates the change in unproductive labor absorbed per unit of (productive) output (the labor displacement effect) and the second term is the real product effect. Finally, the change in total surplus value can be decomposed as follows:

$$\Delta S \equiv S^2 - S^1 = [(\Delta\lambda)Z^1 + (\Delta\text{TULA})\text{FP}^1]$$
$$+ [(\lambda^2 \Delta Z) + \text{TULA}^2 \Delta\text{FP}] \qquad (7.8)$$

where the first term is the labor displacement effect and the second the real product effect.

Table 7.2 shows the percentage decomposition of the change in surplus labor time in total and by component for the three subperiods and the full 1947–76 time period. Panel A shows the movements for the total surplus product. Between 1947 and 1958, the total amount of labor time required to produce the 1947 vector of the surplus product fell by 17 percent from declines in total labor absorption. If the real surplus product had remained unchanged during this period, total surplus value would have fallen by 17 percent. However, the real surplus product increased over the period, and as a result, the labor time absorbed in the surplus product rose by 35 percent from the change in the real product alone. The net impact of the labor displacement effect and the real product effect was an 18 percent (35.0 − 17.4) increase in surplus labor time over the 1947–58 period. Moreover, in order to isolate the relative increase in surplus labor time arising from the expansion in the real surplus product, a so-called expansion factor is computed. This is defined as the ratio of the increase in labor time required for the change in the real product (in second year technology) to the amount of labor time required to produce the year 1 real product with year 2 technology. The numerator is thus the real product effect, and the denominator is the sum of period 1 surplus labor time and the labor displacement effect (which is normally negative). In other words, the ratio shows the expansion of labor resources devoted to increasing the real product relative to the labor time required to maintain the previous level with the new technology.[4] Over the 1947–58 span, the expansion factor was 42 percent.

In the next time period, the statistical breakdown is very similar. The labor displacement and the real product effects were close to their 1947–58 values, the change in total labor content was almost identical, and the expansion factor was 54 percent. The 1967–76 period was characterized by a slowdown in the rate of labor displacement. The labor displacement effect was therefore very small, and the real product

---

[4] A value of zero would thus indicate no change in the real product.

Table 7.2. *Percentage decomposition of change of surplus value into productivity, labor displacement, and real product effects*[a]

Component	1947–58	1958–67	1967–76	1947–76
A. Total surplus product				
1. Productivity change and labor displacement $([(\Delta\lambda)z^1 + (\Delta\text{TULA})\text{FP}^1]/S^1)$	−0.174	−0.220	−0.017	−0.372
2. Change in real product $[(\lambda^2\,\Delta z + \text{TULA}^2\,\Delta\text{FP})/S^1]$	0.350	0.419	0.179	1.008
3. Change in total labor content $[(S^2 - S^1)/S^1]$	0.175	0.199	0.161	0.636
4. Expansion factor $((\lambda^2\,\Delta z + \text{TULA}^2\,\Delta\text{FP})/ [S^1 + (\Delta\lambda)z^1 + (\Delta\text{TULA})\text{FP}^1])$	0.423	0.537	0.182	1.605
B. Total surplus consumption				
1. Productivity change $[(\Delta\lambda)\text{TSC}^1/S_C^1]$	−0.327	−0.229	−0.0	−0.476
2. Change in real product $[\lambda^2\,\Delta\text{TSC}/S_C^1]$	0.345	0.373	0.209	0.884
3. Change in total labor content $[(S_C^2 - S_C^1)/S_C^1]$	0.018	0.144	0.209	0.408
4. Expansion factor $(\lambda^2\,\Delta\text{TSC}/[S_C^1 + (\Delta\lambda)\text{TSC}^1])$	0.512	0.483	0.209	1.688
C. Net capital formation				
1. Productivity change $[(\Delta\lambda)\text{CF}_p^1/S_f^1]$	−0.248	−0.322	0.063	−0.475
2. Change in real product $[(\lambda^2\,\Delta\text{CF}_p/S_f^1)]$	−0.230	0.770	−0.381	−0.009
3. Change in total labor content $[(S_f^2 - S_f^1)/S_f^1]$	−0.478	0.447	−0.318	−0.485
4. Expansion factor $(\lambda^2\,\Delta\text{CF}_p/[S_f^1 + (\Delta\lambda)\text{CF}_p^1])$	−0.306	1.137	−0.358	−0.018
D. Unproductive activity				
1. Labor displacement $([(\Delta\text{TULA})\text{FP}^1]/S_U^1)$	−0.073	−0.212	−0.025	−0.292
2. Change in real product $[(\text{TULA}^2\,\Delta\text{FP})/S_U^1]$	0.477	0.405	0.220	1.294
3. Change in total labor content $[(S_U^2 - S_U^1)/S_U^1]$	0.404	0.193	0.195	1.001
4. Expansion factor $(\text{TULA}^2\,\Delta\text{FP}/[S_U^1 + (\Delta\text{TULA})\text{FP}^1])$	0.515	0.515	0.226	1.827

[a] The residual component of the surplus product, R_p, is excluded from this table.

effect was also smaller than in the two previous periods. The relative increase in total surplus value was 14 percent, slightly smaller than in the two previous periods, and the expansion factor was considerably smaller at 18 percent. Over the full 1947–76 time span, surplus labor time increased by 64 percent. This came about from a 27 percent reduction in labor time from the labor displacement effect and a 101 percent gain from increases in the real surplus product. The expansion factor was 161 percent.

The statistics for surplus household consumption were similar to those for the total surplus product. Over the entire time span, the labor displacement effect, which in this case is the productivity effect, was somewhat larger at 48 percent, the real product effect somewhat lower at 88 percent, the net increase in surplus labor time absorbed in surplus household consumption lower at 49 percent, and the expansion factor slightly higher at 169 percent. The major difference was in the 1947–58 period, when the labor displacement effect was considerably greater for total surplus household consumption and the resultant increase in total labor content considerably lower at 2 percent.

The pattern for investment activity contrasts sharply with that for the total surplus product. The productivity effect for investment was slightly greater in the first two periods than was the labor displacement effect for the total surplus product, but in the 1967–76 period, the productivity effect was actually positive. Over the full time span, the productivity effect for investment was somewhat greater than the labor displacement effect for the total surplus product. The real product effect for net capital formation was actually negative in the 1947–58 and the 1967–76 periods, and over the entire time span, it was very close to zero. The net effect was a sharp decline in the total labor time allocated either directly or indirectly to investment in the first and third periods. Though there was a sharp increase in its total labor content between 1958 and 1967, over the 1947–76 time span, there was actually a *49 percent reduction* in the labor absorbed in net investment. The investment activity was thus a net releaser of surplus labor time. In real terms, moreover, the expansion factor was actually a *negative* 2 percent over 1947–76.

The pattern for unproductive activity also differs from that of the total surplus product, particularly in the first period. Between 1947 and 1958, the labor displacement effect caused a 7 percent reduction in unproductive labor time, whereas the increase in the real product caused a 48 percent increase in unproductive labor time. The net effect was that the labor allocated to unproductive activity increased by *40 percent* during this period, compared to 18 percent for the total surplus product. The expansion factor was 52 percent, compared to 42 percent for the total surplus product. In the next two time periods, the pattern of labor absorption and release for unproductive labor was similar to that of the total surplus product. The percentage change in total unproductive labor time was 19 percent in the second period and 20 percent in the third period. Over the entire 1947–76 period, the surplus labor time absorbed by unproductive activity doubled, compared to a 64 percent increase for total surplus labor time, and the expansion factor was 1.83, compared to 1.61 for the total surplus product. The fact that 92 percent of the increased surplus value between 1947 and 1976 was absorbed as unproductive labor time (cf. Table 7.1) is thus attributable primarily to the real product effect and secondarily to the labor displacement effect.

C.   Distribution of newly added variable capital

A somewhat similar decomposition can be applied to the change in variable capital over time. Let us recall from Chapter 3 that the vector of gross productive consumption per productive worker, m, is given by

$$m = \frac{M}{N_p} = \frac{D_{pp} + G_{pp}}{N_p} \tag{7.9}$$

where D_{pp} is private consumption and G_{pp} is the part of public consumption allocated to productive workers. Then variable capital V^t at time t is given by

$$V^t = \lambda^t m^t N_p^t \tag{7.10}$$

Therefore, the change in variable capital can be decomposed as follows:

$$\Delta V = \lambda^1 m^1 \, \Delta N_p + (\Delta\lambda)m^1 N_p^2 + \lambda^2 N_p^2 \, \Delta m \tag{7.11}$$

where the first term on the right side shows the change in variable capital due to the increase in the number of productive workers (*employment effect*), the second the portion attributable to the change in productivity (*productivity effect*), and the third the portion due to the change in the effective, or Marxian, real wage (*real wage effect*). In like fashion, it is possible to decompose the change in the portion of variable capital that is needed for private consumption. Define

$$V_d = \lambda D_{pp} \tag{7.12}$$

$$d_{pp} = D_{pp}/N_p \tag{7.13}$$

Table 7.3. *Percentage decomposition of change in variable capital into employment, productivity, and real wage effects*

Component	1947–58	1958–67	1967–76	1947–76
A. Private real wage				
1. Employment change $(\lambda^1 d_{pp}^1 \, \Delta N_p / V_d^1)$	−0.051	0.108	0.120	0.151
2. Productivity change $[(\Delta\lambda) d_{pp}^1 N_p^2 / V_d^1]$	−0.335	−0.310	0.005	−0.610
3. Change in private real wage $(\lambda^2 N_p^2 \, \Delta d_{pp} / V_d^1)$	0.156	0.149	0.137	0.353
4. Change in total labor content $[(V_d^2 - V_d^1)/V_d^1]$	−0.229	0.054	0.262	−0.107
5. Expansion factor $(\lambda^2 \, \Delta D_{pp}/[V_d^1 + (\Delta\lambda)D_{pp}^1])$	0.191	0.315	0.256	0.909
B. Total real wage				
1. Employment change $(\lambda^1 m^1 \, \Delta N_p / V^1)$	−0.051	−0.108	0.120	0.151
2. Productivity change $[(\Delta\lambda) m^1 N_p^2 / V^1]$	−0.313	−0.258	0.004	−0.564
3. Change in Marxian real wage $(\lambda^2 N_p^2 \, \Delta m / V^1)$	0.186	0.222	0.150	0.510
4. Change in total labor content $[(V^2 - V^1)/V^1]$	−0.178	0.072	0.274	0.096
5. Expansion factor $(\lambda^2 \, \Delta M/[V^1 + (\Delta\lambda)M])$	0.227	0.398	0.270	1.156

where d_{pp} is the private real wage per worker. Then

$$\Delta V_d = \lambda^1 d_{pp}^1 \, \Delta N_p + (\Delta\lambda) d_{pp}^1 N_p^2 + \lambda^2 N_p^2 \, \Delta d_{pp} \qquad (7.14)$$

Panel A of Table 7.3 shows the decomposition for the private real wage. During the 1947–58 period, the employment of productive workers actually declined by 5 percent. Due to technological change, the amount of variable capital that would have been required to maintain the same private real wage at the new employment level would have declined by 34 percent. However, because of the increase in the private real wage over the period, 16 percent more labor time was required for the new level of worker consumption. The net effect was that the amount of labor time absorbed in providing private consumption to productive workers actually fell during this period by 23 percent. This contrasts sharply with an increase in surplus value of 18 percent during the same period (Table 7.2). The expansion factor for variable capital shows the ratio of the change in labor time required to meet the new consumption of the new number of productive workers to the amount of labor time that would have been required to maintain the original level of consumption of the original number of productive workers with the new technology. In the 1947–58 period, it was 19 percent. This was considerably lower than the 42 percent expansion factor for total surplus value. Moreover, the 34 percent productivity effect for worker consumption was considerably stronger than the 17 percent labor displacement effect for the surplus product. Thus, both the lower real expansion factor and the higher productivity effect contributed to the decline of V_d relative to surplus value during this period.

The employment effects were substantially higher in the next two periods, at 11 and 12 percent, respectively. The productivity effect in the 1958–67 period was somewhat lower than in the first period, and in the third period, it was almost zero. The real wage effects of the last two periods were similar in magnitude to that of the first period. In the 1958–67 period, there was a slight increase in V_d of 5 percent, in contrast to the sharp fall of the preceding period. The major difference between the first two periods was in the change in productive employment, which was negative in the first period and positive in the second. As a result, the expansion factor was considerably larger in the 1958–67 period. However, the change in surplus value between 1958 and 1967 was much greater than that of variable capital, mainly due to the considerably larger expansion factor for the surplus product. In the 1967–76 period, V_d increased by 26 percent. The striking contrast between the second and third periods was the very small rise in productivity in the later period. In fact, V_d increased relative to surplus value during the third period because of its larger expansion factor. Over the entire 1947–76 time span, V_d actually fell by 11 percent. The reason for the decline was that the rate of productivity increase fully outweighed the combined impact of the increase in productive employment and the rise in the private real wage. In contrast, surplus value increased by 64 percent due to its smaller labor displacement rate coupled with a larger real expansion of the surplus product.[5] In fact, the expansion factor for the surplus product was 1.61 in comparison to 0.91 for total private worker consumption.

Panel B in Table 7.3 shows the same set of statistics for the effective real wage of productive workers, which includes both private and public

---

[5] The productivity effect for the private real wage is not strictly comparable to that for the surplus product since the former reflects not only technological change but also the change in employment. Corrected for the change in employment, the private real wage *adjusted productivity effect* was 0.53 for the 1947–76 time span, still significantly greater than the 0.37 productivity effect for the surplus product.

consumption. The first line of panel B is identical to that of panel A since it shows the percentage change in productive employment. The second line shows the productivity effects and is slightly lower than the corresponding line of panel A, reflecting the slower rate of productivity advance in government-provided goods and services. The major difference in the two sets of results is in the real wage effect. The increase in the (total) real wage was consistently greater than the growth of the private real wage, reflecting the more rapid growth of the government sector. As a result, the percentage growth of total variable capital, V, was uniformly greater than that of V_d. Over the 1947–76 time span, variable capital increased by 10 percent, in contrast to an 11 percent decline in V_d but a 64 percent increase in surplus value. In addition, the expansion factor for total worker consumption was greater than that for private worker consumption in each period. Over the entire 1947–76 time span, the expansion factor was 1.16, compared to 0.91 for private consumption. However, the expansion factor for total worker consumption was less than that for the total surplus product, which was 1.61.

D.   Distribution of newly added labor value

Tables 7.4 and 7.5 show the allocation of newly added labor value over all components in each time period. In the first of these, total household consumption is broken down between worker consumption, including that of both productive and unproductive labor, and surplus household consumption. For both groups, private and public consumption are included in total household consumption. In Table 7.5, total private and public household consumption is considered on a per capita basis. As shown in Table 7.4, the increase in labor value (i.e., total employment) was 6.0 million person-years between 1947 and 1958. *Of this, 10.8 million person-years, or 180 percent, of the newly added labor time was absorbed in unproductive uses.* This was the only component that absorbed additional labor time. Total worker consumption (including that of unproductive workers) lost 0.8 million person-years. This change resulted from two movements. First, technical progress allowed 4.7 million person-years of labor time to be released in order to maintain the 1947 real wage level despite the increased employment.[6] Second, 3.0 million new person-years of labor were absorbed to increase private consumption per worker and an additional 0.9 million person-years to increase public consumption per worker. The other

---

[6] Though productive employment declined during this period, unproductive employment rose considerably.

Table 7.4. *Distribution of newly added labor value over components of final demand in millions of person-years (first decomposition)*

Component	1947–58	1958–67	1967–76	1947–76
1. Maintaining total real wage per worker (productive and unproductive) $(\lambda^2 m^1 N^2 - \lambda^1 m^1 N^1)$	-4.74	-1.66	3.61	-3.67
2. Increasing private real wage per worker (productive and unproductive) $[\lambda^2 N^2 (d_{pp}^2 - d_{pp}^1)]$	3.02	2.36	2.16	7.62
3. Increasing public real wage per worker (productive and unproductive)[a] $[\lambda^2 N^2 (g_{pp}^2 - g_{pp}^1)]$	0.94	1.78	1.00	4.51
4. Increasing private and public surplus consumption (excluding that of unproductive labor)[b] $[\lambda^2 (SC_p^2 + G_{sc}^2) - \lambda^1 (SC_p^1 + G_{sc}^1)]$	-0.97	0.33	-0.46	-1.10
5. Increasing net capital formation $(\lambda^2 CF_p^2 - \lambda^1 CF^1)$	-1.35	0.66	-0.68	-1.37
6. Increasing unproductive activity $[(\lambda_{up}^2 Y_p^2 + \lambda_u^2 Y_u^2) - (\lambda_{up}^1 Y_p^1 + \lambda_u^1 Y_u^1)]$	10.78	7.23	8.70	26.71
7. Changing residual $(\lambda^2 R_p^2 - \lambda^1 R_p^1)$	-1.69	0.64	-1.20	-2.25
8. Total change in employment $(N^2 - N^1)$	6.00	11.34	13.12	30.45

[a] $g_{pp} = G_{pp}/N_p$.

[b] $G_{sc} = \dfrac{\sum SC_p}{\sum (D_p + SC_p)} G_p$.

three components of the final product – surplus household consumption (excluding that of unproductive labor), net capital formation, and the residual – also released labor over this period.

In the 1958–67 period, the picture was quite different. Each component of the final product absorbed additional labor time. Again, the largest share went to unproductive activity, which absorbed 7.2 million out of an additional 11.3 million person-years of labor time, or 64 percent. The next largest share went to worker consumption, which accounted for 2.5 million person-years of additional labor time, or 22 percent of the total. Relatively small increases were recorded in surplus household consumption, new investment, and the residual. In the third period, the picture again changed. In this period, as in 1947–58, surplus household consumption, net investment, and the residual all released

Table 7.5. *Distribution of newly added labor value over components of final demand in millions of person-years (second decomposition)*

Component	1947–58	1958–67	1967–76	1947–76
1. Maintaining total real income per capita[a] $[\lambda^2(\bar{d}_p^1 + \widetilde{sc}_p^1 + \bar{g}_p^1)POP^2 - \lambda^1(\bar{d}_p^1 + \widetilde{sc}_p^1 + \bar{g}_p^1)POP^1]$	−4.85	−2.81	2.35	−5.84
2. Increasing private consumption per capita $(\lambda^2 POP^2[\bar{d}_p^2 + \widetilde{sc}_p^2 - (\bar{d}_p^1 + \widetilde{sc}_p^1)])$	2.09	3.45	2.69	7.83
3. Increasing public consumption per capita $[\lambda^2 POP^2(\bar{g}_p^2 - \bar{g}_p^1)$	1.01	2.17	1.25	5.37
4. Increasing net capital formation $(\lambda^2 CF_p^2 - \lambda^1 CF^1)$	−1.35	0.66	−0.68	−1.37
5. Increasing unproductive activity $[(\lambda_{up}^2 Y_p^2 + \lambda_u^2 Y_u^2) - (\lambda_{up}^1 Y_p^1 + \lambda_u^1 Y_u^1)]$	10.78	7.23	8.70	26.71
6. Changing residual $(\lambda^2 R_p^2 - \lambda^1 R_p^1)$	−1.69	0.64	−1.20	−2.25
7. Total change in employment $(N^2 - N^1)$	6.00	11.34	13.12	30.45

[a] $\bar{d}_p = D_p/POP$; $\widetilde{sc}_p = SC_p/POP$; and $\bar{g}_p = G_p/POP$, where POP is the total population.

labor time. Moreover, of the newly added labor value of 13.1 million person-years, total worker consumption absorbed 6.8 million person-years, or 52 percent of the total. This was primarily due to the large increase in employment and the very small rate of technical progress in the production of consumer goods, which caused 3.6 million person-years of new labor time to be absorbed to maintain the 1967 standard of living for the newly added labor force. Increased unproductive activity accounted for 8.7 million person-years, or two-thirds of the total.

Over the whole 1947–67 time span, 30.5 million person-years of labor value were added. Of this, 26.7 million person-years, or 88 percent of the newly added labor time, was absorbed in unproductive activity, and 8.5 million person-years, or 28 percent of the additional labor time, in worker consumption. Of the latter, 7.6 million person-years were accounted for in increased private consumption per worker and 4.5 million person-years in increased public consumption per worker, whereas 3.7 million person-years were released due to technical progress. The other three components of final demand – surplus consumption, investment, and the residual – each released labor value on net.

The allocation of newly added labor value is considered on a per capita consumption basis in Table 7.5. In the 1947–58 period, the amount of labor time devoted directly or indirectly to both public and private household consumption actually declined by 1.8 million person-years. In the next two periods, household consumption had a net addition of labor time. Between 1958 and 1967, it gained 2.8 million person-years, or 25 percent of the total increase, and between 1967 and 1976, it gained 6.3 million person-years, or 48 percent of the net addition of labor time. Over the entire 1947–76 period, 7.4 million additional person-years of labor time were absorbed in household consumption. This accounted for 24 percent of the total increase in labor time, in comparison to unproductive activity, which absorbed 88 percent of the total net addition. Moreover, a larger share of newly added labor time was allocated for increasing private consumption than for increasing public consumption. Yet, the *net increase* in labor absorbed in private household consumption was actually less than that absorbed in public consumption. The reason is that the rate of productivity growth was greater in the production of household consumer goods than in the production of government-provided goods and services. As a result, the reduction in labor time required to maintain the 1947 per capita standard of living was substantially greater for its privately consumed component than for its publicly consumed component. In fact, of the total increase of 7.4 million person-years for total household consumption, only 1.2 million were absorbed in private household consumption, whereas 6.1 million were absorbed in government-provided goods and services. Thus, between 1947 and 1976, over 100 percent of the increased employment was absorbed in government expenditures and unproductive activity. Private household consumption absorbed 4 percent of the increase, whereas investment and the residual were net losers. Insofar as households gained labor resources during this period, it was therefore primarily for the increase in the public portion of their consumption.

E.   Distribution of newly created capital stock

A similar kind of analysis can be done for the allocation of newly added capital stock, as shown in Table 7.6. The picture is quite different for the absorption of newly added capital stock than for newly added labor time. Between 1947 and 1958, the total U.S. capital stock increased by 229 billion dollars (in 1958 prices). Of this, 145 billion dollars, or

Table 7.6. *Distribution of newly added capital stock over components of final demand*[a]

Component	1947–58	1958–67	1967–76	1947–76
1. Increasing private consumption of workers (productive and unproductive) $(\gamma^2 D_p^2 - \gamma^1 D_p^1)$	87.3	85.6	216.1	388.9
2. Increasing public consumption of workers (productive and unproductive)[b] $(\gamma^2 G_{d_p}^2 - \gamma^1 G_{d_p}^1)$	−1.1	63.4	94.4	156.9
3. Increasing private and public surplus consumption (excluding unproductive workers) $[\gamma^2(SC_p^2 + G_{sc}^2) - \gamma^1(SC_p^1 + G_{sc}^1)]$	23.8	43.9	29.7	97.4
4. Increasing net capital formation $(\gamma^2 CF_p^2 - \gamma^1 CF^1)$	−2.4	12.6	−2.0	8.2
5. Increasing unproductive activity $[(\gamma_{up}^2 Y_p^2 + \gamma_u^2 Y_u^2) - (\gamma_{up}^1 Y_p^1 + \gamma_u^1 Y_u^1)]$	144.7	111.7	154.6	410.9
6. Changing residual $(\gamma^2 R_p^2 - \gamma^1 R_p^1)$	−23.4	10.8	−29.1	−41.7
7. Total change in capital stock $(K^2 - K^1)$	228.9	328.1	463.7	1,020.7

[a] Figures are in billions of 1958 dollars.

[b] $G_{d_p} = \dfrac{\sum D_p}{\sum (D_p + SC_p)} \, G_p = N g_{pp}.$

63 percent, was directly or indirectly embodied in expanded unproductive activity, compared to 180 percent of newly added labor time. Worker consumption (including that of unproductive labor) absorbed 86 billion dollars worth of new capital stock, or 38 percent of the total, in contrast to a net loss of newly added labor time. Surplus household consumption (excluding that of unproductive labor) absorbed 10 percent of the new capital stock, whereas net investment and the residual released capital stock. In the next period, 45 percent of the newly produced capital stock was directly or indirectly allocated for total worker consumption, whereas 34 percent was absorbed unproductively, and in the 1967–76 period, the respective figures were 67 and 33 percent. Over the entire 29-year period, the total capital stock increased by 1,020 billion dollars. Of this, 546 billion, or 53 percent, was directly or indirectly allocated for total worker consumption, in contrast to 28 percent of the increased labor time. Of the new capital stock that was directed toward worker consumption, 71 percent was ab-

sorbed in increasing private worker consumption and 29 percent in the increased public consumption of workers. Unproductive activity absorbed 411 billion dollars worth of new capital stock, or 40 percent of the total increase, in contrast to 88 percent of new employment. Surplus household consumption gained 10 percent of the newly added capital stock, in contrast to a net loss in labor time, whereas net investment, which also suffered a net loss in labor time, absorbed 1 percent of the new capital stock.

In regard to total household consumption, 63 percent of the newly added capital stock over the 1947–76 time period was absorbed in this component. In contrast, 24 percent of the newly added labor time was absorbed in household consumption. This result reflects the relative growth in capital intensity in the production of consumer goods. In contrast, unproductive activity absorbed 40 percent of the new capital stock and 88 percent of additional labor time. Moreover, of the 643 billion dollars worth of new capital stock absorbed in household consumption, 72 percent helped increase private household consumption and 28 percent public household consumption. In contrast, only 17 percent of the newly added labor time embodied in household consumption over the 1947–76 period was absorbed in private consumption and 83 percent in public consumption.

F.   Growth in real income

The allocation of resources has direct consequences for the growth of the average standard of living. Several measures of average welfare are presented in Table 7.7. The first two lines use conventional measures of welfare, whereas the last six exclude unproductive activity from the measure of the final product. The first line shows the rate of growth of CFP per worker, or (conventional) average productivity. Its annual rate of growth was 1.8 percent over the full 29 years. During the 1947–58 period, it averaged 2.0 percent; in the 1958–67 period, it climbed to 3.1 percent; and in the 1967–76 period, it fell sharply to 0.2 percent.

The second line shows the growth rate of NNP per capita. It differs from the first line depending on the relative rates of growth of the population and employment. In the 1947–58 period, population grew at an annual rate of 0.9 percentage points greater than employment because of the baby boom. In the second period, the labor force grew 0.4 percentage points faster and in the third period 0.9 percentage points faster, reflecting both the relative aging of the population and increased labor force participation rates. Over the whole time span,

Table 7.7. *Various measures of annual rate of growth of per worker and per capita welfare*

Measure	1947–58	1958–67	1967–76	1947–76
1. Net national product per worker (CFP/N)	1.96	3.05	0.22	1.75
2. Net national product per capita (CFP/POP)	1.11	3.47	1.14	1.85
3. (Productive) final product per worker (FP/N)	0.94	3.34	−0.08	1.39
4. (Productive) final product per capita (FP/POP)	0.09	3.81	0.85	1.48
5. Private consumption per worker ($\sum d_{pp}$)	2.38	2.52	1.88	2.27
6. Average (Marxian) real wage (w)	2.64	2.99	1.85	2.50
7. Private household consumption per capita [$\sum (D_p + SC_p)$/POP]	1.26	2.64	1.92	1.89
8. Total household consumption per capita [$\sum (D_p + SC_p + G_p)$/POP]	1.52	3.11	1.89	2.13

per capita CFP grew at 1.9 percent per year, compared to 1.8 percent per year for CFP per worker.

Line 3 shows the rate of growth of the productive final product, FP, per worker. Over the full 1947–76 period, the growth rate of FP averaged *0.4 percentage points less* than that of CFP, reflecting the relative increase in unproductive output. The discrepancy was particularly pronounced in the 1947–58 period, when FP per worker increased at an annual rate of 0.9 percent, compared to 2.0 percent for CFP per worker. During this period, unproductive activity jumped sharply, and more than 100 percent of the newly added labor time and 58 percent of the increased capital stock was absorbed in expanded unproductive activity. In the second period, FP grew at a somewhat higher rate than CFP, and in the third period, the reverse was true.

In the next line, the rate of growth of FP per capita is shown. In the 1947–58 period, this measure remained virtually constant, whereas CFP per capita increased at over 1 percent per year.

In line 5, the rate of growth of private consumption per worker is shown. During the 1947–58 period, it averaged 2.4 percent per year, considerably above that of the rate of growth of FP per worker and reflecting the more rapid rate of productivity growth in consumption goods than overall (cf. Table 6.4). In the next period, the share of private worker consumption in FP fell and the rate of growth of the private real wage was less than that of FP per worker. In the 1967–76 period, the annual rate of growth of private consumption per worker was 1.9 percent, compared to a −0.1 percent annual growth rate of FP per worker. This difference was not due to differentials in productivity growth rates but rather to a shift in resources away from the surplus final product toward worker consumption. Over the entire 1947–76 period, private consumption per worker grew at 2.3 percent per year, compared to a 1.4 percent growth rate in FP per worker. The difference was due to both a larger rate of productivity growth in the manufacture of consumption goods and a shift in resources toward worker consumption.

In the next line, public consumption is added to private worker consumption to form what has been called the effective real wage, the Marxian real wage, or simply the real wage (w). The difference between this line and the preceding one reflects the growth in government-provided goods and services. In the 1947–58 period, total worker consumption grew at an annual rate of 0.3 percentage points more than private worker consumption, reflecting the relative increase in government-provided consumption. In the second period, the rate of growth of total worker consumption exceeded that of private worker consumption by 0.5 percentage points, and in the 1967–76 period, the two rates were about equal. Over the full time span, the annual rate of growth of the real wage exceeded that of the private wage by 0.2 percentage points. The rate of growth of the real wage was also considerably greater than that of FP per worker in both the 1947–58 and 1967–76 periods and was slightly below that of FP per worker in the 1958–67 period. Over the entire 1947–76 period, the real wage grew at 2.5 percent per annum, almost twice that of FP per worker.

Line 7 shows the average annual rate of growth of private consumption per capita. During the 1947–58 time span, it averaged considerably less than the annual rate of growth of the private real wage because of the faster growth in population than in employment. In the next two periods, despite the fact that the labor force increased relative to population, private consumption per capita grew at about the same rate as the private wage. The reason for this was the relative decline in property income as a source of personal income. Over the whole 1947–76 period, private household consumption per capita grew at an annual rate of 1.9 percent, 0.4 percentage points less than that of private consumption per worker even though the labor force grew slightly faster than the population. The difference was due to the sharp relative increase in labor earnings as a source of personal income and the corresponding relative decline in property income.

The last line shows the growth rate of total (private and public) household consumption per capita. It grew at an annual rate of 2.1 percent between 1947 and 1976, 0.4 percentage points less than that of the real wage. The difference was particularly marked in the 1947–58 period when the real wage grew 1.1 percentage points faster than per capita income, reflecting the more rapid growth in population than in employment. In the next two periods, total household consumption per capita grew slightly faster than the average real wage.

In summary, all eight measures show an increase in the rate of growth of average welfare between the 1947–58 period and the 1958–67 period and then a decline in the 1967–76 period. Moreover, the results suggest three very different episodes in the postwar period in the United States. The 1947–58 period was characterized by relatively high labor productivity growth using traditional measures and a high rate of population growth from the postwar baby boom. In addition, there was a sharp increase in the relative degree of unproductive activity in the economy and an actual increase in the unproductive labor absorbed per unit of (productive) output. As a result, FP per worker grew very slowly and FP per capita was almost unchanged over this period. Despite this, consumption per worker grew in the neighborhood of 2.5 percent per year and consumption per capita around 1.4 percent per year.

The 1958–67 period was characterized by very high labor productivity growth using traditional measures and a fairly rapid growth in employment. Unproductive activity stabilized relative to total output, and the unproductive labor absorbed per unit of productive output fell sharply. As a consequence, FP per worker and FP per capita increased very rapidly over this period, and consumption per worker increased at a rate of about 2.75 percent per year and consumption per capita at about 2.9 percent per year.

In the 1967–76 period, conventional measures showed a very small increase in labor productivity. Employment growth remained high, as in the previous period, but population growth slowed down. Unproductive activity was again stable relative to total economic activity, and the unproductive labor absorbed per unit of productive output again increased, though at a much slower rate than in the 1947–58 period. Despite this, consumption per worker grew at 1.9 percent per year, and consumption per capita also grew at 1.9 percent per year.

CHAPTER 8

Conclusions and speculations

With more than twice the work force and seven times the money, Congress produces about the same volume of legislation it did 20 years ago.

After the close of each two-year session, a box score in the Congressional Record summarizes such items as the number of days, hours and minutes the Senate and House met and the number of bills introduced and enacted.

The box score consists strictly of numbers; thus, it omits a great deal about any Congressional session and the complexity of the issues faced. But the numbers have remained remarkably stable over the years.

In 1977, the first year of the 95th Congress, 15,386 bills were introduced and 1,320 were passed. This year 6,927 measures were introduced and 1,648 passed, some of them holdovers from the previous year.

In the 85th Congress in 1957, 14,013 measures were introduced, and there were 6,591 more in the next year. The totals for bills and resolutions that passed were 2,408 in 1957 and 2,718 in 1958.

In one area, the 95th Congress clearly outstripped the 85th: Its members talked more. In the two years that the 95th Congress was in session, the Senate met for a total of 2,510 hours and the House for 1,897 hours. The record of those sessions filled 66,573 pages. In the 85th Congress the Senate was in session for 1,875 hours and the House for 1,148 hours. Their proceedings filled 33,402 pages of the Congressional Record.

In 1958, the budget for the House was $37.8 million and for the Senate $22.3 million. The figure this year was $282.6 million for the House and $166.4 million for the Senate.

Of course, the Senate is bigger now. There were 96 senators representing 48 states in 1958. That was the year they opened a new building now called the Dirksen Senate Office Building.

Senators and their staffs had no sooner moved into their new quarters when Alaska and Hawaii joined the Union and the size of the Senate increased to 100 members.

An annex to the Dirksen building is under construction to deal with the overcrowded conditions. It will cost $120 million if current estimates hold true. No one thinks they will. (*New York Times*, December 3, 1978, p. 90. Copyright © 1978 by the New York Times Company. Reprinted by permission.)

A.   Review of evidence

The postwar period in the United States was highlighted by a sharp increase in the relative level of unproductive activity. Based on conventional national accounting data, gross output and final output figures in constant-dollar terms were computed for unproductive industries.

164

These results indicate that the gross output of unproductive sectors grew at an annual rate of 4.1 percent over the 1947–76 period, compared to 3.5 percent for productive gross output, while unproductive final output grew at 3.8 percent per year and productive final output at 2.9 percent. Of the six sectors classified as unproductive, the fastest growth in conventionally measured gross output was recorded by the unproductive portion of state and local government activity at 6.0 percent per year, followed by business services at 5.4 percent, the trade sector at 3.9 percent, the finance and insurance sector at 3.7 percent, the real estate sector at 3.3 percent, and the unproductive portion of federal government activity at 3.0 percent.

In regard to the final output components, expenditures on unproductive personal consumption items grew at an annual rate of 3.8 percent (in constant dollars) over the 1947–76 period, whereas productive household spending increased at 3.3 percent per year. Of the former, the most rapid increase occurred in expenditures on finance and insurance services, which grew at 4.1 percent per year, followed by trade services, at 4.0 percent. For government final demand, the opposite was true, with productive spending growing at 4.7 percent per year compared to a 3.8 percent growth rate of unproductive government spending. This was due to a faster growth in state and local government spending, which was characterized by a relatively low level of unproductive spending, than in federal spending. (In fact, the unproductive share of total state and local government spending actually increased over the 1947–76 period, whereas the unproductive share of federal government spending fell very slightly.)

On labor absorption, the results are even more striking. The ratio of those persons directly employed in unproductive sectors to total employment increased from 25 percent in 1947 to 38 percent in 1976. This was largely due to the increase in trade, finance, and business services employment, which increased from 14 to 22 percent, from 2 to 4 percent, and from 1 to 4 percent of total employment, respectively. The fraction of total employment in real estate remained steady at 1 percent, whereas the fraction of employment in unproductive government activity increased slightly from 6 to 7 percent. Moreover, the ratio of workers employed in unproductive occupations within productive sectors to total employment increased very slightly from 13 percent in 1947 to 14 percent in 1976. All told, the proportion of unproductive workers (excluding the armed forces) to total employment rose from 38 percent in 1947 to 53 percent in 1976. In addition, the ratio of unproductively employed labor time to total labor time increased sharply over the 1947–76 period. Defined as the sum of the unproductive labor content of productive final output ($\lambda_{up}Y_p$) and the labor absorbed in fictitious output ($\lambda_u Y_u$), unproductively employed labor time increased from 47 percent of total labor time in 1947 to 61 percent in 1976.

Regarding the absorption of capital stock, the situation was quite different. The ratio of the capital stock directly employed in unproductive sectors to the total capital stock actually fell slightly from 27 percent in 1947 to 26 percent in 1976. Moreover, the proportion of the total capital stock either directly or indirectly absorbed in fictitious output ($\gamma_u Y_u$) rose slightly from 28 to 30 percent. When the share of the capital stock directly employed in unproductive sectors but indirectly absorbed in productive final output ($\gamma_{up}Y_p$) is added to this percentage, the combined fraction increased very slightly from 37 to 39 percent over the 1947–76 period.

Another way of considering the change in the allocation of resources in the postwar period is to look at the absorption of newly added labor time and capital stock. Over the 1947–76 period, employment increased by 30.5 million person-years. Of this, 26.7 million person-years, or 88 percent, was absorbed as unproductively employed labor time and 7.4 million person-years, or 24 percent, for gross household consumption, including both privately and publicly provided goods and services. Moreover, of the 7.4 million person-years added to gross household consumption, only 1.2 million were added for private consumption, whereas 6.1 million were added for government-provided consumption. Thus, between 1947 and 1976, over 100 percent of the increased employment was absorbed either as unproductively employed labor time or in productive government expenditures. Private household consumption absorbed 4 percent of the increased labor time, whereas investment and the residual were net losers. In contrast, of the net increase of 1,021 billion dollars worth of capital goods over the 1947–76 period, 411 billion, or (only) 40 percent, was directly or indirectly absorbed in unproductive uses. On the other hand, 546 billion, or 53 percent, was absorbed in gross household consumption, and of this 546 billion, 71 percent was added for private household consumption and 29 percent for government-provided goods and services. Capital formation, moreover, absorbed 1 percent of the increased capital stock.

Some confirmation is also provided of Baran and Sweezy's (1966) law of the tendency of the surplus to rise. Based on the definition of unproductive activity and necessary consumption developed here, the ratio of surplus value to total labor value increased from 0.80 in 1947 to 0.86 in 1976. This was equivalent to an increase in the rate of surplus value from 4.1 to 5.9. However, the ratio of surplus final product (SFP) to the final product (FP) fell slightly from 0.65 in 1947 to 0.63 in 1976.

The difference in time trends was due to the faster rate of productivity growth in the manufacture of consumption goods than in surplus goods. Moreover, the difference in magnitude between the two ratios was due to the higher labor content of the surplus product.[1]

In regard to unproductive activity, the postwar span from 1947 to 1976 divides into two rather distinct periods: 1947–58 and 1958–76. In the first of these periods, conventional sectoral measures show a sharp increase in the level of unproductive activity relative to the total activity of the economy. Conventionally measured unproductive final output Y_u increased as a share of constant-dollar CFP from 32 to 40 percent, and the component A_{pu} increased from 18 percent of TP to 27 percent in constant-dollar terms. This dramatic change in the structure of conventional final demand was accompanied by major changes in labor force composition. Those directly employed in unproductive sectors increased from 25 to 34 percent of total employment; and those directly employed in either unproductive sectors or occupations increased from 38 to 47 percent. *In absolute numbers, in fact, productive employment actually declined from 35.3 million to 33.5 million person-years.* The ratio of unproductively employed labor time $(\lambda_{up}Y_p + \lambda_u Y_u)$ to total labor time increased from 47 to 59 percent. In fact, of the increase in total employment of 6.0 million person-years over the 1947–58 period, *10.8 million, or 180 percent, were absorbed in unproductive uses.* Finally, the proportion of the capital stock owned by unproductive sectors increased slightly from 27 to 29 percent, and the proportion unproductively employed rose from 37 to 45 percent.

The second period, 1958–76, was characterized by a fairly stable level of unproductive activity relative to total activity according to conventional measures. Unproductive final output as a share of CFP was 40 percent in 1958 and 39 percent in 1976, though there were some fluctuations over the period. On the other hand, the ratio of productive output purchased by unproductive sectors, A_{pu}, to TP did decline over the period from 27 percent in 1947 to 23 percent in 1976. The proportion of the work force that was unproductively employed continued to rise over the period. The percentage directly employed in unproductive sectors increased from 34 to 38 percent, and the fraction directly em-

[1] This definition of surplus product, it should be recalled, excludes that portion of productive government expenditures that is considered part of the necessary costs of reproducing the labor force. If all government expenditure is considered part of the surplus product, the ratio of surplus value to total labor value would have risen from 0.82 in 1947 to 0.89 in 1976. A definition of the surplus product that included total government spending was also used in a statistical appendix provided in the Baran and Sweezy book, which was compiled by Joseph Phillips. They found an increase in the ratio of their measure of surplus to GNP from 0.44 in 1947 to 0.55 in 1963.

ployed in either an unproductive occupation or an unproductive sector rose from 47 to 53 percent. The proportion directly or indirectly unproductively employed $(\lambda_{up}Y_p + \lambda_u Y_u)$ increased from 59 percent in 1958 to 61 percent in 1976. Of the increase of total employment of 24.5 million over the 1958–76 period, 15.9 million, or 65 percent, were absorbed directly or indirectly in unproductive uses. On the other hand, the fraction of the capital stock directly owned by unproductive sectors fell from 29 percent in 1958 to 26 percent in 1976. Moreover, the proportion of the capital stock that was employed either directly or indirectly in unproductive purposes declined from 45 to 39 percent.

The empirical results also provide some confirmation of the predictions of the growth model of accumulation and unproductive labor developed in Chapter 4. The major assumptions of the model held roughly during the period from 1947 to 1976. The first assumption of the model is that the direct absorption of unproductive resources is fixed per unit of (productive) output. The ratio of N_u/X_p fell from 43.0 unproductive employees per million dollars of output (in 1958 prices) in 1947 to 33.1 employees per million dollars of output (in 1958 prices) in 1976. This was equivalent to a decline of 0.90 percent per year. In contrast, the ratio N_p/X_p fell at the rate of 2.92 percent per year, or more than three times as fast as the ratio N_u/X_p. Thus, relative to the direct productive labor requirements, the unproductive labor directly absorbed per unit of productive output was relatively fixed over the 1947–76 period. Moreover, the ratio K_u/X_p was virtually unchanged at 0.300 in 1947 and 0.292 in 1976.

A second assumption of the model is that the ratio of productive inputs purchased in unproductive activities (ΣA_{pu}) is a constant fraction of TP. However, over the 1947–76 period, the ratio did rise from 0.19 to 0.24. A third assumption is that household consumption remain a constant share of TP. Private household consumption $(D_p + SC_p)$ was 57 percent of TP in 1947 and 60 percent in 1976, whereas gross household consumption $(D_p + SC_p + G_p)$ was 0.66 of TP in 1947 and 0.74 of TP in 1976. The fourth condition is that net investment is a constant proportion of TP. The investment (CF_p) share did move cyclically over time, falling from 10.2 percent in 1947 to 5.0 percent in 1958, then rising to 9.1 percent in 1972, and then falling to 4.2 percent in 1976. However, based on National Income and Product Account data, the average ratio of net private domestic fixed investment to NNP was 0.052 in the 1947–58 period, 0.051 in the 1958–67 period, and 0.050 in the 1967–76 period.

The model has five major implications. First, unproductive employment N_u should rise over time as a share of total employment. This ratio did increase steadily over time from 0.38 in 1947 to 0.53 in 1976. Second, the ratio of unproductively employed labor time ($\lambda_{up} Y_{up}$ + $\lambda_u Y_u$) to total labor time should also increase over time. This fraction increased from 0.47 in 1947 to 0.61 in 1976. Third, in the limit, the ratio of unproductive capital stock (K_u) to the total capital stock should approach a positive constant given by $d_2 n/d_3$. The ratio K_u/K fell from 27 percent in 1947 to 26 percent in 1976. The model predicts that this fraction will continue to fall over time until it reaches 0.15. Fourth, the overall rate of labor productivity growth should decline over time. Overall LPG increased slightly from 3.4 percent per year in 1947–58 to 3.6 percent in 1958–67 and then fell precipitously to 0.2 percent per year in 1967–76. (However, many other factors besides the increase in the share of unproductive employment were responsible for the decine in LPG in the last period.) Fifth, the rate of TFP growth for (productive) output should decline over time. This measure averaged 0.9 percent per year in the 1947–58 period, increased to 2.7 percent per year in the 1958–67 period, and then fell to -0.6 percent per year in the 1967–76 period. Finally, the rate of growth of the real wage should decline over time. The annual rate of growth of private consumption per worker (Σd_{pp}) increased slightly from 2.4 percent in 1947–58 to 2.5 percent in the years 1958–67 and then fell to 1.9 percent in the 1967–76 period, and that of gross consumption per worker (w) increased from 2.7 percent per year in the first period to 3.0 percent in the second and then fell to 1.9 percent in the third.

B.   Labor absorption and average living standards

The evidence from the postwar period indicates that there were cyclical movements in both real wages and the rate of displacement of the total labor absorbed per unit of output (TLD). In the 1947–58 period, private consumption per worker (Σd_{pp}) increased at an annual average rate of 2.4 percent, while the rate of total labor displacement averaged 0.9 percent per year. In the 1958–67 period, the private real wage grew at 2.5 percent, whereas TLD averaged 3.3 percent. In the years 1967–76, private real wages grew at 1.9 percent and TLD at -0.1 percent. The average (Marxian) real wage (w), which reflects both private and public consumption, grew somewhat faster than the private real wage during the first two periods at 2.6 and 3.0 percent, respectively. In the 1967–76 period, its annual rate of growth was the same as the private real wage, 1.9 percent.

It is somewhat surprising that the real wage increased at all in the 1947–58 period, since 180 percent of the increase in employment was absorbed directly or indirectly in unproductive uses. Indeed, the amount of productive labor time absorbed in the production of both private and public worker consumption goods declined in absolute amount during this period, and overall TLD averaged 0.9 percent per year. Despite this, the real wage increased over the period because of the very high rate of LPG (4.2 percent per year) in the manufacture of household consumption goods. This high rate of LPG was, in turn, partly due to the fact that a high proportion (38 percent) of the new capital stock was absorbed in the production of private worker consumption goods. Moreover, the rate of LPG for (productive) government output was 1.0 percent per year, which was the highest level achieved in the postwar period.

During the years 1958–67, 64 percent of the newly added labor and 34 percent of the newly added capital stock were absorbed either directly or indirectly in unproductive uses. This was substantially lower than the previous period. Overall TLD was quite high at 3.4 percent per year, as was overall LPG at 3.6 percent per year. LPG for private household consumption was again 4.2 percent per annum, and this component of final output absorbed 26 percent of the newly added capital stock. LPG for government output, on the other hand, was slightly negative. Despite the slow rate of LPG of the government sector, the real wage increased at 3.0 percent per year, the highest level of the postwar period.

In the 1967–76 period, TLD for total productive output was slightly negative, and LPG for productive output averaged only 0.2 percent per year. LPG for private household consumption was also very low, averaging 0.6 percent per year, whereas LPG for government output was zero. Moreover, the rate of growth of employment accelerated to 1.8 percent per annum from 1.3 percent in the years 1947 to 1967. Despite these factors, the real wage increased at 1.9 percent per year because it absorbed a major share of the new resources. Of the newly added labor time of 13.1 million person-years, private and public household consumption absorbed 52 percent, and of the newly added capital stock, it absorbed 67 percent.

The per capita measures of average welfare were similar in pattern to the average wage measures. The rates of growth in per capita welfare all showed increases between the 1947–1958 and the 1958–67 periods and then a decline in the 1967–76 period. The per capita measures were lower than the corresponding real wage measures in the 1947–58 period because of the high rate of population growth in these years. In the last two periods, the opposite was the case because of the rapid growth in the labor force.

Perhaps, the best measure of the average living standard is productive gross household consumption per capita, which includes both privately and publicly financed consumption. The rate of increase of this measure accelerated from 1.5 percent per annum in 1947–58 to 3.1 percent in 1958–67 and then slowed down to 1.9 percent in 1967–76. Over the full 1947–76 period, it averaged 2.1 percent per annum. The best measure of the average *social* level of well-being is probably FP per capita since FP includes not only current consumption but also the net addition to the capital stock and hence provision for future consumption. This measure averaged only 1.5 percent per annum over the years 1947–76. Indeed, in the 1947–58 period, it increased at an annual rate of *only 0.1 percent* per year, which corresponded to the extraordinary increase in unproductive activity. During 1958–67, the rate of growth accelerated considerably to 3.8 percent, and in 1967–76, it fell to 0.9 percent. Finally, perhaps the best available measure of the *potential* level of average well-being is the total net product (TP) per capita since TP is the sum of use values not directly required for the production of other use values (that is, TP is the sum of FP and A_{pu}). TP per capita grew at 1.2 percent per year during the 1947–58 period, considerably faster than FP per capita, reflecting the rapid increase in the use values directly absorbed in unproductive activity. During the 1958–67 period, TP per capita grew at 3.5 percent per year, somewhat lower than that of FP per capita, and during the last period, TP per capita grew at 0.6 percent per year, again somewhat lower than that of FP per capita. Over the full 1947–76 period, TP per capita increased at an annual average rate of 1.7 percent, slightly greater than that of FP per capita.

Though the average Marxian real wage managed to grow in the 1967–76 period, despite the very slow rate of productivity growth and the high absorption of resources in unproductive uses, more recent evidence suggests that this has not been the case since 1976. Based on Bureau of Labor Statistics data and the conventional measure of labor earnings, hourly earnings in 1977 dollars of the private nonagricultural sector *declined* at the rate of 0.6 percent per year from 1976 to 1983.[2] Indeed, average hourly earnings were almost exactly the same in 1983 as in *1968*.

One way of assessing the impact of unproductive activity on the level of well-being is to estimate what the level of per capita income would have been if the resources absorbed in unproductive activity had been absorbed, instead, in productive activity. For this calculation, it is pos-

[2] The source is the *Economic Report of the President, 1983*, Table B-38, p. 264.

sible to use the one-sector model developed in Chapter 4, where it is assumed that there is a single, productive sector in the economy. In this model, the stable equilibrium rate of growth of productivity and the real wage is given by $g^e = w^e = r/\alpha$, where r is the rate of TFP growth in the (productive) sector and α is the average wage share in the economy. Based on estimates for the productive sectors of the U.S. economy in the 1947–76 period, the average annual rate of TFP growth was 1.6 percent, and the average wage share was 0.68. The stable equilibrium values $g^e = w^e = 2.4$ percent per year. This was slightly lower than the actual 2.5 percent annual growth rate of the (Marxian) real wage over the 1947–76 period but considerably higher than the 1.4 percent annual rate of growth of FP per worker. Moreover, g^e and w^e are limiting growth rates for the one-sector economy. In the general, two-sector model, productivity growth and real wage growth both continue to fall over time, as they have since the late 1960s, and in the limit both approach zero.

The long-term implications of the two-sector model are thus rather unsettling. If, indeed, the U.S. economy is heading for the limiting growth path, as the evidence suggests, the United States must look forward to declining rates of increase of real living standards. For reasons peculiar to the post-1965 period, the rate of growth of overall labor productivity declined rather precipitously and certainly more than would be predicted from the logic of the two-sector model.[3] However, even if the United States resumes its normal postwar productivity performance, the structural shift in employment necessitated by the model from a constant absorption of unproductive labor per unit of productive final output will cause a continuous retardation in the overall productivity growth rate. This will be the predominant factor forcing down the rate of growth in real average living standards.

C.   Peculiar logic of capitalism

Unproductivity activity stands as a basic contradiction of capitalism. It exists though it benefits no one; it has grown, though no one is made better off; and it wastes resources that could be used to improve the level of well-being.

Indeed, the contradiction is lodged in the conditions of competition themselves. Competitive capitalism, as Marx argued in *Capital*, has

---

[3] In particular, the post-1965 period was characterized by declines in the productivity growth rates of almost all major sectors of the economy. See Denison (1979), Kendrick (1980), or Wolff (1985), for example.

the potential of engendering a phenomenal increase in worker productivity and thus in average real income. Each capitalist in an industry has the incentive to develop and introduce more productive technology since it thereby reduces unit cost and can increase profit. Moreover, each capitalist, when faced with such an improvement by a competitor, has an incentive to match or better such an innovation if only to ensure the firm's survival. There is thus great incentive for the development of new techniques and their quick dissemination. Viewed from the outside, capitalism seems ideally designed to increase human well-being.

Yet, its logic is such that it sows the seeds for its own destruction. By prompting technological advance and capital accumulation, competitive capitalism also promotes the growth in individual firm size and bankruptcies, thereby increasing concentration. Competitive capitalism thus engenders the *eradication* of competition and gives way to monopoly capitalism. In this stage, the form of competition changes to demand management. There is still an incentive to improve technology, but it is weaker since it is not usually necessary for survival. Moreover, because of the sheer size of the modern corporation, the major source of trouble shifts from the sphere of production to that of "realization" (i.e., demand). Thus, at the level of the individual firm, resources shift away from productive applications toward selling and circulation activity. As a result, an increasing share of resources is absorbed in unproductive uses.

Baran and Sweezy were right to localize the *source* of the rise in unproductive activity in the realization problem. However, for them, it was a *partial* contradiction. On the level of the individual firm, demand management was rational since it ensured the realization of surplus value but from the social point of view it wasted resources and detracted from social welfare. However, they also saw unproductive activity as an ingredient in an *aggregate* demand management strategy. At this level, was it rational not only for the individual capitalist but also for society as a whole since it ensured full employment and thereby stimulated growth and capital accumulation. Yet, their conception grows out of a Keynesian-type effective demand model that is essentially *static* in character. From a dynamic perspective, unproductive activity must be considered irrational from a social viewpoint since it diverts resources away from capital formation. Indeed, though it is true that the realization problem is the source of the contradiction of unproductive activity, capital accumulation is the *locus of its effect*. The evidence presented in this book shows the very strong inverse relation between the two on the cyclical level (both in terms of conventionally measured output levels and in terms of the resources absorbed in capital formation and unproductive activity).

The rise in unproductive activity is seen to be largely rooted in the logic of advanced capitalism. The forces of competition, which in the early stages of capitalism lead to rapid technical change and productivity growth, promote nonproductive and even counterproductive activities in its more advanced stages. The stagnation of American capitalism of the 1970s and early 1980s may thus be largely due to one of the fundamental contradictions of the system.

Yet, is this "cancer" of unproductive activity the final *irony* of capitalism? Is its continually increasing absorption of resources a *necessary* outcome of the forces of competition in a capitalist setting? It is necessary to divide the discussion into two parts. First, on the level of the individual firm, unproductive expenses serve not only to control demand but also to control credit and sources of finance and to protect the firm's surplus from the intrusion of the state. As far as demand management is concerned, it is the existence of individual capitals that are forced to compete with each other that creates the realization problem. Marx calls this the "anarchy of the marketplace," and it is due to the unplanned nature of capitalism. The development of monopoly capitalism *allows* a greater amount of resources to be devoted to advertising, marketing, and trade activities since the surplus is greater. Moreover, the increasing concentration of production and scale of output makes the realization problem more severe since the size of the market in terms of consumers and geography becomes significantly larger.[4] Yet, the concentration of American industries probably peaked in the late 1950s or the early 1960s. As a result, the diversion of resources to marketing must be seen as a historical decision taken by American capital. West German and Japanese companies, for example, have taken the path of improving and advancing their technology. Indeed, their current technological superiority may now force a similar path to be taken by U.S. firms. This is particularly so, since their resulting trade advantage has allowed them to penetrate previously secure domestic markets in the United States.

The growth in resources devoted to financial management and credit control seems to stem from three factors. First, controlling credit is a *form* of competition that gives an advantage to an individual firm over its competitors. Credit is important not only for new investment and

---

[4] There is, perhaps, a "gravity model" type of relation at work, whereby the sales network and the associated costs of circulation grow roughly by the square of the radius of trade.

financing working capital but also as a sales device to lure customers for expensive goods like cars. Indeed, one of the reasons for the increasing concentration of capital is the monopolization of credit sources. Second, the fact that production is concentrated means that the *scale* of production has increased substantially in both physical and value terms. Since this increases the time of circulation due to the greater realization difficulties, the need for credit for inventories of finished goods is thereby increased and so are the resources that must be devoted to financial management. Third, the apparent explosion in financial instruments, due probably to the increasing debt–equity ratios of American corporations, presents added opportunities to increase profits from portfolio management. This has also resulted in an increase of resources devoted to financial management. Yet, here too there is no apparent *necessity* involved in the growth of financial activity, and the increase in resources devoted to this activity seems to stem again from peculiar historical circumstances.

The third source of growth in unproductive activity is in the legal area. The relative size of the legal establishment in the United States compared to a socialist state like the Soviet Union or China stems ultimately from the existence of a particular kind of private property, namely the private ownership of the means of production. Thus, in a capitalist state, more resources must be devoted to maintaining property rights than in a socialist state. Yet, the spectacular rise in the size of the legal profession in the postwar period in the United States seems due to peculiar historical circumstances since other capitalist states, notably Japan, have not had a similar explosion in the size of their legal establishment. One such circumstance appears to be the increasing size of the state. On the one hand, this engendered increasing competition for the surplus generated in the *private sector*, which led, in turn, to the emergence of a legal (and accounting) establishment to protect the surplus from the state. It is perhaps trite to mention the resources that are now devoted to tax avoidance by the corporate and business sector (and also by individuals), but this has become a major industry in the United States. On the other hand, the intrusion of the state in the internal affairs of private business, mainly through legislated regulations and regulatory agencies, has expanded the role of legal departments. Environmental, health, and safety regulations, for example, are vigorously resisted by business because their observance causes a reduction in profits.

This analysis still begs the question of why government and, in particular, unproductive government activity has expanded so dramatically in the postwar economy. There seem to be three reasons. First, the government does provide useful services, such as the construction of highways, sewers, and public transit. The relative rise of the productive portion of government expenditure in total output reflects, by and large, the growing importance of public goods. Second, unproductive general government activity seems to have grown due to the logic of bureaucracy. Like any other surplus activity, there is built into it a certain impetus to expansion. Each member of a bureaucracy has an incentive to build up his own staff in order to raise his position and salary. Thus, bureaucracies have a tendency to expand. In particular, government bureaucrats, whose budgets ultimately come out of the surplus, have become another powerful surplus class who compete with productive capitalists for their share of the surplus. This is one reason that there is so much friction between the state and productive capitalists since they are competitors for surplus value. Interestingly, the neoconservatives implicitly recognize this fact, and their program, as embodied, for example, in the Reagan federal budget proposals, is an attempt to redress the balance in favor of productive capitalists. Yet, they see all government as wasteful (except, ironically, the military), whereas the true culprit consists of all forms of unproductive activity, which are partly from public but mainly from private sources.

The third factor is the expansion of the military and the police in the postwar period. The former may have originally been motivated by the "rational" requirement to protect American capital abroad, but it too has taken on a dialectic of its own, as the "irrational" war in Vietnam gave evidence. The expansion in police power was largely a result of the sharp rise in the crime rate in the United States in the postwar period, a condition that was itself partly engendered by the high rate of poverty and income inequality that characterized the American form of capitalism. Yet, here, too, a comparison with Western Europe and Japan is instructive. Both West Germany and Japan had low levels of defense expenditure during the postwar period, which was largely a result of American foreign policy. This factor was in no small way responsible for the high savings rates in the two countries. Moreover, Japan and most Western European countries had lower poverty rates, income inequality levels, and crime rates than the United States and a considerably lower level of resources per capita devoted to police power. But here, again, there appears to be no necessity for the continued growth in this unproductive activity of the state.

Thus, on the surface, it seems very difficult to argue the case that unproductive activity must rise over time by its own internal logic. Yet, this argument is not necessary for the thesis of the book, which rests only on the presumption that unproductive employment will rise *relative* to productive employment. This condition could be satisfied if there were a high rate of (productive labor) productivity growth (LPG) and the absorption of unproductive workers per unit of (productive) output were fixed over time or declined at a slower rate than the displacement of productive workers. LPG was quite high during the postwar period. Moreover, based on official National Income and Product Account data for the United States, employment in the various unproductive sectors *declined* relative to GNP in constant dollars. The ratio of persons engaged in production to GNP in millions of 1972 dollars declined from 23.4 in 1947 to 12.9 in 1976 in retail and wholesale trade; from 3.9 to 3.4 in finance, insurance, and real estate; from 0.45 to 0.38 in legal services; and from 14.0 to 11.4 in the total government sector.[5] Yet here, too, a rapid rate of displacement of productive workers and a relatively slow rate of displacement of unproductive labor may have been due to special historical circumstances.

In conclusion, then, though it is apparent that unproductive activity may develop according to its own dynamic, it is not an *essential* contradiction of capitalism since its logic is not embedded in the basic structure of capitalist production. Unproductive activity develops in almost all societies when economic surplus is generated. The form it takes depends on the particular characteristics of the society and the particular historical circumstances. In capitalism, the rise of unproductive activity is largely due to the nature of competition and the realization problems it engenders. Yet, its *magnitude* in contemporary American capitalism is due to its particular form of capitalism, which is international monopoly capitalism, and its time path is due more to a rapid displacement of productive labor than to a relative increase in unproductive activity.

D.   Private scarcity/social waste

Yet, the fact remains that unproductive activity is detrimental to capitalism since it reduces the amount of surplus available for accumulation. Though unproductive activity increases the relative share of surplus in the economy, it diminishes the proportion disposable by productive capitalists and thus the proportion available for capital expansion. The product absorbed by other segments of the surplus classes – merchant and financial capitalists, landlords, unproductive workers, and the government – does not aid the accumulation process. Indeed,

[5] The source is *The National Income and Product Accounts of the United States, 1929–76 Statistical Tables*, Tables 6.2 and 6.11. *Persons engaged in production* is defined as the sum of full-time equivalent employees and self-employed persons.

both the empirical evidence and the theoretical evidence strongly indicate a constant drain on investment from unproductive activity.

Unproductive activity thus appears a contradiction of the advanced capitalist system. It threatens the reproduction of the system by reducing the rate of accumulation. Its one apparent virtue is that it absorbs part of the social product and thus alleviates the realization problem. But this product could also be absorbed by increased accumulation (or increased personal consumption). Moreover, unproductive activity is a feature of advanced capitalism that benefits neither workers nor capitalists. Workers (both productive and unproductive) do not benefit from unproductive activity since their real wages are depressed by the increasing share of their money wages "remitted" to the surplus class in the form of taxes and unproductive expenditures. Indirectly, their wages are kept low by the reduced rate of accumulation and the consequently lowered rate of productivity increase. Nor does the individual capitalist benefit from unproductive activity. The portion of the profits paid out in taxes is a loss to the capitalist. The disbursements on unproductive items like business services are a cost from the capitalist's standpoint and reduce the amount available for investment. Unproductive activity thus reduces the amount of surplus at the disposal of the capitalist class.

Why, then, does unproductive activity drain so much resources if neither the capitalist class nor the working class benefits? The reason is that for the individual capitalist such unproductive expenditures are required for competition and constitute necessary expenses. From the social point of view, however, such activity constitutes unnecessary and wasteful uses of the economy's labor power and other resources. It is the capitalist system itself that manufactures needs that provide no useful social function. It is then in the contradictory nature of advanced capitalism that so much of society's manpower and output is devoted to unproductive activities while so many real social needs go unsatisfied.

It is somewhat ironic that the reigning problematic of modern microeconomics is the allocation of "scarce" resources among competing needs. From the vantage of individual capitalists, it is true that resources are scarce. However, from a social point of view, there is an enormous waste of resources. Indeed, the large scale of unproductive activity represents a qualitative change in the character of American capitalism, one where social scarcity is no longer a predominant characteristic. Yet, like the "soft budget line" of the defense sector, unproductive activity can generate excess demand and therefore manufacture shortage on the microlevel of the economy. Thus, phenomenally, individual units in the economy appear to face a condition of scarce resources.

The tremendous slack in the economy created by unproductive labor suggests that the neoclassical paradigm based on the allocation of scarce resources is now outmoded and, indeed, obsolete (if, in fact, it was ever appropriate). Concerns with Pareto-type inefficiencies in regard to the optimal use of resources involve second-order or even third-order effects in comparison to the macroinefficiencies engendered by unproductive activity.

In regard to macroanalysis, traditional national income and product accounts reduce to two components of final demand – consumption and investment. The other three components of standard national accounts are government expenditure, exports, and imports. In conventional analysis, government final demand represents either public goods, and hence consumption, or social capital formation. Exports either directly or indirectly provide consumption or investment to foreign countries. Imports, likewise, directly or indirectly serve consumption or investment needs. In the analysis of this book, a third outlet of the national product is added – namely, unproductive uses. This component is not reducible to either consumption or investment. As a result, traditional concepts and measures of income and product must be radically altered (as was argued in Chapter 3) in order to maintain an identity between the two. The "crisis" of modern macroeconomics – both Keynesian and non-Keynesian forms – may stem, in part, from the failure to recognize this third component of final output. Moreover, the poor predictive performance of Keynesian-based macromodels over the last half dozen years or so may be due, in some measure, to the failure to appreciate the qualitative change American capitalism has undergone since World War II and the modification of national accounting categories such a change entails.

Appendix: Data sources and methods

The data for the components of the standard input–output accounting framework were assembled from a variety of sources described below. All estimates are reconciled with the National Income and Product Accounts where possible. The basic data can be divided into six components: (1) the commodity flow table, (2) labor coefficients, (3) capital matrix, (4) sectoral price deflators, (5) personal taxes, and (6) industry by occupation matrix.

A.   Commodity flow tables

The standard 87-sector Bureau of Economic Analysis (BEA) scheme is shown in Table A.1. Sector 74, research and development, exists as a separate sector in only the 1947 and 1958 tables. Sector 78, federal government enterprises, and sector 78, state and local government enterprises, are government-owned facilities that sell their services or products directly to the public – such as the post office in the case of the former and electrical utilities in the case of the latter. Sector 80, transferred imports, records the purchase of imports that are nonclassifiable in one of the other 86 sectors by intermediate and final users. (Imports that are "competitive" with domestic products are recorded in the row in which there are close domestic substitutes.) Column 80 is therefore blank. Sectors 84–7 (government industry, rest of the world industry, household industry, and inventory valuation adjustment) are value-added sectors that record wages and salaries and profits in the respective activities. All flows are recorded in current producer prices.[1]

Value added by sector is broken down into three components: (1) employee compensation, (2) property-type income, and (3) indirect business taxes. The second component, property-type income, consists of the sum of proprietors' income, rental income of persons, corporate

---

[1] Producer prices show the price paid for each input or commodity net of its trade markup. The total sum of the trade margins on the whole column vector of inputs is then shown as a single entry in the trade row in each industry (column).

180

Table A.1. *The 87-sector input–output classification scheme*

1 Livestock and products	45 Construction, etc. machinery
2 Other agricultural products	46 Materials-handling equipment
3 Forestry and fishery products	47 Metalworking machinery
4 Agricultural services	48 Special industrial equipment
5 Iron and ferroalloy mining	49 General industrial equipment
6 Nonferrous metal mining	50 Machine shop products
7 Coal mining	51 Office machines
8 Crude petroleum and gas	52 Service industry machines
9 Stone and clay mining	53 Electrical industry equipment
10 Chemicals mining	54 Household appliances
11 New construction	55 Electric lighting equipment
12 Repair construction	56 Radio and TV equipment
13 Ordnance and accessories	57 Electronic components
14 Food and kindred products	58 Miscellaneous electrical equipment
15 Tobacco manufactures	59 Motor vehicles
16 Fabrics, yard and thread	60 Aircraft and parts
17 Miscellaneous textile goods	61 Other transport equipment
18 Apparel	62 Professional instruments
19 Fabricated textiles	63 Optical equipment
20 Lumber and wood products	64 Miscellaneous manufacturing
21 Wooden containers	65 Transportation and warehousing
22 Household furniture	66 Communications
23 Other furniture	67 Radio and TV broadcasting
24 Paper and allied products	68 Utilities
25 Paperboard containers	69 Wholesale and retail trade
26 Printing and publishing	70 Finance and insurance
27 Chemical products	71 Real estate and rental
28 Plastics and synthetics	72 Personal and repair services
29 Drugs and cleaners	73 Business services
30 Paints and allied products	74 Research and development
31 Refined petroleum	75 Auto repair and services
32 Rubber and allied products	76 Amusements
33 Leather products	77 Medical and educational services
34 Footwear	78 Federal government enterprises
35 Glass products	79 State and local government
36 Stone and clay products	enterprises
37 Primary iron and steel	80 Noncompetitive imports
38 Primary nonferrous metals	81 Business travel
39 Metal containers	82 Office supplies
40 Structural metal products	83 Scrap and used goods
41 Screws, bolts, and nuts	84 Government industry
42 Other fabricated metal	85 Rest of the world
43 Engines and turbines	86 Household industry
44 Farm machinery	87 Inventory valuation adjustment

profit and inventory valuation adjustment, net interest, business transfer payments, and the capital consumption allowance less the difference between subsidies and the current surplus of government enterprises. The sum of the three value-added components is equal to the gross national product. The column vector of final demand is broken down into seven components: (1) personal consumption expenditures, (2) gross private domestic capital formation, (3) net private inventory change, (4) federal government purchases of goods and services, (5) state and local government purchases of goods and services, (6) exports, and (7) imports (recorded as a negative flow). The sum of components 2 and 3 is gross private domestic investment and the sum of 6 and 7 is the trade balance or net exports. The sum of the seven components is equal to gross national product.

The data sources are as follows:

1947: The 1947 transactions table, final-demand vectors, and total value added by sector were provided by Beatrice Vaccara of the Bureau of Economic Analysis and are described in Office of Business Economics (1970). This table is a reworking of the original Bureau of Labor Statistics 1947 input–output table. The revision was done to make the 1947 sectoring scheme consistent with the later years and to integrate the table with the National Income and Product Accounts (NIPA). The value-added row was divided as follows: A partial list of employee compensation coefficients by sector (the ratio of total employee compensation to gross domestic output by sector) was provided by Anne Carter and Peter Petri of the Brandeis Economic Research Center (BERC, for short). Supplementary data were obtained from the Bureau of Labor Statistics (1979b) *Employment and Earnings, 1909–66*, for employee compensation in the private sector and from *Economic Report of the President, 1979*, Table B-20, p. 206, for government employee compensation. Total employee compensation was then aligned to the NIPA total (Table B-20). The residual value added was then treated as the sum of property income and indirect business taxes. In order to separate the two components, the same indirect business tax coefficients were used as for 1963 (see below) to obtain a preliminary estimate of total indirect taxes by sector. This row was then multiplied by a scalar to sum to the NIPA total for indirect business taxes (Table B-17, p. 202).

1958: The transaction matrix, the final-demand vectors, and the value-added row were obtained from BERC on computer tape in standard

87-sector BEA format. In order to decompose the value added into its three components, employee compensation coefficients for the first 83 sectors were obtained from Marty Marimont of BEA (mimeo). Government employee compensation was added from NIPA (*Economic Report of the President, 1979* Table B-20, p. 206, ibid.), and total employee compensation was then aligned to the NIPA total (Table B-20, p. 206) by multiplying the row by a scalar. The residual value added was then treated as the sum of property income and indirect business taxes. In order to separate the two components, as in the case of the 1947 table, the indirect business tax coefficients were used from the 1963 table. The row was then adjusted by a scalar to sum to the NIPA total for indirect business taxes (Table B-17, p. 202). The residual value-added row was then treated as the property income row (by construction, its sum equaled the NIPA total).

1963: The transactions matrix, the final-demand vectors, and the value-added row were obtained from BERC on computer tape in standard 87-sector BEA format. The decomposition of the value added on the 87-sector level into employee compensation, indirect business taxes, and property-type income was obtained in Walderhaug (1973). Alignment with NIPA totals was already done in this study.

1967: The transactions matrix, the final-demand vectors, and the three value-added rows (employee compensation, indirect business taxes, and property-type income) were obtained from BERC on computer tape in standard 87-sector BEA format. The data are fully described in Interindustry Economics Division (1974).

1972: The transaction matrices, the final-demand vectors, and the three value-added rows (employee compensation, indirect business taxes, and property-type income) were obtained from Philip Ritz of BEA on computer tape in standard 87-sector BEA format.[2] The data are described in Ritz (1979) and Ritz, Roberts, and Young (1979). One major innovation in the 1972 input–output table is the treatment of so-called secondary products (for example, coal produced and sold by a steel manufacturer). In previous tables, such a secondary product was treated as though it were sold by the producing industry to the industry to which it is primary and then added to the output of the primary industry for distribution to users. This creates some distortions in both capital and labor coefficients. In the 1972 table, two separate matrices

---

[2] Actually, two sectors were eliminated in the 1972 scheme – business travel and office supplies – that were essentially artificial sectors in the earlier tables.

were produced. The first, called the use matrix (or the commodity-by-industry matrix), shows the actual commodities purchased by each industry as inputs in production. The second, called the make matrix (or the industry-by-commodity matrix), shows the commodities produced by each industry. For (reasonable) consistency with earlier years, an industry-by-industry matrix was constructed from these two basic matrices showing what each industry sells to each of the other industries and to final demand irrespective of the particular commodities produced.[3]

1976: The so-called RAS method, or method of biproportional adjustment, described below, was used to estimate a 1976 total flow industry-by-industry input–output matrix by updating the 1972 total flow industry-by-industry matrix. The procedure used was as follows: First, each industry row of the 1972 input–output table was multiplied by its 1976/1972 sectoral price inflator to convert the table to 1976 prices. (See Section D for a description of the sectoral price deflators.) Second, estimates of gross domestic output for each of the 87 sectors were obtained from the following sources. Totals for sectors 1–79 and 86 were provided in the Bureau of Labor Statistics (1979a) *Time Series Data for Input–Output Industries.* For sector 80, noncompetitive imports, noncompetitive import coefficients (the ratio of noncompetitive imports to total output) for 1972 adjusted for 1976 prices were used for each of the 87 endogenous sectors and each of the final-demand components. Multiplying each of the coefficients by the total output or final demand of its respective sector yielded not only an estimate of total noncompetitive imports but also an estimate of the row.

Sectors 82 and 83 were excluded from the 1976 table, as they were from the 1972 table. For sector 84, government industry, the percentage of total purchases spent on sector 84 by the federal government and by the state and local government components of final demand in 1972 was used. Multiplying these coefficients by the respective final-demand totals yielded an estimate of the total output of industry 84. For sector 85, the rest of the world industry, the percentage of total expenditures spent on this sector by each of the components of final demand in 1972 was used. Multiplying these coefficients by the respective final-demand

---

[3] The construction of the industry-by-industry matrix requires the assumption that the market shares of the primary and secondary industries producing each commodity be constant. The column coefficient matrix of the make matrix can then be constructed, showing what percentage of the output of each commodity (the market share) is produced by each industry. Finally, the coefficient make matrix is post-multiplied by the total flow use matrix to yield the industry-by-industry total flow matrix.

totals yielded an estimate of the total output of sector 85. The estimate for sector 87, inventory valuation adjustment, was obtained in *Economic Report of the President, 1979*, Table B-19, p. 204.

For the construction of the final-demand matrix, totals for each of the seven components were obtained from *Economic Report of the President, 1979*, Table B-1, p. 183. For all the components except imports, it was assumed that the distribution of purchases over the 87 sectors was the same in 1976 as in 1972.[4] Adjusting for the change in price by sector yielded the final-demand flows. For the import column, it was assumed that the ratio of imports to total sales (that is, the market share of imports) remained the same for each industry between 1972 and 1976. This assumption yielded a first round estimate of the new import column in final demand. This column, with the exclusion of noncompetitive imports, was then multiplied by a scalar to sum to the final-demand total for competitive imports. The last component, the value-added matrix, was estimated by using the wage and salary, property income, and indirect business tax coefficients in 1972 and multiplying each column by 1976 gross domestic output. Each row of the value-added matrix was then multiplied by a scalar to sum to its NIPA total (Tables B-17 and B-19, pp. 202, 204).

The last step was then to balance the resulting commodity flow matrix. Since the input–output matrix is a form of double-entry bookkeeping, the vector of row sums of the matrix must equal the vector of column sums, which must be equal to the vector of gross domestic output. Since the final-demand totals and value-added totals agreed with the NIPA accounts for 1976, it was assumed that the final-demand and value-added matrices were correct. It was also assumed that sector 80 (the noncompetitive import row), which has a zero column, and sectors 84–87, which are value-added sectors with zero columns, were all correct. The difference between gross domestic output and estimated value added by sector was then used as the control totals for the column sums, and the difference between gross domestic output and estimated total final demand by sector was used as the control totals for the row sums. The RAS method was then applied over sectors 1–79. This method operates by iteratively distributing the row control totals proportionately over the row cells followed by distributing the column control totals over the column cells until convergence is reached.

[4] The only exception was the new construction row in the final-demand matrix, where separate estimates for federal government, state and local government, and private construction were obtained. The source was *Economic Report of the President, 1979*, Table B-43, p. 232.

B.   Labor coefficients

Data on employment by input–output sector also came from a variety of sources. In each case, the total employment was aligned to the total employment figures provided in *Economic Report of the President, 1979*, Table B-27, p. 214. For 1947, labor coefficients for 76 out of the first 83 sectors were provided by BERC. The missing entries in the first 83 sectors were estimated using data from the Bureau of Labor Statistics, *Employment and Earnings, 1909–66*. For 1958 and 1963, a complete list of labor coefficients for the first 83 sectors was provided by BERC. For 1947, 1958, and 1963, employment in sector 84, government industry, was obtained from *Economic Report of the President, 1979*, Table B-34, p. 222. For sectors 85 and 86, rest of the world and household industries, employment was estimated by first computing the mean earnings in the economy and then dividing total earnings in each of these two sectors by mean earnings.[5] For both 1967 and 1972, employment for each of 125 sectors was obtained in the Bureau of Labor Statistics (1975) *The Structure of the U.S. Economy in 1980 and 1985*. The 125-order scheme was then aggregated to obtain the first 83 sectors of the 87-sector BEA scheme. Employment for sectors 84–86 was estimated in the same way as the earlier years. For 1976, estimates of employment by sector for 154 sectors were obtained in Bureau of Labor Statistics (1979a), *Time Series Data for Input–Output Industries*. These were aggregated to obtain estimates of employment for each of the 87 BEA sectors, except government (84) and rest of the world (85). These two sectors were estimated as in previous years.

C.   Capital stock and depreciation

The 1947, 1958, and 1975 capital coefficient matrices for the United States were obtained from BERC.[6] These matrices, which were also 87-order, show the dollar value of capital stock of each of 87 commodity types[7] owned by each sector as a ratio to the total dollar output of that sector.[8] In the 1947 and 1958 tables, data on capital stock ownership were missing for sector 13 (ordnance), sector 74 (research and devel-

---

[5] Sector 87, inventory valuation adjustment, has no employment.
[6] The 1958 and 1975 matrices were originally constructed by the Battelle Memorial Institute, with some modifications later done by BERC.
[7] More specifically, the capital stock is classified according to the industry that produced it. As a result, only about 50 of the 87 rows have any entries.
[8] For 1947 and 1958, separate data were provided on the capacity utilization of the capital stock owned by each sector.

opment), sector 78 (federal government enterprises), sector 79 (state and local government enterprises), and sector 84 (government industry). In the 1975 table, data were missing for sectors 78–80. The missing information was estimated as follows: For sector 13, the same capital coefficients as for column 60 (aircraft and parts) were used. For sector 74, the column coefficients for column 73 (business services) were used. For sector 78, a weighted average of the coefficients for column 68 (utilities) and 69 (trade) was used. The weights used were derived from the relative magnitudes of the secondary outputs produced by the government sector, which fell into the trade sector and the utilities sector in 1958. The respective weights were 0.389 and 0.611. For sector 84, the average capital coefficients for the private economy were used. Information was available on the total dollar value of the capital stock owned by the government sector (excluding government enterprises), which was provided by John Musgrave of the Bureau of Economic Analysis (worksheets) and used to estimate the capital stock column.

The 1975 capital coefficients were used for the 1976 capital coefficient matrix. For the 1963, 1967, and 1972 capital coefficient matrices, each column of the matrix was constructed by using a straight-line interpolation between the respective columns of the 1958 and the 1975 matrices. Thus, for the 1963 capital coefficient matrix, each column j was computed as a weighted average of column j of the 1958 matrix and column j of the 1975 matrix, where the weights were $\frac{12}{17}$ and $\frac{5}{17}$, respectively. For the 1967 matrix, the respective weights were $\frac{8}{17}$ and $\frac{9}{17}$; and for the 1972 matrix, the weights were $\frac{3}{17}$ and $\frac{14}{17}$.

In order to obtain a consistent set of capital stock estimates, the preliminary capital stock matrix estimates in each year were then aligned to estimates of the total capital stock owned by each input–output sector provided in the BLS (1979c), *Capital stock estimates for input–output industries: methods and data*. Some modification of the BLS data was first necessary. First, the data series by sector extended only as far as 1974. The 1974 capital–output ratio was therefore used to compute the total capital stock owned by each sector in 1976. Second, the four agricultural sectors (1–4) were aggregated into one sector in the BLS data. The BLS total agricultural capital stock estimate was therefore distributed over these four sectors proportionately to the preliminary estimates. Third, the new construction sector (11) and the repair and maintenance construction sector (12) were aggregated into one sector in the BLS data. The BLS estimate was distributed proportionately to the preliminary estimates in these two sectors. Fourth, only the business sectors were covered in the BLS data. The total capital stock in sectors 78, 79, and 84 was computed as described above. The alignment of the capital stock matrices to these column control totals was accomplished by multiplying each column of the matrix by a scalar.

Depreciation: Estimates of the average depreciation rates of the plant and equipment owned by each sector were obtained for each business sector except 13 and 74 for years 1947 and 1958 from BERC. Sector 13, the ordnance sector, was assigned the same depreciation rate as sector 60, the aircraft sector, whereas sector 74, research and development, was assigned the same depreciation rate as sector 73, business services.

Depreciation rates for the years 1963, 1967, and 1972 were obtained from data supplied from *Internal Revenue Service Corporation Income Tax Returns* for each of these years. The estimates in these publications are statistical estimates derived from a sample of unaudited income tax returns filed by corporations. Because of the aggregated nature of the Internal Revenue Service data, in many cases the same depreciation rate was assigned to more than one input–output sector. For year 1976, the same depreciation rates by sector were used as for 1972.

For the business sectors, the depreciation rates were then adjusted by a scalar for each year so that the estimated total depreciation of the capital stock agreed with the NIPA capital consumption allowance (source: *Economic Report of the President, 1979*, Table B-17, pp. 202–3). Depreciation rates for the government sectors were computed as follows: For sector 78, federal government enterprises, a weighted average of the depreciation rates of utilities (sector 68) and trade (sector 69) were used, with weights of 0.389 and 0.611 (see the discussion of capital stock above). For sector 79, state and local government enterprises, the same depreciation rate was used as for utilities (68). For the government sector (84), an unweighted average of all the depreciation rates of all the other sectors was used.

D.   Sectoral price deflators

Price deflators for each of 81 sectors for years 1947/1958 were obtained from BERC. For the missing sectors (80, 82, and 84–7), price indices were obtained in Office of Business Economics, (1970). The 1963 sectoral price deflators for all 87 sectors except noncompetitive imports (80) and household industry (86) were also obtained from BERC. Price deflators for 1967 were also obtained from BERC on an 125-order level and were aggregated to 82 BEA standard sectors using output weights. The missing sectors were 80 and 84–7. Price deflators for 1972 were supplied by Philip Ritz of BEA for all sectors except 80, 84, 85, and 87.

Missing price indices, including those of the depreciation sector, were estimated in the following way (sectors 80, 84–7, from *Economic Report of the President, 1979*):

Sector 80: Noncompetitive imports: the GNP import deflator, Table B-3, p. 187.

Sector 84: Government industry: the GNP total government deflator, Table B-3, p. 187.

Sector 85: Rest of the world industry: the GNP export deflators, Table B-3, p. 187.

Sector 86: Household industry: the GNP personal consumption expenditures on services deflator, Table B-3, p. 186.

Sector 87: Inventory valuation adjustment: the ratio of total inventories in 1972 dollars to total inventories in current dollars, Tables B-15 and B-16, pp. 200–1.

Sector 88: Depreciation: a weighted average of the price deflators of the other 87 sectors, with total capital stock by type of capital good as the weight.

E.   Personal taxes

Data on personal tax and nontax payments as a percentage of total personal income were obtained from *Economic Report of the President, 1979*, Table B-21, p. 208.

F.   Occupation-by-industry matrices

The basic data sources were occupation-by-industry matrices compiled from decennial U.S. census data in census years 1950, 1960, and 1970 and a breakdown of employment by occupation for 1980. The specific sources were as follows:

1. U.S. Bureau of the Census, *U.S. Census of Population: 1950*, Vol. II, *Characteristics of the Population*, Part I, Chapter 6, Occupation by Industry, U.S. Government Printing Office,

Washington, D.C., 1953. The statistics are for the employed labor force, 14 years old and over.

2. U.S. Bureau of the Census, *U.S. Census of Population: 1960, Subject Reports, Occupational Characteristics*, Final Report PC(2)-7C, U.S. Government Printing Office, Washington, D.C., 1963. The statistics are for the employed labor force, 14 years old and over.

3. U.S. Bureau of the Census, *U.S. Census of Population: 1970, Special Reports*, Final Report PC(2)-7C, Occupation by Industry, U.S. Government Printing Office, Washington, D.C., 1973. The statistics are for the employed labor force, 16 years old and over.

4. U.S. Bureau of the Census, *U.S. Census of Population: 1980*, Supplementary Report PC 80-51-8, *Detailed Occupation and Years of School Completed by Age, for the Civilian Labor Force by Sex, Race, and Spanish Origin: 1980*, U.S. Government Printing Office, Washington, D.C., March 1983, Table 1. The statistics are for the civilian labor force, 16 years old and over.

The U.S. census industry classifications were aligned to those of the input–output classification scheme. The occupational classifications in each of the four census years were aggregated to the following categories:

Productive occupations:

1. Professional and technical
2. Clerical
3. Craft
4. Operative
5. Service
6. Nonfarm labor
7. Farmers
8. Farm labor

Unproductive occupations:

9. Professional and technical
10. Clerical
11. Managerial and administrative
12. Sales
13. Protective services

The 1947 occupation-by-industry matrix was formed from 1947 industry employment totals and 1950 occupational coefficients by industry. The 1958 occupation-by-industry matrix was based on 1958 industry employment totals and 1960 occupational coefficients by industry. The 1963 occupation-by-industry matrix was based on 1963 industry employment totals and 1960 occupational coefficients by industry. The 1967 and 1972 matrices were both based on 1970 occupational coefficients by industry and each on industry employment totals of their respective years. The 1976 matrix was formed in the following manner: First, 1976 occupational totals were estimated by interpolating between the 1970 and 1980 totals by occupational category. Second, the RAS method was applied to the 1970 occupation-by-industry matrix based on 1976 employment totals by industry and occupation.

References

Adler, Hans J., and Oli Hawrylyshyn (1978), "Estimates of the value of household work, Canada, 1961 and 1971," *The Review of Income and Wealth*, Series 24, No. 4, December, pp. 333–56.

Baran, Paul (1957), *The Political Economy of Growth*, New York: Prometheus.

Baran, Paul, and Paul Sweezy (1966), *Monopoly Capital*, New York: Modern Reader Paperbacks.

Baumol, William (1967), "Macroeconomics of unbalanced growth: the anatomy of urban crisis," *American Economic Review*, Vol. 57, No. 3, June, pp. 415–26.

Becker, James (1971), "On the monopoly theory of monopoly capital," *Science and Society*, Winter, pp. 415–38.

Becker, James (1977), *Marxian Political Economy*, Cambridge: Cambridge University Press.

Blaug, Mark (1968), *Economic Theory in Retrospect*, Homewood, Illinois: Richard D. Irwin, Inc.

Bullock, Paul (1973), "Categories of labour power for capital," *Bulletin of the Conference of Socialist Economists*, Autumn, pp. 82–99.

Bureau of Economic Analysis (1981), *The National Income and Product Accounts of the United States, 1929–76: Statistical Tables*, September, Washington, D.C.: U.S. Government Printing Office.

Bureau of Labor Statistics (1975), *The Structure of the U.S. Economy in 1980 and 1985*, Bulletin 1831, July, Washington, D.C.: U.S. Government Printing Office.

Bureau of Labor Statistics (1979a), *Time Series Data for Input–Output Industries: Output, Price, and Employment*, Bulletin 2018, March, Washington, D.C.: U.S. Government Printing Office.

Bureau of Labor Statistics (1979b), *Employment and Earnings, United States, 1909–78*, Bulletin 1312–11, July, Washington, D.C.: U.S. Government Printing Office.

Bureau of Labor Statistics (1979c), *Capital Stock Estimates for Input–Output Industries: Methods and Data*, Bulletin 2034, September, Washington, D.C.: U.S. Government Printing Office.

Council of Economic Advisers (1979), *Economic Report of the President, 1979*, Washington, D.C.: U.S. Government Printing Office.

Denison, Edward (1979), "Explanations of declining productivity growth," *Survey of Current Business*, Vol. 59, No. 8, Part II, August, pp. 1–24.

Eisner, Robert (1978), "Total incomes in the United States, 1959 and 1969," *The Review of Income and Wealth*, Series 24, No. 1, March, pp. 41–70.

193

Fleanor, C. Patrick, David L. Kurtz, and Louis E. Boone (1983), "Changing profile of business leadership," *Business Horizons*, July–August, pp. 43–46.

Gilman, Joseph (1957), *The Falling Rate of Profit*, London: Dennis Dobson.

Gough, Ian (1972), "Marx's theory of productive and unproductive labour," *New Left Review*, December, pp. 47–72.

Harrison, John (1973), "Productive and unproductive labour in Marx's political economy," *Bulletin of the Conference of Socialist Economists*, Autumn, pp. 70–81.

Hunt, E. K. (1979), "The categories of productive and unproductive labor in Marxist economic theory," *Science and Society*, Vol. 18, No. 3, Fall, pp. 303–25.

Institut National d'Etudes Démographiques, ed. (1958), *Francois Quesnay de la Physiocratie*, Paris: Institut National d'Etudes Démographiques.

Interindustry Economics Division (1974), "The input–output structure of the U.S. economy: 1967," *Survey of Current Business*, Vol. 54, No. 2, February, pp. 24–56.

Kendrick, John (1976), *The Formation and Stocks of Total Capital*, New York: National Bureau of Economic Research.

Kendrick, John (1980), "Productivity trends in the United States," *in* Shlomo Maital and Noah M. Meltz, eds., *Lagging Productivity Growth*, Cambridge, Massachusetts: Ballinger.

Landes, David (1969), *The Unbound Prometheus*, Cambridge: Cambridge University Press.

Mage, Shane (1963), "The law of the falling tendency of the rate of profit," Unpublished Ph.D. dissertation, Columbia University.

Marx, Karl (1963), *Theories of Surplus Value*, Moscow: Progress Publishers.

Marx, Karl (1967), *Capital*, New York: International Publishers.

Morishima, Michio (1973), *Marx's Economics*, Cambridge: Cambridge University Press.

Morishima, Michio, and Francis Seton (1961), "Aggregation in Leontief matrices and the labor theory of value," *Econometrica*, Vol. 29, No. 2, April, pp. 203–20.

Myint, Hla (1962), *Theories of Welfare Economics*, New York: Augustus M. Kelley.

O'Connor, James (1975), "Productive and unproductive labour," *Politics and Society*, Vol. 5, No. 3, pp. 297–336.

Office of Business Economics (1970), "The input–output structure of the United States economy: 1947," mimeo, March, Washington, D.C.

Quesnay, Francois (1968), *Economical Table*, New York: Bergman Publishers.

Ritz, Philip (1979), "The input–output structure of the U.S. economy: 1972," *Survey of Current Business*, Vol. 59, No. 2, February, pp. 34–72.

Ritz, Philip, Eugene Roberts, and Paula Young (1979), "Dollar value tables for the 1972 input–output study," *Survey of Current Business*, Vol. 59, No. 4, April, pp. 51–72.

Roll, Eric (1956), *A History of Economic Thought*, 3rd ed., Englewood Cliffs, New Jersey: Prentice-Hall.

Ruggles, Patricia (1979), "The allocation of taxes and expenditures to households," Ph.D. dissertation, Harvard University.

Ruggles, Richard, and Nancy D. Ruggles (1982), "Integrated economic accounts for the United States," *Survey of Current Business*, Vol. 62, No. 5, May, pp. 1–53.

Schumpeter, Joseph A. (1937), *History of Economic Analysis*, New York: Modern Library.

Seton, Francis (1957), "The transformation problem," *The Review of Economic Studies*, Vol. 24, No. 65, June, pp. 149–60.

Smith, Adam (1937), *The Wealth of Nations*, New York: Modern Library.

Solow, Robert M. (1956), "A contribution to the theory of economic growth," *Quarterly Journal of Economics*, Vol. 70, February, pp. 65–94.

Walderhaug, Albert J. (1973), "The composition of value added in the 1963 input–output study," *Survey of Current Business*, Vol. 53, No. 4, April, pp. 34–41.

Wolff, Edward (1975), "The rate of surplus value in Puerto Rico," *Journal of Political Economy*, Vol. 83, No. 5, October, pp. 935–49.

Wolff, Edward (1977a), "Unproductive labor and the rate of surplus value in the United States, 1947–67," *in* Paul Zarembka, ed., *Research in Political Economy*, Vol. 1, Greenwich, Connecticut: JAI Press.

Wolff, Edward (1977b), "Capitalist development, surplus value and reproduction: an empirical examination of Puerto Rico," *in* Jesse Schwartz, ed., *The Subtle Anatomy of Capitalism*, Santa Monica, California: Goodyear Publishing.

Wolff, Edward (1979), "The rate of surplus value, the organic composition, and the general rate of profit in the U.S. Economy, 1947–67," *American Economic Review*, Vol. 69, No. 3, June, pp. 329–41.

Wolff, Edward (1981), "The accumulation of wealth over the life-cycle: a microdata analysis," *The Review of Income and Wealth*, Series 27, No. 2, June, pp. 75–96.

Wolff, Edward (1983), "The distribution of household disposable wealth in the United States," *The Review of Income and Wealth*, Series 29, No. 2, June, pp. 125–46.

Wolff, Edward (1985), "The magnitude and causes of the recent productivity slowdown in the U.S.," *in* K. McClennan and W. Baumol, eds., *Policies for the Stimulation of U.S. Productivity Growth*, New York: Oxford University Press.

Index